A hell of a lot of
GLASS

Achieving gender equality in the workplaces of Australia

KATE RAMSAY

With contributing authors Dr Anne Hartican,
Lindsay Mackay and Megan Young

I dedicate this book to Jessica, Isabella, Phillipa, Alexandra and Lila – may you face no barriers as you achieve your hopes and dreams.

First published in 2023 by Kate Ramsay

© Kate Ramsay 2023

The moral rights of the author have been asserted

A catalogue entry for this book is available from the National Library of Australia.

ISBN: 978-1-923007-10-9

Printed in Australia by McPherson's Printing
Project management and text design by Publish Central
Cover design by Pipeline Design

The paper this book is printed on is certified as environmentally friendly.

Contents

Foreword

A hell of a lot of glass makes an important contribution to the ongoing conversation about how to achieve true gender equality in the workplaces of Australia.

It explores answers to questions about why there are still so few women CEOs in the top 200 ASX listed companies, why there is still a gender pay gap, and why, after more than 4 decades of anti-discrimination, equal opportunity and affirmative action legislation and policy in Australia, we still do not have gender equality in our workplaces. Importantly, the book includes practical ways to address these challenges.

Kate Ramsay was motivated to write this book after providing decades of leadership coaching for women had made her realise that the glass ceiling is still not only there, but that there's also a 'hell of a lot' of other glass impeding women's progress; such as the glass cliff and the glass labyrinth, and even double glazing for women of colour, women with a disability and women from the LGBTQI+ communities.

This book is a must read for leaders keen to create a gender diverse workforce, for change agents with the inclusion and diversity portfolio in their workplaces, for women juggling work and family responsibilities and for all of us who want equality at work. What sets it apart from other books on this subject is the fresh approach: it combines solid research with sometimes disturbing interviews, but always offers hope.

Kate Ramsay's experience, integrity, insight and passion, the hallmarks of an extensive career in leadership coaching and mentoring, shine through this engaging and inspiring vision for the future.

The Honourable Dame Quentin Bryce AD CVO

Biographies

Kate Ramsay is a leadership coach, mentor and writer. She is Managing Director of AnD Leadership Consulting, a boutique business that provides coaching and mentoring support to leaders and emerging leaders, and many of her clients are women. She has previously worked as an equal opportunity consultant, a hospital nurse, a midwife and a community nurse. She is the author of *Go with love – a memoir about love, loss and learning* (2015), and co-author with Patricia Bellamy of *Barriers to women working in corporate management* (1994). Kate also produces the *Value Adding Newsletter*, a quarterly newsletter about how coaching can add value to life. She has just distributed edition # 93 of this newsletter.

Lindsay Mackay is a lawyer who is currently a legal counsel in an international finance firm. She has expertise in the application of anti-discrimination law in a corporate context and an interest in the history and practice of gender-based anti-discrimination and affirmative action legislation.

Megan Young is a social ecologist, leadership and life vision coach, researcher and writer. Megan's earlier incarnation was a corporate career that included being equal opportunity coordinator in a large corporation. Megan's work received awards in the 1994 Affirmative Action awards and the 1993 Business Council of Australian Work and Family awards. Megan has a Masters of Applied Science (Social Ecology). Since leaving corporate life she has worked in a range of roles for small business, not-for-profit, social enterprise and as a business consultant.

Dr Anne Hartican is a leadership and organisational development consultant and researcher. Over the years Anne has conducted in-depth interviews with a number of senior women leaders for publications and conference presentations. She co-authored *The character of leadership: what works for Australian leaders – making it work for you* (2006) and *Inspirational women in Asian business and government: what makes them succeed?* (2010). She has also published articles in *Leadership and Organization Development Journal* and the *Monash Business Review*.

Introduction

'This is the book I didn't believe I was capable of writing', I heard Markus Zusak say in a television interview in 2018 about his then recently released book, *Bridge of clay*.[1] Zusak is an author I much admire, and this sentence was his gift to me because *A hell of a lot of glass* is the book I didn't believe I was capable of writing. The fact that Zusak wrote a superb book has been a motivator to keep me working on mine.

As every author knows, writing a book is a huge undertaking. So, what was the catalyst for me back in 2018 to sit down and embark upon another book? In short, it was because I wanted to make sense of the ongoing resistance to the achievement of a gender diverse workforce in Australia – which is about having an equitable representation of both women and men throughout every organisation.

This remains a mystery to me: the research shows that a gender diverse workforce is good for business and that there are now more women graduating from many university faculties than men. This means the feeder pool of available women is there, and surely the ongoing dearth of female talent at senior levels is bad for business. So why has the change still not happened? Is it fear, or is it good old-fashioned misogyny? I needed to find out why the patriarchy still seems to be holding onto the status quo, particularly in larger organisations, rather than embracing what seems to me to be a logical change for the good. I also wanted to think deeply about what more could be done so that the Australian workplace becomes a truly safe and equal place for women.

So, the purpose of this book is to answer these questions, as well as to record in parallel, the history of gender-based anti-discrimination and affirmative action legislation in Australia, all of which is intended to achieve equality of opportunity for women.

To contribute to this dialogue, I plan to explore what I've learnt during my second and third careers as an equal opportunity consultant and a leadership coach and mentor, during which I've consulted to dozens of organisations and coached hundreds of women leaders and emerging leaders.

Next, and complementing my own story, will be my research about how patriarchal control continues to dominate in many organisations – particularly the larger ones – how women have experienced this, and what they've done and might further do to resist it. My intention is that this book will read as a case study of how sexism operates in organisations, and what more needs to be done to eliminate it.

As part of my research, I've conducted in-depth interviews with 22 women who've worked in senior roles in public and private organisations, universities, and even one retired politician, to find out about their gender-related employment experiences. I've also interviewed three men from a range of backgrounds to enquire about whether patriarchy has helped or hindered them in their careers and lives. I'm aware that my female interviewees are either in, or have previously been in, senior positions in large Australian organisations, so they could well be described as a privileged sample group. My reason for this choice is twofold. First, at a practical level these are the women I've known, coached and supported to reach more senior positions. Second, and I believe more importantly, my interviewees are in positions of influence, which hopefully means they will be spurred on by this book to continue to do all they can to contribute to an improvement in the status of women in all sectors of the Australian workforce.

It's only now as I reflect on my three careers spanning over six decades that I can see a theme running through my choices. In my first two working decades I was a general nurse, then a midwife and finally a community health nurse. The values encouraging me on to be the best nurse I could be, were *caring* and *service*. In my next decade, I was an equal opportunity (EO) consultant with a commitment to supporting organisations to remove the barriers to their women's full contributions. The core values driving me through these challenging years were *equity* and *fairness*. In the last three decades I've been a leadership coach and mentor, with the values of *support* and *service* motivating me. This feels almost like I've returned to the place where I first began, because I can now see that underlying each of my career choices has been the theme of making a positive difference to people in their lives. And now, as an author, I've set out to record this history, and hopefully to answer the questions I've posed to myself above.

I tell the story of how I came to make the huge leap from my first career in nursing to my second as a self-employed consultant specialising in equal employment opportunity (EEO) and affirmative action (AA) in chapter 4. My motivation for reinventing myself into my third career as a leadership coach and mentor was two-fold: as an EO consultant I'd truly believed that the combination of legislation and policy were going to result in the necessary changes for the Australian workplace to become equal for women. Then, in the early 1990s, a recession hit and EEO/AA budgets were slashed, and as a result, I saw my thriving consultancy rapidly diminishing and my optimism crushed. It turned out that providing equal employment opportunities for women was a 'nice thing' to do in healthy economic times only. So, as well as needing to make a shift for economic survival, my second motivation to walk away from EO consulting, was my disillusionment with the ability of the CEOs and senior managers of Australia's larger organisations to effect real change for their women.

By the early 1990s my mentor was offering leadership coaching support to organisations. In response to my complaints about my dwindling bank account, he suggested I combine the counselling skills and experience I'd gathered as a community health nurse, with my more recent consulting experience, and put out my shingle as a leadership coach as well. Spurred on by his encouragement, I signed on my first leadership coaching client at the end of 1990, and I continue to have a small coaching practice over 30 years later.

What are leadership coaching and mentoring? Definitions vary but to me, leadership coaching involves providing one-on-one support to my clients from a belief that their answers lie within themselves, and that my role is to be a catalyst to their self-discovery. I don't give advice. Instead, I provide regular time out for disciplined reflection. This involves me asking open-ended questions and listening keenly to my clients' responses. I coach clients in safe, supportive environments and encourage them to explore the barriers stopping them from being the best that they can be in the context of their vision, purpose and values, and I encourage them to set plans to overcome these barriers. Conversely, my mentoring is a pro bono service for small business-women needing support. As a mentor, my support can and does at times include giving clients advice on the probable best ways forward. And it's a given that both services are enshrined in confidentiality.

Of course, the responsibility for making change in organisations must not rest with women alone. This book is also about what leaders – both men and women – can do differently to create organisational cultures that enable, and indeed welcome, gender diversity in their workplaces.

I also believe that the time is right to look once again at the much-examined issues of sexism, misogyny and the patriarchy, but through a fresh lens. Why? Because courageous, high-profile younger women are all demanding change: Grace Tame, the 2021 Australian of the Year, chosen for her work on behalf of survivors of child sexual abuse; Chanel Contos, consent education advocate; and Saxon Mullins, the 2018 recipient of the Australian Human Right Commission's Young People's Human Rights Medal for her work in raising the issue of consent. Also, because hundreds of thousands of women and men Australia-wide participated in the March4Justice in the autumn of 2021 chanting 'enough is enough'.

The book has been a collaborative effort, not only because of the generous contributions my interviewees have made, but also from three co-writers:

- Lindsay Mackay, a lawyer, writes about the history of the development and the proclaiming of gender-based anti-discrimination and affirmative action legislation in Australia. Her chapter immediately follows my second chapter because I believe Lindsay's legislative framework sets the scene for the remainder of the book.

- Megan Young, who has been an equal opportunity practitioner in corporate Australia, shares her extensive research about the patriarchy and matriarchy in Chapter 19.

- Dr Anne Hartican is a leadership and organisation development consultant and researcher. In chapter 21 she has written in-depth case studies of three women CEOs from different sectors of the Australian workforce who have overcome the so-called 'glass ceiling'.

Each chapter is intended as a stand-alone essay on a wide range of topics relevant to the book's purposes. My chapters include what I learnt as I pursued my passion for supporting women as a consultant, coach and mentor, as well as all that I've gathered from my research and through my interviews. In each of my chapters I begin with my personal reflections, then cover the relevant research and what my interviewees have to say on that topic. I end each chapter with suggestions about how progress can continue to be made towards Australian workplaces becoming fully gender equal, and the conclusions I've reached about that topic.

My hope is that my readers will include:

- women, to remind them that it's time they claimed their place in the public arena
- human resources and people and culture practitioners – especially those who are given the inclusion and diversity portfolio
- consultants with the brief to devise programs and processes to help leaders break down any unconscious biases in their workplaces, and in so doing to create more female friendly cultures
- committed leaders, both men and women with power, who understand the challenges that many women still face as they have the courage to claim a fair go.

My focus in this book is on achieving gender equality in large organisations in the public, private and higher education sectors in Australia, because this is where my experience has been, and it's also where cultures are much more resistant to change than in smaller more entrepreneurial organisations. As you will read, many of the women who've left these large organisations are now leading or contributing to smaller businesses and not-for-profits.

I've chosen not to explore the hideous ongoing rates of family and domestic violence, nor the ongoing racism in Australia, including towards our own Indigenous people. There are others writing wisely and well on these challenging topics – for example, see Jess Hill's book *See what you made me do*, Stan Grant's books *Talking to my country*, *Australia Day* and *On identity*, and Aileen Moreton-Robinson's book *Talkin' up to the white woman*.

Chapter 1

Why women too?

B efore I dive into the technical challenges of achieving a gender equal workforce and the history of my contribution to meeting this challenge, let's reflect awhile on why this is a good idea.

For the over 35 years that I've been working in the field of equal employment opportunity, affirmative action and gender diversity, I've been putting forward the business case for a gender balanced work-force, as well as the obvious equity case for achieving such an outcome. Having a workforce that reflects the population within which any business operates to best understand their customers' needs, has been my main argument, as well as the obvious loss of talent when there are barriers to women's advancement. I've always thought these were compelling arguments, but in the dozens of EO awareness seminars I facilitated to hundreds of managers Australia wide in the late '80s and early '90s, this logic seemed to mostly land on deaf ears.

As a leadership coach, I provide confidential one-on-one sessions, usually of two hours duration over an initial contract of 12 hours of coaching, followed by an evaluation and review. One of my golden rules has been to provide sessions offsite in a convenient location with parking. My reason for asking my clients to meet with me offsite was twofold: first, it maintained confidentiality for them, and second, it meant they could separate from the demands of their busy lives and, in a safe setting, focus on themselves for those two hours.

Once my clients felt they could trust me, many would express the difficulties they were having in convincing their senior managers of the value to the business of the inclusion and diversity program that they, my client, were responsible for implementing. They would share their frustrations about the fact that the words all sounded good, and the glossy documents outlining the program looked good. However, when there was only a miniscule budget allocated for the proposed changes, they just knew that most, if not all, their senior leaders were, at best, only paying lip service to the program. I could see the despair on their faces as they would share the latest roadblocks they were meeting, and they quite often looked exhausted. During our sessions, these women and I would brainstorm yet more clever ways that they might influence their leaders to change, and they would commit to a plan that we would review at their next session.

Research

For the purposes of this book, I set about searching for both qualitative and quantitative evidence of the value of a gender diverse leadership team and workforce. Here's what I found:

In September 2018, the findings of a collaboration between organisational consulting firm Korn Ferry and the Australian Institute of Company Directors (AICD) were released in a research report called *Australian women CEOs speak*. The researchers conducted structured interviews with 21 Australian women – current and former CEOs and women who had headed up professional services firms, government departments and universities. The study aimed to discover which aspects of these women's careers and life trajectories helped them reach a top job. The findings of this report are being used to rework development programs to support women who aspire to be leaders, as well as to inform organisations that are aiming to increase the number of women at their senior levels.

The final page of the report titled 'A future that embraces women at the top', refers to a management consulting firm, McKinsey & Company, study that showed a 'statistically significant correlation between a more diverse leadership team and financial outperformance'. The Korn Ferry/ AICD researchers concluded that:

> Women's success is unique and differentiated by leaders with high levels of agility and resilience who collaborate to gain influence. These women are motivated by the opportunity to make a difference, rather than power for its own sake. We need to value these skills as a profound contribution to C-suite strength.[2]

As his contribution to arguments about the value of a diverse workforce, Richard Denniss, the chief economist at the Australia Institute wrote in the *Guardian Weekly* on October 11, 2019:

> There are lots of reasons why our parliaments, our company boards and our media feeds should be as diverse as the communities that we live in ... The main one is fairness ... and then there is performance.

To support the latter claim Denniss quotes the *International Monetary Fund*:

> Our analysis springs from the observation – supported by considerable microeconomic evidence – that women and men bring different skills and perspectives to the workplace, including different attitudes to risk and collaboration. Studies have also shown that the financial performance of firms improves with more gender-equal corporate boards.[3]

On June 19, 2020 an exciting thing happened that further added to my collection of data about the value of a diverse workforce: a link to an ABC News article written by journalist Annabel Crabb landed in my Inbox. Crabb's article announced some 'electrifying new research' that is 'a world first because of the causal role it identifies between greater gender diversity and business success.'[4]

The study was conducted over six years by the federal Workplace Gender Equality Agency (WGEA) and led by researchers Rebecca Cassells and Alan Duncan from the Bankwest Curtin Economics Centre. They found that increasing equal representation of women across each of the key leadership roles in an organisation added market value of between $52 million and $70 million per year for an average sized organisation. In other words: more women in leadership results led to better business performance. The researchers tracked organisations and their leadership appointments, and their specific findings established direct proof that:

> Companies who appointed a female CEO increased their market value by 5 percent – worth nearly $80 million to an average ASX200 company.

> Increasing the number of women in other key leadership positions by 10 per cent or more … increased a company's market value by 6.6 per cent or an average of $105 million.[5]

Further, the researchers found what we women already knew: that women have differing leadership styles from men – they tend to be more democratic, more collaborative and to have a greater sense of corporate social responsibility. As well, they found that women are less likely to participate in fraudulent behaviour than men.

Cassells and Duncan also explored what practitioners in the EEO field like to call 'homo-social reproduction' and what these researchers call the 'tyranny of incumbency'. This is about senior people recruiting their own kind, while leaving an 'untapped talent pool' of women in less senior roles.[6]

Another text that helped me explore the value of a gender diverse workforce was the book *Women and leadership* written by Julia Gillard and Ngozi Okonjo-Iweala. These authors interviewed eight international female political leaders including Hillary Clinton and Jacinda Ardern. The book was structured in eight rather quirky hypotheses about issues relating to women as leaders, and the authors used their research to test these hypotheses. On the topic of the value women bring to organisations, Gillard and Okonjo-Iweala tell their readers that the fifth of the UN's 17 goals to guide activities on sustainable development from now until 2030 is about achieving gender equality, 'for hard-headed, not feel-good reasons'.[7]

And finally, from former Sex Discrimination Commissioner Kate Jenkins in her opening address to The Beijing Platform for Action, 25 years on: Progress, Retreat and the Future of Women's Rights conference that was held online in Australia on December 3, 2020:

> As we know, women's rights are first and foremost a question of justice. But achieving gender equality also makes good sense for

everyone. Progressing gender equality not only promotes the rights of women, it also increases the efficiency and productivity of our business economy and community. And, in turn, the absence of women from the paid economy acts as a thorny roadblock to the healthy and robust economy for which almost every country strives.[8]

Interviewees

Here is what my interviewees had to say about what women want (and don't want), and their thoughts about the value of a gender diverse workplace.

LM, a legal counsel in an international finance company, brought her training in the law to her argument about the value of a diverse workforce. She explored the need for senior people to bring what she called 'diversity of thought'. LM concluded that:

I believe that more diversity will lead to better corporate conduct, fewer scandals, greater whistle blowing, fairer outcomes and an equal society for all.

DP, a consultant in leadership and organisational change told me that 'what women want is to be taken seriously'.

PM, a former health professional and politician who is now a cattle breeder, was quite clear in her answer: 'what women want is equality at work and at home'.

DD, a former senior corporate HR executive who now runs her own international motorcycle adventure soul safari company, shared her frustrations with me about what she'd both observed and experienced in her younger years:

Completely unprofessional, disrespectful and unacceptable behaviours between a boss and his subordinate/direct reports. Emotionally I now feel angry that I (and other young women were and are) subjected to inappropriate behaviour, and then are inclined to internalise it, and take on that I/they have done something to cause/ create the situation. I am also disappointed that the culture of the organisations at the time condoned, in some way subtly sent messages to bosses that this behaviour was OK.

AN is a younger woman who'd worked in communications/marketing, business development and sustainability in organisations and now consults online in personal development from Australia for a UK based firm. Hers is an example about the loss of talent in organisations that don't provide women with what they want. AN told me that she'd voluntarily left two organisations without a job to go to. Why?

> *Because I wanted to try new things, be more independent with my time, have more control over my day and how I am in the world, and to be able to define my own life.*

Conclusions

As I've already explained, in over 30 years as a leadership coach, I've provided support to leaders in large corporations, professional services firms, and the higher education and not-for-profit sectors. Most of my clients have been women – either in senior positions, or those who'd been identified as emerging leaders, and were offered coaching support to help them further develop their careers.

Some of these women were in line roles in a profit-making centre, but most were working in either organisation development (OD) or human resources (HR), which are both seen as cost centres to business. The responsibilities for OD and HR professionals inevitably mean they are change agents, and many of the women I've coached over the years have been in the especially tough change agent roles that used to be called equal opportunity managers but are now inclusion and diversity (I&D) managers.

The sometimes subtle, yet stubborn, resistance to change that so many of my clients have told me about has led me to conclude that, despite all the research cited above about the benefits of a gender diverse workforce, the hearts and minds of many senior leaders remain resistant to making the changes still needed to fully open the way for women in their workplaces.

So, why women too? I've lost count of the number of intelligent capable women I've coached, who've walked away from organisations to set up their own businesses because they were not being valued, nor given the opportunity to further develop and contribute their full potential. Thus, my conclusion from my own experiences, my research, and my interviewees in response to this question is, that it is this waste of talent that is the most compelling argument for why organisations need to change to tap their women's full potential.

I'm relieved that there is now dollar/bottom-line data from places like the Bankwest Curtin Economics Centre and McKinsey & Company to convince the sceptics of the need for this change. But come on gents, get your act together, the message is now clear that, quite aside from the fairness argument, it's dumb business to be only tapping half the pool of your available talent.

Chapter 2

The gang of three – sexism, misogyny, and patriarchy

I n the last chapter I looked at some of the research arguing for the value, both qualitative and quantitative, of a gender diverse work-force. In this chapter we unpick the three thorny topics of sexism, misogyny, and patriarchy – what I'm choosing to call the 'gang of three' – all of which create barriers to women's opportunities.

I rarely listen to, or watch parliament in session, but I happened to be tuned into ABC TV on October 9, 2012, when then Prime Minister Julia Gillard stood up and delivered what became known as her 'misogyny speech'. With no notes, Gillard spoke slowly and deliberately – as was her way – and although I could sense the rage within her, she remained calm and clear as she told the Parliament that she would not be lectured to on sexism and misogyny by the then Leader of the Opposition, Tony Abbott. I watched in awe because in those 15 minutes she told Parliament and the women of Australia that she, too, had experienced both overt and covert sexism. Furthermore, she used neither the victim nor the gender card, as she said emphatically that these behaviours had to stop.

The political press reported Gillard's speech as a 'dud', accusing her of 'playing the gender card', and predicting that it would backfire on her. They were wrong. Gillard's speech went viral – when I last checked there'd been almost three million views on YouTube, and one of my sisters even gave my other two siblings and me a tea towel for Christmas that year with the speech printed on it. Lucky me – I can now reminisce about that superb speech as I dry my dishes.

Sir Humphrey's words in an episode of *Yes Minister* keep coming to my mind as I ponder my thoughts regarding sexism, misogyny, and patriarchy. The minister was arguing for greater equal opportunity for women, to which Sir Humphrey, the senior bureaucrat, replied, 'I think this is a good idea in principle, Minister. After all, some of my best friends are women.' True to form, Sir Humphrey was resisting the idea that his department or, heaven forbid even he, needed to change for women to show up in greater numbers in the British political system. I used to get a lot of laughs from my mostly male participants when I showed a small section of this episode at my equal opportunity seminars for managers back in the late '80s and early '90s. But in that one short sentence Humphrey was of course expressing the entrenched attitudes of many well-meaning men who continue to enjoy the status quo in both their organisations and lives and are not keen to see this destabilised.

As I've heard said, 'to the privileged, equality feels like oppression', so I guess it stands to reason that those who currently hold the power want to hang onto it for fear of the consequences to them should they have to share this with others.

Men can, of course, be the victims of sexism too. I well remember the hard time we female nurses gave the first few men who dared to enter 'our' profession. They'd had the courage to challenge a long-held stereotype that nursing was women's work. Once there, however, they soon soared to senior positions while we female nurses stood around wondering how this had happened. On reflection I've realised that their conditioning as a male meant they were ambitious for promotion, whereas the conditioning of we women meant that we simply wanted to do a good job and please our patients. And on further reflection, I would add that despite nursing having at the time an almost exclusively female hierarchy, a disproportionate number of male nurses were promoted, which suggests that the powers that be assumed men were more suited to supervisory and management positions than my female colleagues and me.

What about my experiences of the gang of three? I was born in 1946 – the cusp of the Baby Boomer years in Australia. I was raised in a happy family that conformed to the patriarchal model: my mother was a (mostly) stay at home mother and housewife and did the bulk of raising us four kids, while Dad earned the money to feed, clothe and educate us. I married young, changed my name to his, and was quite unconsciously repeating the model of my parents until I took a dangerous step – I attended an assertiveness training course. For a while after that I tried to juggle between being a good wife and mother to our two kids and an emerging feminist, but that assertiveness training course was my moment of awakening. Once I'd learnt that I was entitled to state my needs and expect to have these met, I found I could no longer remain silent. Looking back, I could well have been labelled a 'radical feminist' for a few years, as I flexed my womanly muscles in, at times, clumsy ways. My marriage didn't survive this turbulence, and I launched into a new career with a driven urge to improve the status of women in Australia (more about that in chapter 4, EEO and me).

In my new independent life, I assumed I'd left the patriarchy behind, but I certainly bumped up against a fair bit of resistance over the next few years, both in my business and personal life. I can recall an example of being treated in a sexist way – which I can now see was a repeating pattern for me – that went like this: I would be in the early stages of interacting with a man – be that a client in my business or a prospective suitor. I would appear warm and charming, and he would assume I was a pushover and that he would be able to 'have his way' with me, whether that was in negotiating down my charge out rate, or my willingness to go to bed with him. When I would then express my outrage to him about this assumption, my prospective client or suitor would look hurt and baffled and withdraw in a sulk.

Now in my eighth decade, I believe that that strident woman has found a sense of her own self. Further, that the negotiating skills I've learned over the years mean I am easier to relate with at work and at play, while continuing to stay true to my feminist beliefs.

As I write this chapter, I find myself trawling back through my memory for examples of sexism and the domination of patriarchy that I saw during my years of consulting, coaching, and mentoring. The examples that come to mind are of the subtle ones that were, and are, more about the way work is structured than because men set out to deliberately discriminate against women in their workplaces. For example, how, after a woman had announced the happy news that she was pregnant, she began noticing that she was no longer invited to key meetings, and that she was being left off the list of participants for the next professional development program. And, how a woman's career would stall when she refused her next promotion, because it involved a move interstate or overseas, and she felt she couldn't derail her husband's career or pull her kids out of school. And for a third example, of women being a minority voice in meetings and finding their suggestions only gained traction when one of the men repeated it. The list could go on, but I trust these examples illustrate how current work practices can, and still do, stall women's progression without anybody overtly setting out to disadvantage them.

Finally, before I move on to what my research on the gang of three has found, I wish to put in a word of reassurance to the men in my life. Like Sir Humphrey, but in reverse, some of my best friends are men, and I want to assure my readers that this is not an anti-men book. Far from it – I've seen first-hand some of the constraints that patriarchy has put upon my dear brother and, to a lesser extent, my beloved son, both of whom I regard as two of my best friends. In fact, I'm hopeful that the changes I'm arguing for in this book will benefit not only us women, but also all those men who are yearning to make a bigger contribution to their family life, and to live a fuller life than the current, old-fashioned notion of 'male breadwinner' that has burdened them until now.

Research

When I reflect on my decades of experience as an EO consultant, leadership coach and mentor, I realise that the words sexism, misogyny and patriarchy were rarely, if ever, used. The statistics that employers of over 100 people were required to gather and report on under the *Affirmative Action (Equal Employment Opportunity for Women) Act 1986* (Cth) and that I used to present at my EO awareness seminars for managers, painted a picture of a gender-stereotyped workforce. Women were clustered in the services and support roles, and either missing or in a tiny minority, at a senior level. But no one, including me, the so-called expert in EEO and AA, ever said that these statistics were a clear demonstration of a culture that was patriarchal and infused with sexism and misogyny. A wise man I once knew used to say that 'if you go in the water, you can't help getting wet', to describe the pervasive nature of corporate culture. And it's only now that I can see that all of us were similarly encultured, and sadly many continue to be so.

So, how to unpick what the research tells us about what I'm choosing to call this gang of three?

Author, journalist and feminist Anne Summers in her book *The misogyny factor* has helped me understand the link between sexism and misogyny. She tells her readers that these two go hand in hand, and that sexism provides the rationale for misogyny, which in turn comes from an attitude towards women that excludes them, treats them as inferiors, and denies them respect:

> *Sexism, like racism, ascribes attributes to people on the basis of a single inherited and immutable characteristic – a person's sex or their race – without regard to their individuality, and is then used as the basis for treating them differently and unfavourably. ….*
> *If misogyny is the theory of women's inferiority and unworthiness and, therefore, unsuitability to be equal players in our society, sexism is the everyday expression of it.*[9]

Summers proposes that it is because of the misogyny factor that, despite a raft of sex discrimination and affirmative action legislation in Australia over the past few decades, the efforts of several generations of feminists, and myriads of well-meaning change programs in the Australian workplace since the mid '80s, we still live in a society in which women do not have real equality with men.

Robert Jensen, a professor of journalism in the USA in his 2017 book *The end of patriarchy* helped me understand the role of patriarchy in the gang of three. Jensen defines patriarchy as 'a system of social structures and practices in which men dominate, oppress and exploit women'.[10] He writes that it has taken several thousand years to embed institutionalised male dominance in our world and that this has come to define virtually all our interactions within the family and between humans and the larger living world.

Further Jensen believes that 'patriarchy turns the biological differences between men and women into social and political gender inequality, that institutionalised male dominance continues to structure our lives and influence our understanding of ourselves, and that the ultimate goal is to achieve a society that transcends patriarchy'.[11] He sees feminism as a crucial element of any program that is created to achieve social justice, which is why patriarchal forces do their best to eliminate or marginalise feminist ideas; and he goes on to say that a 'just society that guarantees dignity for women is impossible' in a patriarchal society.

Like me, Jensen believes that patriarchy can be tough on men as well as women. In fact, he admits that patriarchy meant that he was raised in a culture of such 'toxic masculinity' that not only subordinated women but also 'crippled' his capacity to be fully himself. Jensen suggests that the goal is to build a 'just society' with a gender system that guarantees the dignity of both women and men. And he argues that as we strive to achieve this goal, we must hold onto our core values of dignity, solidarity, and equality.[12]

I next turn in my research to a good read called *Sapiens: A brief history of humankind* by Yuval Noah Harari.[13] Harari helped me to make sense of patriarchy from an historical perspective.

Harari asks his readers why is it that since the Agricultural Revolution, most human societies have been patriarchal ones in which men are valued more highly than women. He tries without success to come up with a biological reason why patriarchy continues to rule the world. He looks at, but then challenges the assumption that it's about male muscle power, or that men are more aggressive. Another explanation Harari explores is a biological one: that over time the masculine genes that thrived were those belonging to the most ambitious, aggressive, and competitive men, whereas the feminine genes that made it through, belonged to women who were and are the more submissive caretaker types.

Harari, the author of this long yet fascinating book, remains unconvinced of any logical explanation for patriarchal societies. He concludes by reassuring the reader that gender roles have undergone a massive change over the past century. Yet why then, I ask, is sexism still alive and well and so seemingly entrenched in our so-called modern societies?

Irrespective of its cause, I found confirmation of the fact that the patriarchal system is still alive and well from reading the master thesis of a friend called Margaret Kelly. Completed in 2017, her thesis is titled *Turning the spotlight on the 'wizard behind the curtain'. How do transgender women experience and navigate male privilege and entitlement, pre- and post-transition?* The thesis summarises Kelly's findings from qualitative interviews with 12 transgender women to find out their experience of privilege in the Australian society as a man, and then as a woman.

Two key findings stand out for me from this extraordinary piece of research:

> *Participants who had privilege when they lived as men were largely unaware of the advantage at that time. However, on transition, they became acutely aware of the loss of privilege.*

> *All participants, post-transition, reported a newfound fear for their personal safety. This was particularly so for participants who had enjoyed privilege when they lived as men.*[14]

In her conclusion Kelly wrote about how the study participants who'd enjoyed authority and privilege when they lived as men, were surprised and shocked at its loss when they transitioned. And further, that three participants even expressed shame about how they now realised that they'd abused their privilege and discriminated against some men, and all women, when they lived as a man.

Although a small sample, I believe Kelly's findings confirm Jensen's reflections about the fact that many men continue to act in ways that perpetuate the patriarchy which in turn harms women.

I felt dejected as I read in the December 17, 2018, edition of *The Conversation* that research by Lisa Heap and two other academics at the then Institute of Religion, Politics and Society, at the Australian Catholic University found that current workplace laws that are aimed to protect women are not achieving their goal. These laws include the histori-cally significant sex discrimination and affirmative action laws that are described in detail in the next chapter. As these authors wrote:

> *Workplace laws designed to protect women are ineffective because they fail to address the gender inequality, disadvantage and dis-crimination due to caring responsibilities, and being subjected to gendered violence.*[15]

21

Journalist David Leser in his book *Women, men and the whole damn thing* writes about the 'alphabet soup' of patriarchy that we are all exposed to every day whether we're aware of this or not. In a skype interview Leser had with Eve Ensler (famous for her play, *The vagina monologues*), she posed a question about what men can do to challenge the impact of patriarchy in their lives and allow their feminine sides to flourish. Leser unpicks answers to Ensler's question throughout his book.

Former Prime Minister Julia Gillard is now an author as well as a board member on some national and international organisations spanning the education and health sectors. From her book *Women and leadership* co-authored with Nigerian leader Ngozi Okonjo-Iweala I learnt a new word – 'intersectionality'. They explain that this is a word used to explain that every day millions of women confront more than one form of discrimination – not just sexism but also racism and disadvantage based on things like their sexuality, their gender identity, their disability and their health status – in particular their mental health status.[16]

One form of discrimination that women continue to experience in the Australian workplace is the gender pay gap. I've written more about this in chapter 15.

As I was doing a final edit of this chapter about the gang of three, I found out about the work of two psychologists, Susan Fiske and Peter Glick, who together have reconceptualised sexism. Fiske and Glick have differentiated sexism into two categories: hostile sexism and benevolent sexism. They define hostile sexism as anything that demeans women and is typically a form of 'subtle hostility', whereas they explain that benevolent sexism is paternalistic and includes protective behaviours towards women such as chivalry.[17]

In an article at *neuroleadership.com* called The Science of How 'Benevolent Sexism' Undermines Women, Glick explains that an example of benevolent sexism is when a male boss doesn't give a female team member a challenging assignment because he fears it might be too stressful or demanding for her. Another example is when a male boss doesn't give a woman honest critical feedback because he worries it might hurt her feelings. It's easy to see that a possible outcome of both scenarios might be that women miss out on a promotion because they haven't proved themselves through a challenging assignment, and/or haven't had the opportunity to learn from some frank and fearless feedback.[18]

Benevolent sexism can therefore undermine women's equality and lead them to doubt themselves, and these two researchers believe that this can be even more damaging to women in the workforce than hostile sexism. Why? Because where a woman can call out hostile sexism, it's more difficult for her to name benevolent sexism because it's highly likely that her boss believes he's 'only trying to be kind and helpful'.

And a shout out to any chaps who might be reading this book: I enjoy a bit of chivalry as much as the next woman, but not when it assumes I can't do something myself, or if it limits my opportunities – what we might call paternalistic chivalry.

Interviewees

TT has been a federal public servant and now consults to, and coaches senior leaders. She suggested to me that political correctness is often a 'mask for sexism':

> In the Commonwealth Public Service overt sexism is less obvious. Respect for all is a part of their values framework and necessary to guide public sector behaviour. But what I see more often than not, is countless displays of 'political correctness' and not necessarily deeply held representations of gender equity. The overt language isn't there, it's very much frowned upon, but the visibility of entitlement most certainly is. To a large extent, this 'correctness' often masks sexism and keeps it from being truly challenged. It's a pervasive sense – and the simple examples are demonstrated on a daily basis: the majority of voices heard in meetings are generally male, regardless of gender ratio. The first to answer a question, male; be the first to talk, male; be the first to ask questions; male. The casual conversations represent the broader community...throw away sexist lines are there as much as anywhere. If you believe in women, and all people having an equal opportunity, you don't presume entitlement based on 'maleness'. You create space for all people to contribute equally. When there is a disconnect between what is said, and what is truly believed, it shows. And in my experience, most of my male colleagues didn't really believe in equity, not deep down.

> *They were definitely being politically correct but it lacked depth and*
> *real sincerity.*

MY who worked in an equal opportunity role in the oil industry for a number of years over 30 years ago, gave me a fascinating example of sexism in action from back in her oil industry days:

> *A sales manager once told me that he'd never select a woman to*
> *work for him. When I asked him why he said, 'Because if a service*
> *station manager was rude to her and she cried, I would have to*
> *intervene.' I shared this example with the marketing director who*
> *said his team shouldn't have people like that working for it. To which*
> *I said, 'Well, you wouldn't have very many people working for you,*
> *because there are so many that think like that.'*

JKR, a historian, academic and then a federal and state public servant (a so-called 'femocrat') told me that she believes that sexism is the 'tool of patriarchy'.

JKR also lamented the fact that:

> *After the exciting and productive years of the late '80s and early '90's*
> *when affirmative action programs were common and the Australian*
> *government was taking UN Conventions for women seriously, we've*
> *seen from the mid '90s a 'systematic whittling away of these kinds of*
> *achievements, from the Howard years and beyond.*

EM, a retired CIO, stressed the point that true equality for women will only be achieved once there is a recognition that 'this will involve treating women differently from men because we are different'.

PS, an agriculturalist and one of my male interviewees, said in response to my question about the patriarchy:

> *Yes, I'm well aware of patriarchy still existing. There are most cer-*
> *tainly 'boys' clubs' in sport, politics, industry etc.*

What more can be done?

I believe that sex discrimination and affirmative action law and policy remain an essential base from which a range of innovative programs and processes must now be added. These laws were legislated in the early

'80s in the context of a (debated) decision that such legislation was a useful strategy to move change in workplace practices and attitudes to women. There's more about the history of this, and the Acts now in place, in the next chapter.

So, what else needs to change for the gang of three to be eliminated so that women can achieve a fair go in the Australian workplace? Drawing on my own experience, my research and the opinions of my interviewees, I believe that there needs to be a two-pronged approach for further change to happen: one, targeting the senior executives in organisations to require them to make the necessary systems and policy changes that will break down both the overt and covert barriers to women; and the other, targeting women themselves to be supported to reclaim their power.

In my role as an EO consultant I worked hard for several years to do my bit to help achieve the first of this two-pronged approach through facilitating EO awareness seminars for managers and leaders in the public, private, higher education and not-for-profit sectors. For more detail about these seminars, see chapters 4 and 6. For now, suffice to say that, at the time I was running them (the late '80s and early '90s), I could see that my participants were intelligent people. I sincerely believed that information sessions such as these would serve to change their hearts and minds, such that they would return to their workplaces fully committed to making the changes needed for them to become a true equal opportunity employer. Sad to say, time has proved me wrong.

Also, in my role as an EO consultant, and with the goal of supporting women to reclaim their power, I developed and facilitated dozens of career development programs for women in my client organisations, as well as public workshops in several of Australia's larger cities. These programs included practical things like goal setting, how to create a network of support with other women, as well as the importance of accessing mentors and sponsors. At the core of each program was an opportunity for participants to explore their vision and values, to learn assertiveness skills to negotiate for what they now wanted to achieve and, most importantly, to explore how to challenge any self-limiting thinking they had, and so to grow their self-confidence and step into their personal power.

There was always a degree of pushback about running a program for women only. 'What about the men?' was the common refrain, not only from men, but from women as well, who felt uncomfortable about being given this special opportunity. For these programs to succeed, what was needed was the public sponsorship of the CEO or managing director, and where this occurred, I saw women growing in confidence before my eyes. I still hear from women who tell me that attending one of these programs was a profound turning point in their career.

So, what more can be done? In terms of the first of my so-called two-pronged approach – that of requiring senior executives to make the change – I understand that unconscious bias workshops for managers and leaders are now in vogue. However, from my research and anecdotally as well, I'm discovering that these are being proven to have limited effectiveness. As I've suggested elsewhere in this book, retirement is helping to move things along. Older leaders with entrenched attitudes hand over to younger leaders, some of whom have been raised and educated in a feminist world, and many of whom probably have professional partners and even daughters, who they absolutely assume will experience a fair go at work.

On the second of my two-pronged approach – that of helping women reclaim their power – I believe programs like the ones I used to run could be readily adapted to the digital age to help achieve this goal.

In terms of how to measure the effectiveness of the change that is currently needed, there were a wide range of opinions among my interviewees about whether it's time for organisations to set quotas or targets as a goal to work towards. One of the more common arguments for setting a measure, whatever it gets called, is that this is done for all other change programs, so why not in relation to equity in the workplace programs? To me this is a no brainer: of course, organisations must measure the effectiveness of their change initiatives, and how else to do this but to set some measures whatever these get called? There's more about the controversial quota question in chapter 8.

In terms of what further change is needed for women, Gillard shares some wise counsel to other women striving for senior leadership positions in *Women and leadership*. She wrote that the longer she served as prime minister, the worse the sexism became, so that on reflection she would have done two things differently: she would have named it sooner, and she would have encouraged community leaders, especially men, to comment publicly on the sexism she experienced because they would have been seen as having a more objective opinion.

I'll give author and journalist Anne Summers the final word about what needs to be done to fully overcome the gang of three of sexism, misogyny and patriarchy in Australia:

> *It's time to stop asking nicely for what is rightfully ours. It's time to demand equality. And that means confronting, head-on, the continuing and entrenched bias … towards women in this country.*[19]

Conclusions

Having unpicked the gang of three in this chapter, my first conclusion is at a personal level. My own journey towards fully believing that I'm entitled to have an equal place with men on planet earth has been about doing my best to exorcise the influence of sexism and misogyny from my life. However, I realise that in spite of my best efforts to achieve this, patriarchy still lurks, and I need to remain ever alert to avoiding its influence.

Another conclusion is that my passion for supporting other women through my coaching and mentoring services over the last three decades, has been driven from the desire to help them to do the same. And when I hear about how my clients are thriving in their chosen worlds, I'm filled with joy.

At an organisational level, my conclusions are that there is no longer the overt resistance to making the Australian workplace fair for women that I had to face in my early years of EO consulting. It is now the more covert things, like the way work is structured and the unconscious biases of some of those still at the top, that continue to hold up progress for change. This topic will be discussed at length in chapter 14 *What on earth is going on?*

I fear I won't see the end of the insidious influence of the gang of three in my lifetime; nor perhaps will my daughter and son in theirs. Nevertheless, my hope is that in my five granddaughters' lifetimes, the patriarchy will at last have been found wanting, and will have faded into oblivion with perhaps more a whimper than a bang.

Chapter 3

What does the law say?

Now that we've unpicked the three 'bad guys' of sexism, misogyny and patriarchy in the previous chapter, in this chapter Lindsay Mackay, a friend and colleague, will outline the history, and nature, of the laws that have made these 'bad guys' unlawful in Australia.

Introduction

Australia has, at times, been a leader for law reform on gender equality: it was the second jurisdiction to grant white women the vote and the first to grant white women the right to hold elected office.[20] History tells us that many of these reforms were hard won through social movements led by women but were often only successful when the reforms also reflected the interests of those in power, when there was a convergence of interests.[21]

This history of anti-discrimination and affirmative action in Australia has been a story of social movements driving parliaments to enact laws prohibiting certain behaviour rather than finding enshrined rights and principles of equality or duties. This has resulted in a complex matrix of prohibitions enacted by individual parliaments at different times in different jurisdictions. Even in 2021 and beyond, the public discourse on sexual harassment, sexual assault, violence against women and '#MeToo' can be traced back to specific incidents where individuals spoke up or took action.[22]

Along the way the social movements were met with responses that change was not necessary and in fact would harm others who already had rights.[23] The question asked was, what damage would this do to the status quo? This resonates with the more recent movements and the fear articulated in the public discourse that people would be wrongly accused of sexual harassment, defamed and reputations would be damaged.[24]

In 2022, Australia ranked 43rd out of 146 countries in the Global Gender Gap Index, 38th in terms of women's economic participation and 50th in political empowerment.[25] Have our laws focused too much on the individual cases of misconduct and not enough on rights, and too much on specific instances of discrimination and not enough on what we must do to achieve equality? Do we rely too much on individuals and groups of women to bring about change?

Anti-discrimination legislation

Anti-discrimination laws seek to prohibit unfair treatment of particular groups of people in society who share a common identity or 'attribute', such as race, gender, sexuality and disability, which has been specified in the law for protection.[26]

Protected attributes generally include age, race, religious belief, sex, sexual orientation, pregnancy or potential pregnancy, breastfeeding, having caring responsibilities, having a disability, employment activity, gender identity, industrial activity, irrelevant criminal conviction, lawful sexual activity, marital status, parental status, physical features, political belief or activity or having a personal association with someone who has one of these characteristics. Generally, the laws make it unlawful to directly or indirectly discriminate against a person with a protected attribute.

Direct discrimination is treating a person or group less favourably than another because they have a protected attribute or characteristic, such as refusing to hire someone who is pregnant.[27]

Indirect discrimination is a practice that results in a person or group being disadvantaged because they have the protected attribute.[28] For example, the police requirement for police officers to be a certain height indirectly discriminated against females because females are generally shorter than males, so this rule indirectly resulted in fewer females in the police force. It is usually a defence if the discrimination is justified by the inherent requirements of the role or there would otherwise be unjustifiable hardship, as well as specific legislative exemptions.

In Australia, protection from discrimination is not enshrined in a constitutional or statutory bill of rights or as a fundamental principle of law identified by judges in cases before the courts. Following the pressure of social movements and international influences, state and federal parliaments have legislated for protection from discrimination, choosing to protect different attributes at different times and in different ways in the various statutes. This has resulted in eight different state and territory anti-discrimination laws and four Commonwealth anti-discrimination laws. While the laws are similar, there are technical differences which create complexity and there have been calls for consolidation and reform,[29] most recently in the *Respect@Work: Sexual Harassment National Inquiry Report (2020) (Respect@Work Report)* issued on 5 March 2020,[30] and the *Free & Equal: A reform agenda for federal discrimination laws Position Paper*[31] issued by the Australian Human Rights Commission in December 2021.

The Constitution

While Australia does not have any specific constitutional protection for human rights (unlike the United States, which has recognition of certain human rights of its citizens in its constitution) protection from discrimination was considered in the drafting of the Australian Constitution.

After the 1890 Federation Convention, the Attorney-General of Tasmania Andrew Inglis Clark included a right to equal protection under the law in his preliminary draft of the 1891 Constitution Bill. At the 1898 Federation Convention he then sought to expand this to explicitly say that the state should not be able to deprive a person of the equal protection of its laws, based on the 14th Amendment of the Constitution of the United States.[32] This stemmed from a desire to create a federal citizenship based on the experience of the United States.[33]

These proposals were attacked on the basis that they could limit laws of certain colonies that restricted the employment of workers based on race.[34] For example, the colony in Western Australia restricted mining employment of people of African or Asian descent as well as having immigration restrictions. There was also clearly a desire in the Constitution to discriminate against First Nations Australians, with discriminatory references to Indigenous Australians included.[35]

It was considered to be unnecessary to include human rights or statements about equality in Australia. It was not common in constitutions other than in the United States at the time to include statements about human rights and equality. It was expected that these goals would be achieved through government institutions.[36] As a result, there were limited rights against anti-discrimination enshrined in the Australian Constitution. Section 117 protects residents of one state from discrimination by another state on the basis of residence.[37] This was the final formulation of Clark's proposal for protection from discrimination.

It was not until 1967 that the discriminatory reference to Indigenous Australians was removed from the Constitution by referendum. The High Court later found that there is no implied right of equality in the Australian Constitution.[38]

The lack of protection of individual rights in the Constitution has forced governments to rely on various indirect powers in order to legislate anti-discrimination laws. These include the power to legislate for external affairs (to implement international treaties), and the power to make laws related to the activities of corporations and trade and commerce (or a combination of several powers or as many as possible).[39] There have been several challenges seeking to invalidate anti-discrimination laws.[40]

Certain states and territories have since established charters or legislation for human rights: the ACT since 2004, Victoria since 2006 and Queensland since 2019.[41] This requires their governments to consider human rights in formulating law and policy and gives people the opportunity to seek justice if their rights are violated. While an Australian Bill of Rights was first proposed in 1973,[42] there is no federal charter of human rights at the time of writing. In December 2022 following several years of consultation, the Australian Human Rights Commission issued a Position Paper[43] recommending that the Australian Parliament enact an Australian Human Rights Act and setting out its recommended model. The Australian Human Rights Commission cited human rights concerns associated with Australian governments' responses to the COVID-19 pandemic as demonstrating why a legislated bill of human rights is required in Australia.[44]

Judge-made law

Australian common law, where judges interpret the law in cases before them, historically did not establish a principle against discrimination. For example, judges historically did not recognise the equality of men and women. Early Australian courts considered that women were 'not persons' able to vote or to enter many professions.[45] In Australia, this continued even after women had won the right to vote.

Similarly, before World War I, arbitration judge Judge Higgins referred to tailoresses as 'invaders of the workforce'[46] and another judge, Judge Heydon, would not find a right to equal pay because men were the main breadwinners in a family and should be protected by the court.[47] At the time both employers and judges considered it to be within their rights to examine a woman's family life and circumstances in order to determine employment matters.[48] They would ask questions about whether a woman was married, where her husband was and who was looking after the home, and then base employment decisions on this.

In 1882 tailoresses in Melbourne formed the first women's union at a meeting in Trades Hall on 15 December, which led its members on strikes. There were women's unions formed in the 1880s and 1890s by tailoresses, barmaids, waitresses, teachers and public servants.[49] First Nations women had also gone on strike before this time seeking to be paid for their labour.

While in some industries there were female rates of pay, women were not allowed in the union and therefore not covered by the award. Therefore, the union branded these employers as 'anti-union' for hiring women at all and women had to lead the struggle for their equal pay.

For example, in evidence given in response to the tailoresses strike of 1901, one employer of Sydney firm Anthony Hordern and Sons – who referred to the women striking as 'little girls' – reported that he had done the right thing when a woman sought employment by enquiring what her husband was doing. The husband had previously sought work from Hordern but Hordern had refused to give him a job. Hordern resolved the situation by employing the woman for 15 shillings and her husband for 25 shillings, which was just under one labourer's wage at the time of 42 shillings. Hordern described this as doing a kindness to the couple, when in fact he was getting two employees for the price of one.[50]

In the equal pay cases, such as the 1907 'Harvester case', the Commonwealth Court of Arbitration determined the minimum wage based on a male and what he would need to support a family.[51]

From around 1912, in the 'Fruit Pickers case' before Arbitration Courts, Judge Higgins determined that employers should consider that an adult male has dependants and women are provided for, either by their fathers or their husbands. Judge Higgins inferred that women were not under obligations to care for dependants 'unless perhaps in very exceptional circumstances'.[52] However, the reality was that women often did have to care for dependants, when their husband had passed away or was unable to work or they had to care for their parents or relatives. Justice Higgins felt that employers should not have to take into account specific employee circumstances where women unusually did have to provide for others. Therefore, in an industry like fruit picking, where the workers were mostly female, he set a rate for women based on their own food, clothing and shelter needs but not that of providing for a family as was the case for males.

In 1902 women telegraphists and postmistresses briefly won equal pay and status in the Commonwealth Public Service Act[53] (through an Act of legislation, not common law made by judges). The victory was short-lived as two years later, in 1904, a ban was imposed on married women being employed in the public service. Many of the very women activists who had achieved equal pay for public servants, were now no longer able to work at all. Repeal of this provision did not take place until 1948 in New South Wales (earlier in that state due to the continued opposition by women teachers) and 1966 in other states.

The first Commonwealth Conciliation and Arbitration Commission ruling to secure equal pay for women performing the same roles as men in traditionally male roles did not come until 1969. It was not until 1972 that women and men undertaking similar work were eligible for the same pay. In 1973 there was a ruling granting an equal minimum wage to all Australians regardless of sex and in 1974, the breadwinner component of a male wage was finally removed.

In November 2022, there is still a wage gap of 13.3% of male average earnings with women earning, on average, $253.50 per week less than men.[54] This has been affected by the COVID-19 pandemic, which saw the gender pay gap widen as a higher proportion of women reduced their working hours to meet caring responsibilities and growth occurred in the traditionally male-dominated construction industry.[55] Before this the trend was downward, although at the previous trend rate it may take another quarter of a century to reach parity.[56]

International influences

After the Second World War, in an effort to prevent the human rights atrocities that had occurred from happening again, the United Nations established treaties to protect human rights with the fundamental principle of non-discrimination.[57] The United Nations Charter of 1945 included promoting 'universal respect for, and observance of, human rights and fundamental freedoms for all without distinction as to race, sex, language, or religion'.[58]

In 1946 the United Nations Commission on the Status of Women (UNCSW)[59] was established 'to raise the status of women … and to eliminate all discrimination against women in the provisions of statutory law, in legal maxims or rules, or in interpretation of customary law'.[60] The UNCSW contributed to the Universal Declaration of Human Rights to include gender inclusive language.

The Universal Declaration of Human Rights of 1948 provides that 'everyone is entitled to all the rights and freedoms set forth in this Declaration, without distinction of any kind, such as race, colour, sex, language, religion, political or other opinion, national or social origin, property, birth or other status'.[61]

It was adopted and guaranteed women the right to vote, hold public office and exercise public functions.[62]

The International Labour Organisation (ILO) developed treaties on labour rights, including defining discrimination in the ILO Convention Concerning Discrimination in Respect of Occupation and Employment

(1958) as 'any distinction, exclusion or preference made on the basis of race, colour, sex, religion, political opinion, national extraction or social origin, which as the effect of nullifying or impairing equality of opportunity or treatment in employment or occupation...'[63]

This was then followed by a specific ILO treaty against racial discrimination in 1965.[64] The United Nations General Assembly then approved the International Covenant on Civil and Political Rights[65] and International Covenant on Economic, Social and Cultural Rights,[66] which further expanded on the rights in the Universal Declaration, including introducing a right of equality that 'all persons are equal before the law and are entitled without any discrimination to the equal protection of the law'.[67]

In addition to the international bodies, several countries were enacting anti-discrimination laws throughout this time. In Canada, Ontario introduced a Racial Discrimination Act in 1944, followed by a Canadian Bill of Rights in 1960.[68] In the US, the civil rights movement led to the Civil Rights Act of 1964, which dealt with discrimination based on sex in certain spheres including voting and employment and allowed a person to bring a civil action against the person who discriminated against them.[69] It was then through judicial interpretation of these laws in the US, that the concept of direct and indirect discrimination was introduced. This then led to these concepts being first legislated in the *Sex Discrimination Act 1975* (UK).[70]

The United Nations decided to make 1975 'International Women's Year' and the decade from 1976 to 1985 the 'Decade for Women'. Then the Convention on the Elimination of All Forms of Discrimination Against Women (the Women's Convention) adopted in 1979 and in force in 1981 imposed obligations on ratifying states to provide effective legal protections of the rights.[71]

In Australia, local legislation is required to give effect to ratification of international treaties in order for them to take effect in Australia – the treaties do not automatically apply. However, the recognition of non-discrimination by the United Nations and the UK legislating the Sex Discrimination Act in 1975, combined with local social movements campaigning for rights to protection against discrimination provided an impetus for anti-discrimination legislation in Australia.[72]

Beginning in South Australia

The first anti-discrimination legislation in Australia was enacted in South Australia and assented to on 1 December 1966 with the *Prohibition of Discrimination Act 1966* (SA). This legislation made it a criminal offence to discriminate in employment on the grounds of race, skin colour and country of origin. The intention was to protect the rights of First Nations Australians and non-British migrants who had settled in South Australia after World War II. The legislation also made it an offence to refuse entry and service and to refuse to let or sell land on the basis of race.[73]

These reforms were introduced by Don Dunstan, who had a legacy of promoting the rights of Indigenous Australians and equal opportunity for women. Having been raised in Suva, Fiji, he was appalled by conditions for Aboriginal residents and began campaigning to abolish laws that discriminated against Aboriginal people in South Australia.

As the law made racial discrimination a criminal offence, to be successful, the police had to prove beyond a reasonable doubt that there was intention and a racial motive to discriminate. This was the same approach taken in the earlier Ontario, Canada laws. As a result, cases of discrimination were hard to prove and only one case was successful. The successful case involved $100 fines to a hotel company and barman who refused to serve Indigenous Australians. Another case failed because the police could not prove beyond a reasonable doubt that the refusal of service was based on race. However, some commentators have said that the legislation was successful in its psychological effect on South Australia in that there was a right not to be discriminated against and a duty on the police to enforce this.[74]

An opinion piece in *The Bulletin* at the time entitled 'Insurance against hatred'[75] reported that this law was introduced to protect the rights of those who were discriminated against. It argued that otherwise they would have no recourse given the established notion of 'freedom of commerce', i.e. the freedom to choose who to trade with. The article gave the example of an Aboriginal woman who was falsely accused of stealing money on the basis of her race and the article noted that legislation was needed to influence behaviour.

In August 1973, Liberal backbencher and eye surgeon Dr David Tonkin, who was the child of a widowed mother during the Depression, introduced a private member's bill against sex discrimination in employment, services and the provision of credit.[76] He would go on to become the leader of the Liberal Party in 1975 and then became Premier in 1979, overseeing three years of an economically conservative but socially progressive government.

When Tonkin's mother was widowed when he was five, the family struggled to make ends meet. Tonkin's mother could not get suitable employment due to a lack of training and because it was not considered the 'done thing'. The story is that his mother died on the night before he was to present the Bill in Parliament and was keen for him to go ahead as she thought it was very important to South Australia.[77] The Bill was referred to a committee, which concluded that there was discrimination but that the legislation should be presented as a government Bill so as to provide funding for the establishment of a Sex Discrimination Board.[78]

In 1975, Don Dunstan introduced the government's Sex Discrimination Bill into Parliament.[79] This Bill was broader and established the Sex Discrimination Board with the power to award damages to provide a means for complainants to have an avenue to obtain a remedy without having to prove discrimination before a court.[80] Dunstan announced that this would be a 'signal advance' that would hopefully create a 'climate in which public opinion would be mobilised against this form of discrimination'.[81] Part of the Bill was modelled on the UK Sex Discrimination Act of 1975 and prohibited both direct and indirect discrimination on the grounds of sex or marital status.[82]

This Bill was also referred to a committee who took evidence from employees and employers and found that there were discriminatory practices based on sex and marital status.[83] The Bill received Royal Assent on 4 December 1975 and was proclaimed on 12 August 1976. It protected people against discrimination on the grounds of sex or marital status and against being victimised for raising complaints about sex discrimination. From August 1976 to 30 June 1977, 154 complaints were made under the Act including around 80% from women. The Act also established an Office of the Equal Opportunity Commissioner, which was created on 12 August 1976.

The Act was repealed by the *Equal Opportunity Act 1984*, which was designed to consolidate anti-discrimination legislation in South Australia under one Act and one agency, following the recommendation of a working group on anti-discrimination legislation.[84]

South Australia had a legacy of firsts in equal opportunity legislation, including allowing white women to petition for divorce in 1858, to legally own and manage property in 1883 and to vote in 1894. It was also the home state of the first female political candidate in 1897, first women elected to a University Council in 1914, first female police officer in 1915 and first female judge appointed to the Supreme Court in 1965. In July 1965, the South Australian Industrial Court awarded pay increases for female teachers in South Australia heralding a landmark 'equal pay for equal work' judgement. This was then extended to the State Public Service in 1966.[85]

These achievements can be understood in the context of South Australia having been freely settled with roughly equal numbers of men and women and been the first jurisdiction where white women won the right to vote (after New Zealand) and the first to win the right to stand for parliament. Interestingly, the right of South Australian white women to stand for parliament was actually introduced into the suffrage Bill by conservatives. They thought that by adding the right to stand as candidates for parliament as well as to vote would be so ridiculous that it would cause the whole Bill to fail and continue to deny women the right to vote. However, to their surprise, on 18 December 1894 following the strong social momentum behind the suffrage Bill, the Bill was passed 31 votes to 14. South Australian women were granted both the right to vote and the right to stand for political office. Women came out in force to vote at the first election in 1896 and the informal vote was unusually low, seen as a mark of success.[86]

In 1899, to undermine the vote of incoming gold rush miners from the eastern states, Western Australia granted women the right to vote.[87] When federalism approached in the 1890s, South Australian women could vote on the referendum, and the convention itself was held in Adelaide.[88] Following concerns raised by Frederick Holder, former Premier of South Australia, a provision was included in the Constitution among other goals to reassure South Australians that women would not be disenfranchised, without saying so directly.[89]

The next state to legislate against sex discrimination was New South Wales in 1977 with the *Anti-Discrimination Act 1977* (NSW), which covered discrimination on the basis of race, sex and ethnic origin.

At the federal level

The first federal anti-discrimination legislation was the *Racial Discrimination Act 1975* (Cth). It was enacted by the Whitlam Government using the power in the Constitution to legislate for external affairs to implement Australia's commitment to the United Nations' International Convention on the Elimination of all forms of Racial Discrimination (1965).[90] Unlike the South Australian *Prohibition of Discrimination Act 1966, the Racial Discrimination Act 1975* (Cth), provides for a civil cause of action. Complainants can bring a claim to the tribunal and prove the civil burden of proof of the balance of probabilities.[91]

The *Racial Discrimination Act 1975* (Cth) protects the attributes of race, colour, descent or national or ethnic origin. The Act bases its definition of discrimination on the United Nations Convention[92] and, unlikely other Australian anti-discrimination legislation, did not use the concepts of direct and indirect discrimination as it was enacted before these concepts were developed in the UK.[93]

The Whitlam Government also legislated for no-fault divorce, made the contraceptive pill more affordable, established the Family Court and successfully lobbied the Australian Conciliation and Arbitration Commission to establish the principle of 'equal pay for equal work' in 1972.

Australia signed the Convention on the Elimination of All Forms of Discrimination Against Women (CEDAW) on 17 July 1980 and this was ratified by the Australian Parliament on 28 July 1983.[94] CEDAW provides that parties should adopt appropriate legislation.[95] This provided the constitutional basis for federal sex discrimination legislation under the 'external affairs' power in the Australian Constitution as well as several other powers including trade and commerce and corporations.

CEDAW requires the member states to take measures to realise the principle of sex equality and to eliminate discrimination in a range of areas from not just political and public life, education and employment, but also to 'cultural life' and marriage. It was wide-ranging in its efforts to advance equality in all facets of life and 'condemn discrimination against women in all its forms'.[96] When Australia did implement its federal anti-discrimination laws, it did not extend this to the private sphere, to 'cultural life' or marriage.[97]

Australia also did not agree to the requirement to introduce paid maternity leave on the basis that it would cause unacceptable outlays in the private sector.[98] Australia also did not accept application of CEDAW to exclude women from combat positions in the defence force. Nor did Australia accept the 1999 Optional Protocol, that allowed individual claims of violations of CEDAW to be made to a Convention Committee, until 2008.[99]

On 26 November 1981, ACT Labor Senator Susan Ryan, a former teacher and academic, introduced the Sex Discrimination Bill into Parliament as a private member's Bill while in opposition. The purpose of the Bill was to implement Australia's treaty obligations under CEDAW and prohibit and eliminate sex and marital status discrimination and promote affirmative action in employment.[100] The Bill applied to Commonwealth employment and employment in the private sector where there is constitutional power. The Senator cited the volume of complaints received under state legislation as evidence that the legislation would create opportunities for women and that it would break down prejudice in the community and be used as a model for the anti-discrimination provisions.[101] It provided for limited exceptions for insurance and superannuation for a period of two years.

The Bill was adjourned without a vote. It did not have the support of the coalition government of the day and was not debated. Senator Ryan explained in the second reading speech that this was because the Bill was complex and the Senate and the community should have time to consider it before voting. She said that she did not seek leave to proceed with a debate on the Bill for several months.[102]

On 2 June 1983, Senator Ryan introduced the Sex Discrimination Bill 1983 (Cth) into the Senate as a government Bill, but without the affirmative action provisions. The Hawke Government announced the legislation dealing with discrimination on the basis of sex or marital status at the opening of Parliament in March 1983. The *Sex Discrimination Act 1984* (SDA)[103] was one of the first laws passed by the Hawke Government. It received Royal Assent on 21 March 1984 and commenced on 1 August 1984.

At the time there was vocal opposition from some politicians and public interest groups. The government did not control the Senate and some members, including independent MP Brian Harradine, had objections. Part of the opposition was to Australia signing CEDAW, as well as the Bill itself, as there were concerns about the number of non-Anglo-Saxon countries signing CEDAW, that abolishing sex discrimination was more relevant for third-world countries and that this was an overreach by the federal government.[104]

There were also concerns about the extension of constitutional powers.[105] However, the High Court decision in the 'Tasmanian Dam'[106] case had previously confirmed the Commonwealth's power to make domestic laws to implement treaty obligations. This was coupled with continued Cold War rhetoric and the rise of conservative groups including the 'Women Who Want to be Women' group concerned about the breakdown of the family and seeking to advocate for 'silent women' who had chosen to work in the home raising children.[107] The term 'silent women' reminds me of the term 'quiet Australians' referred to in political discourse in the 2020s).[108] There was also concern addressed in thousands of petitions that women might be given the right to demand an abortion, although this was not the subject of the Bill. As a result, an amendment was included to clarify that the Bill did not apply to services that can only be provided to members of one sex.[109] Another factor was that there were very few women in Parliament at the time, with only six women of 125 members of the House of Representatives and 13 women in the Senate.[110]

Despite these objections, the legislation passed by 86 votes to 26.[111] Fourteen Liberal and 12 National Party members voted against the legislation. The National Party were concerned about the effect of the bill on 'traditional family values' as the Leader said that it would 'make it more difficult for women to follow a traditional role in the home and the raising of their children, should they wish to' and preferred education as the better way of dealing with the discrimination.[112] Many amendments, as many as 53, were negotiated to the Bill, including a two-year exemption for non-government schools, including permitting discrimination on religious grounds, sport, clubs and exemptions for superannuation and insurance. Senator Ryan's judgement was that it was better to have the major provisions legislated and then address exemptions later on.[113]

This legislation made it illegal to discriminate on the basis of sex, marital status, pregnancy or potential pregnancy, breastfeeding and family responsibilities[114] (both direct and indirect discrimination) in employment or enrolling in education, renting or buying property and accessing services. It also made sexual harassment illegal in Australia for the first time and set up the Office of the Sex Discrimination Commissioner. This then opened up opportunities in employment for women.

Unlike other anti-discrimination legislation, the SDA did not bind a state or territory government unless expressly provided for; for example, a state workplace was not bound in relation to the prohibitions against sex discrimination in the workplace.[115]

One of the aims of the SDA is to 'eliminate, as far as possible discrimination involving sexual harassment, and discrimination involving harassment on the grounds of sex, in the workplace, in educational institutions and in other areas of public activity'.[116] Sexual harassment under the *Sex Discrimination Act 1984* (Cth) is any unwelcome sexual advance, request for sexual favours or other unwelcome conduct of a sexual nature in circumstances where a reasonable person would have anticipated the possibility that the person would be offended, humiliated or intimidated.[117] Circumstances to be considered include the sex, age, sexual orientation, relationship status, race, ethnicity or disability of the person harassed, the relationship between the person harassed and the person who engaged in the conduct and any other relevant circumstance. Similar to anti-discrimination, it covers conduct in employment, education and provision of goods and services. In 1992 the SDA was amended to change the definition of sexual harassment, including to remove the requirement that the complainant show disadvantage and to expand the areas where it is unlawful to include the provision of goods and services, Commonwealth programs and the provision of accommodation.[118] An employer can be held liable for unlawful acts of employees in connection with their employment.[119]

The federal anti-discrimination laws are enforced under the *Australian Human Rights Commission Act 1986* (Cth). The *Fair Work Act*

2009 (Cth) protects workplace rights, freedom of association and protection from workplace discrimination.

Unlike the *Racial Discrimination Act 1975* (Cth), which implemented the Racial Discrimination Convention, the Sex Discrimination Act did not go as far as the Women's Convention. In Elizabeth Evatt's assessment of the Act in 2004, the 20th anniversary, she found that the Act was limited to discrimination in certain fields – such as employment, education and services. While this provided for private individual actions, the Act did not provide for actions against systemic discrimination, such as enshrining rights of equality.[120]

Exemptions include where a role can only be performed by a person having a particular attribute, where employment is within a private household, for single sex educational institutions, for religious bodies and charities (i.e. in relation to ordination of priests), clubs where membership is only available to persons of a particular sex (taking into account the purpose for which the club was established), sporting activities, accommodation and combat duties.

States and territories

After 1975, the states and territories adopted anti-discrimination legislation providing for a civil cause of action rather than a criminal offence. Legislation was adopted in South Australia in 1975 with the *Sex Discrimination Act 1975* (SA) and the *Racial Discrimination Act 1975* (SA), in 1977 in New South Wales and Victoria, in 1984 in Western Australia, 1991 in Queensland and the Australian Capital Territory and in 1998 in Tasmania. Most states first adopted legislation against racial and sex discrimination and were then broadened to cover disability, sexual harassment, sexuality, religious belief and industrial action, with new attributes being added over time, such as age.

The states and territories followed the model of direct and indirect discrimination based on UK legislation rather than the *Racial Discrimination Act 1975* (Cth) model.

Now Australia has eight different anti-discrimination laws at state and territory level and four at Commonwealth level as well as the *Australian Human Rights Commission Act 1986* (Cth). This matrix of laws makes compliance difficult and there have been cases seeking to invalidate certain laws that were inconsistent. The Commonwealth legislation has been amended to allow the laws to operate concurrently, but for the complainant to choose a forum to prevent double dipping. Unlike the state tribunals, the Australian Human Rights Commission cannot give a binding resolution of a complaint. This means complainants find they must then go to the court if their complaint remains unresolved.[121]

There have been several reviews[122] considering consolidation of anti-discrimination laws to improve consistency and make it easier for people to understand, and for the law to more effectively contribute to its stated goals of equality and removal of barriers as well as the objectives of global conventions. These reviews have generally found that discrimination continues to be an issue and that barriers to access to justice remain. The reviews also consider that addressing the gender pay and employment gap is also likely to have a significant impact on the economy.

More recently the *Respect@Work Report* recommended that the Australian Government work with state and territory governments to achieve greater consistency with the federal Sex Discrimination Act without reducing protections.

While the SDA has made discrimination and sexual harassment unlawful and has given a voice to these issues through the Office of the Sex Discrimination Commissioner, its effectiveness depends on individuals or groups bringing claims and how those claims are interpreted by the courts, rather than necessarily being a force for systemic changes.[123] Would there be a difference in outcome if we focused on upholding the civil rights of the person who may be harassed? Focusing on the action against the perpetrator brings a focus upon individuals, the reliability of evidence and reputation rather than on prevention of harassment.

It has also been argued that the anti-discrimination laws fail to consider intersectionality – how different characteristics, such as a combination of gender, race, disability could expose individuals and groups to overlapping and forms of discrimination that may need to be specifically addressed within this context. Also, that the damages have been too low to have a powerful effect on systemic change.[124]

For more systemic change, can we look to the influence of affirmative action and equal opportunity laws as Senator Ryan had originally intended?

Affirmative action

While anti-discrimination legislation seeks to prevent discrimination against a group of people because of protected attributes, affirmative action seeks to address entrenched discrimination (i.e. the effects of long periods of discrimination in the past). Anti-discrimination laws provide an avenue for individuals to seek redress once they have proved their case. Over time this may improve equality of opportunity by the standards set in society and efforts undertaken to be compliant and avoid legal action. In contrast, affirmative action laws seek to make progress towards equality by setting a planned systemic method for progress.

CEDAW provides that 'temporary special measures' to accelerate equality between men and women would not be considered discrimination.[125] Governments could establish legislation or policies to seek to increase the representation of women in the workforce and leadership positions. Australia already had some affirmative action legislation including the requirement for the public service to have an equal opportunity plan for women and 'persons in designated groups'[126] and the NSW Anti-Discrimination legislation required government departments and statutory bodies to prepare equal opportunity management plans.[127]

On 26 November 1981, Senator Ryan told Parliament that she included affirmative action provisions in her 1981 Private Member's Bill to address structural discrimination by creating equal employment opportunity for women.[128] It would have required Australian Government and private sector employers with more than 100 employees or with significant federal government contracts to implement affirmative action management.[129] In her second reading speech, Senator Ryan explained that structural discrimination would only be eliminated by implementing goals and targets.[130]

The provisions were based on the New South Wales provisions and experience in the US. The requirements were targets and not quotas. This was intentional as it was considered that genuine progress 'can only be made if jobs are awarded on merit'.[131]

These affirmative action provisions that had been included in Senator Ryan's Private Member's Bill in 1981 were not included in the *Sex Discrimination Act 1984* (Cth). The government instead wanted to ensure that unworkable provisions were not imposed on employers but wanted to consult extensively on proposals that employers would see in their interests to implement.[132] This has meant that in Australia, affirmative action legislation is separate from anti-discrimination legislation, unlike in the United States.

The Hawke Government decided instead to consult and issued a green paper 'Affirmative Action for Women: A Policy Discussion Paper' presented to Parliament by Bob Hawke PM on 5 June 1984.[133] The government's view was that the anti-discrimination laws could not by themselves improve equality of employment. It was intended that employers would analyse their workforce, design a strategy to improve women's participation rates and monitor and evaluate the success of the strategy over time. The purpose of the legislation was to impose an obligation on employers to develop these programs. As part of this process, a pilot was established with 28 large private sector companies and three higher education institutions participating and ran for 12 months.

The government also established a Working Party on Affirmative Action Legislation to monitor the pilot and make recommendations to Government. It was made up of representatives of different groups and was chaired by Senator Ryan. In November 1985, the working party recommended that legislation be introduced to require all higher education institutions and private sector employers with 100 or more staff to implement affirmative action programs for women.[134] The main objection from the private sector was that there should not be 'prescriptive legislation' and that appointments should continue to be made based on 'merit'.[135]

On 19 February 1986, Prime Minister Bob Hawke introduced the Affirmative Action (Equal Employment Opportunity for Women) Bill 1986 (Cth) to require certain employers to promote equal opportunity for women in employment and establish the office of Director of Affirmative Action.[136] It was unusual and notable for a Prime Minister to introduce the Bill. The Act commenced on 1 October 1986.[137] Employers with more than 100 employees were required to implement an affirmative action program and submit annual progress reports.[138]

There was criticism that the legislation needed stronger enforcement mechanisms and demonstrated progress by employers.[139]

Following a government review, this Act was replaced by the *Equal Opportunity for Women in the Workplace Act 1999* (Cth), which came into effect on 1 January 2000.[140] This legislation changed references to 'affirmative action' to 'equal opportunity for women in the workplace' and gave employers an outcomes-focused reporting format and longer reporting period. Education and consultation became key objectives.

The Act was reviewed in 2009–10 with the review[141] finding that it was an issue that the legislation only focused on women and that the coverage of the Act should be extended and reporting format clarified. The review found that all employees (of all genders) working in female dominated industries tended to be paid less than in male-dominated industries and – women generally – were less likely to be in leadership positions and more likely to have lower earnings.

The legislation was again amended in 2012 to the *Workplace Gender Equality Act 2012* (Cth), to change the name of the Act and the agency to focus on improving outcomes for both men and women in the workplace.[142] A new reporting framework required employers to report against gender equality indicators to be developed by the Workplace Gender Equality Agency in consultation with employers and employee organisations. This reporting would be made public and would include reporting on board composition. There was specific recognition of equal remuneration and family and caring responsibilities. A failure to comply may affect eligibility for government contracts.[143]

The Workplace Gender Equality Agency reported in 2020 that there has been a strong increase in employer action on gender equality, more women in leadership roles and a decline in the gender pay gap.[144] However, the gender pay gap persists, women continue to be under-represented in leadership positions and many important industries and sectors. Data released on 26 November 2020 showed that employer actions on gender equality had stalled.[145] Following a recommendation by the Workplace Gender Equality Agency that the legislation be reviewed to drive further progress towards the attainment of gender equality, in October 2021, the Australian Government announced a review into the *Workplace Gender Equality Act 2012*. The report was released in December 2021 and contained 10 recommendations to drive change, including to require reporting of gender equality data at the employer level rather than industry level and setting targets for large employers.[146] On 30 March 2023, the Commonwealth Parliament passed the *Workplace Gender Equality Amendment (Closing the Gender Pay Gap) Bill 2023*,[147] which requires certain employer pay gaps to be published and employers with more than 500 employees to have a policy for each of six gender equality indicators. Sexual harassment and discrimination are now gender equality indicators.

More recent developments

Recently, the #MeToo movement and similar international social movements have highlighted public attention on sexual assault and harassment.[148] #MeToo was started by activist Tarana Burke in the US to empower vulnerable women by letting them know they are not alone, following widespread allegations of sexual abuse in the entertainment industry. The movement has had a global impact.[149]

In June 2018, the Sex Discrimination Commissioner and Minister for Women the Hon Kelly O'Dwyer MP announced the National Inquiry into Sexual Harassment in Australian Workplaces to be undertaken by the Australian Human Rights Commission. The final report, *Respect@ Work: Sexual Harassment National Inquiry Report* was issued on 5 March 2020 by Kate Jenkins, Sex Discrimination Commissioner, Australian Human Rights Commission.

The report found that making a complaint puts a burden on the complainant's career, reputation and relationships. The report also found that gender inequality in our workplaces has been a driver for sexual harassment and has also hindered prevention. It considers sexual harassment to be a 'form of gender-based violence'.[150]

Among 55 recommendations, the report proposes a regulatory model that recognises a right of workers to be free from sexual harassment as a human right, workplace right and a safety right. It recommended that the Commonwealth Sex Discrimination Act be amended to include a positive duty requiring employers to take reasonable measures to eliminate sexual discrimination, harassment and victimisation as far as possible with enforcement powers to assess compliance.[151] This would require employers to take proactive steps.

The report recommended amendments to provide the Commission with powers to enforce compliance with the positive duty as well as powers to inquire into systemic discrimination or harassment issues.[152] It recommended that the exemption for state and territory public servants be removed (as had previously been recommended in 1992).[153] The Australian Government released a Roadmap in response to the Report on 8 April 2021, committing to implement regulatory reforms to reduce complexity.[154]

As recommended by the *Respect@Work Report*, the Sex Discrimination Act was amended in September 2021[155] to clarify that it extends to all members of state and federal parliament, judges and their staff and consultants and state and territory public servants. The changes also expanded the coverage of protections for volunteers, students and self-employed, who are now specifically protected from sex discrimination in their workplace.

The *Sex Discrimination and Fair Work (Respect at Work) Amendment Act 2021* legislates a new 'affirmative action' type objective of the Sex Discrimination Act: 'to achieve, so far as practicable, equality of opportunity between men and women' [note that the AHRC's recommendation of an aim of achieving 'substantive equality' was not included]. The *Respect@Work Report* found that gender inequality was a key driver of workplace sexual harassment and that this would be consistent with Australia's international human rights obligations.

The *Respect@Work Report* recommended that sex-based harassment (conduct which is not of a sexual nature and therefore is not sexual harassment but is sex discrimination) should be expressly prohibited under the SDA. Sex-based harassment is now specifically prohibited in the SDA; for example, inappropriate comments or jokes based on a person's sex, display of materials that are sexist or requesting someone to engage in degrading conduct based on their sex. A person who instructs, aids or permits sex-based sexual harassment or sex-based harassment may also be liable.

The then Coalition Government determined not to introduce a positive duty on employers to take measures to eliminate sex discrimination and harassment in the workplace on the basis that there is already a positive duty to prevent work health and safety risks in the model Workplace Health and Safety Act (legislation that has been adopted in all states and territories except Victoria and Western Australia).[156] These laws require employers to prevent sexual harassment as part of the broader duty to manage workplace health and safety risks. However, the *Respect@Work Report* recommended that these laws also needed to be amended to recognise psychological health risks as recommended by the independent Boland Review of these laws, as well as amending the SDA to ensure that sexual harassment is addressed in a systemic way.[157] In Victoria, there is a preventative duty in equal opportunity legislation and under workplace health and safety laws to eliminate sexual harassment and other unlawful discrimination, however, there is no mechanism for enforcement.[158]

The *Respect@Work Report* found that 'a lack of a positive duty in the SDA to prevent workplace sexual harassment means that employers place a higher priority on compliance with employment law and work health and safety laws than discrimination law. This also places a heavy onus on individuals to complain'.[159]

The positive duty recommended by the *Respect@Work Report* reflects previous recommendations by discrimination law experts that a positive duty is more likely to produce systemic change than a focus on individual conduct.[160] Focusing on individual conduct also requires an admission of wrongdoing rather than on change to drive equality.[161]

The positive duty was legislated effective January 2023 by the *Anti-Discrimination and Human Rights Legislation Amendment (Respect at Work) Act 2022*.[162] Employers are now required to take reasonable measures to eliminate certain forms of sex discrimination, including sexual harassment.

The Respect@Work Inquiry also received evidence that Australian defamation laws discouraged people from making complaints about sexual harassment. The report recommended further review of defamation laws and protections for alleged victims who appear as witnesses in proceedings.[163] At the time of writing, a review of the model defamation provisions is underway.

In June 2020 the Chief Justice of the High Court of Australia, the Hon Susan Kiefel AC made a statement that allegations of sexual harassment had been made against a former Justice, the Hon Dyson Heydon AC QC and an independent investigation found that six former Court staff members had been harassed by the former Justice.[164]

In November 2021, the Australian Human Rights Commission released *Set the standard: Report on the independent review into Commonwealth parliamentary workplaces*. The report was a review into sexual harassment and sexual assault at a particular category of workplaces: those of Commonwealth parliamentarians and their staff.[165] The review, led by the Sex Discrimination Commissioner Kate Jenkins, was established by the Australian Government following alarming allegations of sexual assault in Parliament House.

The *Set the standard* Report recommends affirmative actions, including targets and specific actions to achieve gender balance among both parliamentarians and staff and the tabling of an annual report in Parliament on gender representation across specific roles.

Also in 2021, affirmative consent laws were passed in NSW[166] and Victoria.[167] The *Crimes Act 1958* (Vic) was amended to require a person to take active steps to confirm they have received consent for sexual activity. The removal of protection during sexual activity was also explicitly made a crime. The *Crimes Act 1900* (NSW) has been amended to require consent by words or actions.[168] Queensland also strengthened its consent laws in March 2021.[169]

Conclusions

It is interesting to reflect on the above having recently read historical accounts of the equal pay cases where there was found to be a duty on employers to consider male breadwinner status and the need to provide for family at home when setting pay rates. Following the *Respect@Work Report*, we now have a positive duty on employers to take action specifically to address discrimination and harassment in the workplace.

In 1966 *The Bulletin* heralded the first Australian anti-discrimination legislation as establishing a civil right and protecting those who might be discriminated against.[170] But that is not the history of anti-discrimination law in Australia. The history is not a story of established civil rights or principles of equality, but of individual parliaments at different times being influenced to prohibit certain behaviour.

Reading this history resonates with the current #MeToo debate. The fears expressed in the past were not so much about whether or not women should have equal rights or be treated equally, but about what the resulting damage would be to the status quo. Would a publican be able to attract customers if they could not discriminate by race? Would men receive a living wage if women were paid equal wages? Would men have their reputations damaged if women are able to bring claims of sexual harassment? The focus has not been on protection and the damage being done by the unequal or unfair treatment, but the level of damage to the status quo by change. This has been exacerbated by not having enshrined rights or judicially established principles of equality, and our law becoming a matrix of prohibitions.

Australia was once a world leader in terms of gender equality legislation. Are we still a leader? The pace of reform has picked up in 2020–23 with recent events initiated once again by individual actions culminating in legislative change. Historian Professor Clare Wright has equated this time with the movement that brought about the world leading suffrage reform of the early 1900s.[171] If that is correct, then Australia may be returning closer to the lead, but there is undoubtedly also going to be strong opposition as there has been throughout history.

Behaviour that was deemed socially acceptable has changed over time. This means that in a time of change, it is difficult for those in positions of power to condemn the behaviour, because they themselves or their colleagues and friends may have acted that way or did not call it out. This forces them to have to admit responsibility or wrongdoing either personally or publicly in order to take action against the behaviour. It also damages the reputation of our institutions where this behaviour was accepted (e.g. the reputation of the High Court following allegations against former Justice Heydon). It may require generational change to avoid this while our legislation continues to focus more on individual instances of conduct and discrimination rather than positive duties and 'affirmative actions' to drive change.

What level of damage will we continue to accept to preserve the status quo, where Australia lags in terms of gender equality? Or what level of damage to the status quo will we push through to once again be a leader for reform?

Summary of legislation at the time of writing

Federal

- *Age Discrimination Act 2004* (Cth)
- *Australian Human Rights Commission Act 1986* (Cth)
- *Disability Discrimination Act 1992* (Cth)
- *Fair Work Act 2009* (Cth)
- *Racial Discrimination Act 1975* (Cth)
- *Sex Discrimination Act 1984* (Cth)
- *Workplace Gender Equality Act 2012* (Cth)

State and territory

- *Anti-Discrimination Act 1977* (NSW)
- *Anti-Discrimination Act 1991* (Qld)
- *Anti-Discrimination Act 1996* (NT)
- *Anti-Discrimination Act 1998* (Tas)
- *Equal Opportunity Act 1984* (SA)
- *Equal Opportunity Act 1984* (WA)
- *Equal Opportunity Act 2010* (Vic)
- *Discrimination Act 1991* (ACT)
- State workplace health and safety laws are based on the Model Work Health and Safety Act in all states and territories, except Victoria and WA, which have their own schemes.

International conventions

- *International Labour Organisation Convention (No. 100) Concerning Equal Remuneration for Men and Women Workers for Work of Equal Value*, adopted in Geneva 29 June 1951, 34th session (entered into force 23 May 1953).
- *International Labour Organisation Convention (No. 111) Concerning Discrimination in Respect of Employment and Occupation*, opened for signature 25 June 1958, 362 UNTS 31 (entered into force 15 June 1960).
- *International Convention on the Elimination of All Forms of Racial Discrimination*, opened for signature 21 December 1965, 660 UNTS 195 (entered into force 4 January 1969).

- *International Covenant on Civil and Political Rights*, opened for signature 16 December 1966, 999 UNTS 171 (entered into force 23 March 1976).
- *International Covenant on Economic, Social and Cultural Rights*, opened for signature 16 December 1966, 993 UNTS 3 (entered into force 3 January 1976).
- *Convention on the Elimination of All Forms of Discrimination against Women*, opened for signature, 18 December 1979, 1249 UNTS 13 (entered into force 3 September 1981).
- *Convention on the Rights of the Child*, opened for signature 20 November 1989, 1577 UNTS 3 (entered into force 2 September 1990).
- *Convention on the Rights of Persons with Disabilities*, opened for signature 30 March 2007, 2515 UNTS 3 (entered into force 3 May 2008).
- *International Labour Organization, Ending Violence and Harassment in the World of Work*, Report V(1), International Labour Conference, 108th session, Agenda Item 5 ILC.108/V/1 (2019).
- Australia voted in favour of the International Labour Organisation adopting a new Convention and accompanying Recommendation Concerning the Elimination of Violence and Harassment in the World of Work (ILO Convention 190) in June 2019.

Chapter 4

Equal employment opportunity and me – bringing the legislation to life

The last chapter provided a summary of the history and details of anti-discrimination and affirmative action legislation in Australia. In this chapter I'm aiming to bring this legislation to life by outlining how it changed my career and my world. So, to begin, why did I take a huge career risk in my fifth decade by establishing a consultancy that aimed to help break down barriers to women at work, and why am I at it again in my eighth decade of life, by writing this book?

I've spent a lot of time reflecting on what has driven me to put myself through such challenges. My sense is that some of my strong desire to improve things for women goes right back to my childhood. My mother and father met and fell in love at the Adelaide Teachers College. On graduation they were appointed to teach at country schools in vastly different parts of rural South Australia. They missed each other desperately, my father proposed, and my mother said 'yes' long before she'd taught out her teacher training bond.

My three siblings and I grew up with the story that our parents had a wonderful traditional wedding. In fact, I have a photo of them beside me as I'm writing – she's looking glowingly beautiful in a long white dress and antique lace veil, and he's looking proud and handsome in a tuxedo. However, a dampener to their joy, was that the policy of the time meant that our mum had to resign as a teacher on marrying, and that our dad had to pay off her outstanding bond. When I got old enough to think about such things, I used to ponder on what a dreadful start this must have been for two young people who presumably wanted to have an equal relationship in their marriage.

In hindsight, I think it was no coincidence that my two sisters and I all built careers that have involved improving the status of women in Australia: my older sister first in academia and then in government, my younger one in education, and me primarily in the private sector. (Our brother was also inspired to improve the status of women throughout his long career as a GP, particularly in his, at the time, radical obstetrics practice.) I think our parents' story led we three sisters, mostly uncon-sciously, to roles that would help to break down the kinds of barriers to women that our mother had experienced in such an overt way all those years before. Our mum was proud of her three daughters' professional achievements, but this always seemed to come tinged with some form of resentment that we were able to have careers while she was robbed of hers. Looking back, I can well understand why.

It's only now that I'm realising that my career also stalled when I was newly married. I became pregnant while working as a midwife in 1970. I submitted my resignation to Matron; she unquestioningly accepted it, and I left a job I loved a week or so before my baby girl was born. Maternity leave as a right was still a long way ahead, and I accepted that leaving to have a baby was the appropriate thing to do. Further, affordable childcare and paid parental leave provisions were non-existent, so I was forced to become a full-time at-home mother, whether I wanted to or not.

It's also now, over three decades later, that I've finally joined some dots about another factor that gave me the impetus and courage to embark on such a huge career risk in my early 40s. This was the fact that our parents instilled in my three siblings and me a deep core belief in the importance of fairness. A simple example about how this was lived in practice was when, after our father died, our mother was deciding which of the few valuable paintings she and he had collected that she would leave to each of my three siblings and me. Mum asked us which painting we each wanted, but before agreeing to our wish, she first had the paintings valued to ensure that the dollar value we each received was equitable. Only when she was reassured that we were inheriting art works of a similar value, did she set about writing four small notes with our names on them, that included the then dollar value of our chosen painting. She put these in small plastic bags and stuck them to the back of each painting. My inheritance hangs just inside the front door of my home, with the wee note in her beautiful, and oh so familiar handwriting, still attached to the back of the frame.

I've now concluded that my memories about both my mother's and my experiences of stalled careers – hers by marriage and mine by childbearing – and my conditioning about fairness, all contributed to me throwing caution to the wind by leaping into the unknown world of self-employed consulting all those years ago.

So, what were the steps by which I established a consultancy specialising in equal employment opportunity (EEO) in the mid 1980s? My career until then had been in nursing: I trained as a general nurse, then as a midwife and I finally moved into community health nursing, first at the Family Planning Association (FPA) and then at a regional health centre in suburban Adelaide.

By then I was a newly divorced single mother of two teenagers. I spent two years working as a community health nurse in the Christies Beach Community Health Centre. I loved working in that sector because it focused on prevention being better than cure. However, I soon worked out that community health was at the bottom of the budgets and priorities of the South Australian Health Department. Further, I learnt that we nurses were the least well-paid of the community health team, and that we had virtually no career path ahead of us.

In the midst of these two years I met a man who became not only my lover, but also my first ever mentor. His name was Des, and he was the kind of mentor who was better at giving me a 'kick in the pants' than listening to my complaints. When I began moaning to him about the plight of community health nurses, he challenged me with the question, 'What are you going to do about this then, Kate?'

As described in the previous chapter by Lindsay Mackay, in 1984 the new Hawke Labor Government had established a program to assess the need for legislation in the private sector to improve the status of women. Twenty-eight corporations were invited to participate in an Affirmative Action Pilot Program to advise government on whether they believed legislation was needed to break down any barriers to the women they employed.

This was when the important legislative changes outlined by Lindsay in the previous chapter became part of my own story. This was when I chose to become one of those who set about bringing the affirmative action legislation to life.

By luck, Simpson Pope, one of the companies in the pilot program, was Adelaide-based and, by more luck, Des knew the woman at Simpson Pope who'd been given the role of equal opportunity officer to liaise between the company and the Federal Government's pilot group. Des gave me this woman's contact details and I gave her a call. Her name was Jan and she and I agreed to meet for lunch. We instantly clicked. Jan shared some of her observations about what was happening in the pilot program, and we chuckled as she talked about management resistance versus the almost full support of the designated EO officers, all of whom were women. I liked this honest open woman, and as our conversation flowed, an idea began percolating in my mind.

With Des's challenging question spurring me on, I resigned as a community health nurse in early '85, and in March that same year I put out my shingle as one of Australia's first EO consultants. I didn't know what this meant, but luckily, neither did the market. I set about networking and researching what services might help industry implement equal employment opportunity programs for their female employees.

Over way too many coffees, I picked the brains of people who worked in the EO sector in government and education, where legislation already existed, about their knowhow and experiences of EEO and AA. It was then time to decide what services I could offer the hopefully, soon to be legislated, private sector.

I combined the experience in training and facilitation I'd gained as a nurse educator at the FPA, and the information I'd gathered through my research and networking. I developed two programs: an EO awareness seminar for managers to help them understand their responsibilities and liabilities under EEO/AA law and practice, and a career development program for women to help them set goals and plans to benefit from the barrier-free workplace I'd naively thought the new legislation would enable.

I set about marketing these programs. This sounds like an easy enough thing to do, but the reality could not have been further from that. It was in fact a very scary time for me. All my old self-doubts bubbled to the surface as I put myself way outside the comfort zone of nursing. A bad habit of mine of grinding my teeth in my sleep worsened. The little voices in my head were yabbering away about me 'not being good enough'. And it was lonely. I'd taken for granted the wonderful support I got from my peers in the community health team, until it was missing. Only then did I realise that I'd have to build my own network of support in my new chosen career in consulting.

Nonetheless, to my delight and despite the negative submissions from most of the 28 pilot companies who'd said they could self-regulate, the Affirmative Action (Equal Employment Opportunity for Women) Act was proclaimed in federal parliament on October 1, 1986 – my 40th birthday – how auspicious! Thank you, Bob Hawke, although really thank you Senator Susan Ryan, who at that time was the Minister assisting the Prime Minister on the Status of Women, and who'd persuaded Hawke that AA legislation in the private sector was needed. Thanks are also due to Anne Summers, who assisted Minister Ryan as the first head of the new Office of the Status of Women in the Department of the Prime Minister and Cabinet.

As outlined in chapter 3, this new Act required employers of more than 100 people to implement a nine-step AA change program in their organisations and to report annually to the AA Agency. The larger corporations typically appointed an HR person to set up and monitor their program, and it was to these people – again almost exclusively women, including my, by now friend Jan from Simpson Pope – that I marketed my EO training services. To my further delight and relief, by the end of the '80s I'd built a successful EO consultancy with a growing number of clients in Adelaide, Sydney and Melbourne.

All these experiences, together with my later work as a leadership coach and mentor, have incrementally contributed to my understanding of the barriers between women and an equal workplace. This has shaped the rest of my professional life and led me to write this book.

As I reminisce about the heady days of my early years as an EO consultant, three examples of how challenging this proved to be come to mind.

The first occurred when I presented my first ever EO awareness seminar to the executive team of South Australia's public power utility.

I sought help from my 15-year-old daughter about what to wear, and we agreed on a pale blue two-piece outfit and a string of pearls, for a soft and feminine look. Before the seminar I introduced myself to the CEO. He looked at me suspiciously and asked, 'Are you an activist?' I paused, gulped, and the goddess of good answers must have been with me, because I smiled warmly and replied, 'I'll let you decide that for yourself.' At the end of the seminar, I shook his hand again and asked him how the seminar had been for him. This time he was smiling as he said he'd found it 'informative'. Phew!

The second story took place a few months later when I was leading a similar session in Perth for the state managers of two corporations in the male-dominated industries of building and manufacturing. Again, I dressed in a feminine way and wore my, by then hard-working, pearls. I covered the legislation in the first session of the day. At the morning tea break one of the participants had to be restrained. It seems he wanted to 'physical' me because he thought I was from the government, and he was enraged that these laws were daring to tell he and his colleagues that they had to change the way they were doing business. The organisers of the seminar had to settle this man down by explaining that I was a private consultant whom his company had engaged to provide him and his fellow participants with this important information. Phew again!

I'm not sure why, but most of my early clients were from what I call 'blokey' industries, such as building and construction, manufacturing and trucking. The third example of the challenges I faced presenting to managers in these industries was when I was engaged by a national trucking company to facilitate my one-day seminar to all the senior managers in the business, in a five-day back-to-back block at their head office in Sydney. I remember flying home to Adelaide at the end of that week feeling totally exhausted, and when I stepped onto the scales the next morning, I discovered I'd lost 5 kg in weight that week. It seems that those truck drivers, turned managers, had taken their 'pound of flesh' from me!

As I've already mentioned, the second program I developed was a career development program for women. This aimed to help women make use of the opportunities opening in their organisations because of its AA change program. Included in these programs was time for participants to clarify their vision, purpose and values and to set goals to achieve these. Also covered were models to assist them build their assertiveness skills and self-confidence. Another aspect of the content was a chance for them to build their networks of support, not only through networking, but also by finding themselves mentors and sponsors. Women typically loved the networking opportunities they gained from attending these programs.

I loved running these programs, and my sister recently reminded me that I'd once told her I would leave the seminars for managers feeling like I had holes gouged into my body, and when I worked with women, I felt as if those holes were refilled.

So why am I 'at it' again in my eighth decade by writing this book? I've asked myself this question any number of times as I researched the topic of gender workplace inequalities, as I interviewed dozens of women and some men, and now as I sit and write. I've often feared that the topic is past its used-by date. Perhaps it's just me who still rages quietly about things like gender pay inequities, women's insecurity in part-time employment, and the lack of affordable childcare – not to mention the more subtle forms of sexual harassment in the workplace that I continue to hear about from my clients.

I felt encouraged to keep going with the book when the Human Rights Commission's report *Respect@Work*, was tabled in Parliament in March 2020. The report made 55 recommendations designed to shift the current reactive, complaints-based approach to sexual harassment to one that focuses on prevention which requires positive action from employers. I discuss this report in detail, including the patchy progress made in response to it since March 2020, in chapter 13.

Research

What did I find out from my research about equal employment opportunity in the Australian workforce?

When I was first building my EO consultancy, Australia had a highly sex-segregated workforce. Female workers were primarily clustered in the community services and wholesale and retail sectors, and most women were employed as clerks, salespeople or personal service workers. Women were conspicuously under-represented in management and the average female wage was about 60% of the male wage.

'At the time of publication, things have improved for Australian working women, although the COVID-19 pandemic brought into sharp focus the ongoing sex segregation in our workforce. Women are still clustered in the lower paid caring roles, showing that we're still a long way from achieving true equality. For example, I've learnt that:

- There are currently only 21 women CEOs leading an ASX200 company in Australia. And an anecdotal story I enjoy telling is that there are still more CEOs called Peter in these companies than there are women.
- Australian women typically lose 90% of their wages for every extra day they use childcare, and in many cases, women pay to work because of the high cost of childcare.
- The perverse results of the intersection of the taxation and Family Benefits system mean that a woman earner with children under 18 carries a marginal tax rate so high – particularly when combined with childcare costs – as to make it not worth her while to work in other than part-time or casual work.
- Women still carry the domestic burden while their men 'help'. Add to this the fact that women bear the children and, because of the way work is currently structured, this affects women's career progress.
- On retirement, of a male and female who graduated in law on the same day, the male will have earned $1million more than the female during their legal careers. This of course means the female's superannuation will also be less than the male's.

On reflecting back in her 2013 book *The misogyny factor*, Anne Summers, journalist, tireless feminist and formerly head of the Office of the Status of Women expressed a regret about what could have been done differently in the early stages of establishing EEO and AA for women:

> We should have realised the need for a powerful external lobby organisation, as unions, farmers, miners and almost every industry group you can think of has, ... we put our faith in government. Some of us actually went to work inside the system, persuading ourselves that we could make changes from within. And, on the outside, we relied on our own amateur persuasive efforts to influence the direction of policies that would foster women's equality.[172]

I fear I was one such soul who was relying on my 'amateur persuasive efforts' to change the hearts of minds of our leaders about the value of a gender diverse workforce.

Interviewees

To gain an understanding of the employment experiences of my female interviewees, I asked each of them to share with me the advantages and disadvantages of their being a woman in the Australian workforce during the past two to three decades.

JKR, a retired academic and bureaucrat, began by telling me that her gender was an advantage in one way, yet not in others, during her career in the late 1980s:

> At that point state and Commonwealth governments were thinking about improvements in gender and were looking for people who could do that – and my academic study of women's history was one of the things that got me the jobs that made my public sector career.

> Later, however, that advantage could become bitter-sweet when being seen as a 'women's stuff' specialist was less valued in terms of advancement than 'real jobs' in 'proper' or 'hard' policy. Some women deliberately stayed out of the women's units for that reason.

> I therefore worked out subsequently that what had given me an advantage could result in disadvantages, as women who chose to work on policy for women found themselves 'pigeonholed' when they sought mainstream promotions.

TA, formerly in recruitment in the accounting sector and now an executive coach, explored the pros and cons of her gender as her career was developing:

> As the only female in the sector at the time, an advantage was that I was sometimes able to use my gender as a point of differentiation. Conversely, I felt that there were more hoops created for we [sic] females to get to the next level than our male counterparts.

EM, a retired CIO told me:

> My gender has probably more hindered than helped [my career]. I've often been the only woman in the room and it's hard to be heard.

> *And jumping to the unconscious bias issue, being the only woman, you're often asked to take the minutes. It's such a tired example but it's still true.*

SA has been an allied health practitioner, an academic and leader in the higher education sector, and is now the managing director of a small business that provides information, resources and advice to the allied health sector. She said:

> *I think that the career I first chose [in allied health] was probably framed by my gender … because it gave me the chance to have a 'little career' while I worked part-time and had kids. However, I don't think I was aware of gender bias until I moved to senior roles. … I've sat on boards where strong women are not listened to in the same way that men are … they were almost demonised and passed as a witch. I now sit on a board where it's part of the culture that if I'm not being heard a colleague will say to the chair, 'S is trying to say something'.*

JS, a former scientist and now business manager at a university, with previous experience as a board member on two boards, told me:

> *I got one of my biggest breaks when I was appointed to the Fire Brigade Board because I was a female in a male-dominated environment. Also, because organisations (including at senior board level appointments) are now looking for more balanced leadership teams, and I think my appointment was partially because (of my skills and experience) but also because I balanced the gender on the team.*

JS then went on to tell me:

> *I think being a woman can be positive, as it can mean you can be noticed (if of course you have the required ability). The issue, however, is [that] the Margaret Thatcher syndrome is still alive and well in situations where there are only a few places for females and strong competition to get these. It depends on the type of overall culture that is prevalent. If gender issues are not the predominant or underlying aspect, then usual workplace issues apply. If, however, there is a hyper-competitive environment for female representation, the added risk for females is strong competition with other females.*

> *Senior leadership is tough and mentoring is needed. The risk for*
> *females is that this may be even harder to obtain – just because*
> *there are other females does not of itself mean a supportive environ-*
> *ment exists.*

I also asked my interviewees whether they thought things had improved
for women over the years. LM, a legal counsel told me:

> *I almost feel that what I'm hearing at work and in the media are*
> *about the last gasps of resistance. I feel that because I think there's*
> *maybe some generational change coming through – they're younger*
> *and not prepared to follow the old models of joining the old boys'*
> *networks … and the younger men are wanting to spend time with*
> *their children or doing other things.*

What more can be done?

Can the requirements of EEO/AA legislation achieve the goal of gender
equality at work in Australia? History thus far suggests not. However,
I do believe that current legislation could be better contributing to
achieving this goal if governments, both state and federal were prepared
to allocate decent budgets to those who administer the relevant acts.
Also, given we humans sometimes seem to respond better to sanctions
than rewards, I believe that EEO/AA legislation would probably lead to
more measurable change, if it were amended to strengthen the consequences of non-compliance.

Aside from these proposed legislative changes, what more can be
done? For real gender equality to be achieved in the Australian workforce, I believe that it's now beyond time that the primary focus of
responsibility for achieving this goal needs to shift to the leaders of this
land. I'll write more about this later.

Conclusions

One conclusion I've reached from my own experience, and through my
research and interviews in this chapter, is that things have improved for
women since my dear mum had to resign as a teacher when she married
my dad. And on my good days, I believe that the combination of both
anti-discrimination and more recently affirmative action legislation, has

helped to speed up the changes needed for the Australian workplace to be truly gender equal.

But have they? On my less optimistic days I find myself wondering why the gender statistics at the executive and board levels remain stubbornly male-dominated. Both my EO consulting clients and I were so optimistic in those heady days of the late '80s after the AA legislation was enacted in 1986. Now I'm doubting whether this change-based legislation has had much of an impact on making the Australian workplace fairer for women. Thirty-five years is a long time, and as I write, I find myself wondering whether legislative changes relevant to other areas of our society have taken so long to effect change. I doubt it.

Ever since I launched my EO consultancy in the mid '80s, I've been convinced that real change will only be achieved for working women in Australia through cultural change led by the leaders of each organisation. This sounds so simple, yet both my EO clients and I have wracked our brains about how to convince leaders that legislation alone is not enough, and that it was and is their job to make the necessary changes to break down the barriers to women in their organisation.

When I felt like I was hitting a brick wall in the EO awareness seminars for mostly male groups, I would hear myself say, 'You know, you have to walk in another Indian's moccasins for a day to know how it feels to be that Indian.' And over the many years of doing this work, I've concluded that until each leader does the equivalent of wearing another (disadvantaged) person's shoes, it seems that they just don't know how it feels to be disadvantaged in some way. For some leaders, this epiphany has occurred because either their partner or daughter was discriminated against in some way. For others, it has been because of the resignation of a high potential woman from their team whose exit interview said that she was at times overlooked, not listened to, and not taken seriously.

So, another conclusion I've reached at the end of this chapter, is a confirmation about the degree of resistance that this legislation and the policies to enact it have met. I was and still am perplexed about what the problem is. Why is there such resistance to what is both fair to workers, and beneficial to the workplaces of Australia? I will continue to explore this question as this book unfolds.

Chapter 5

Changing hearts and minds

I n the previous chapter I outlined why and how I set about establishing an EO consultancy in Australia. In this chapter, I explain how I went about helping managers and leaders understand their responsibilities and liabilities under EO and AA legislation through my EO awareness seminars.

Presenting the EEO/AA legislative framework to resistant managers, and then attempting to convince them that it was in their best interests to create a barrier free workforce for their women was, as I've already written, a huge challenge.

At most of my one-day EO seminars the client organisation would arrange for the sex discrimination commissioner in that state to give a presentation to participants at the beginning of the day to explain management responsibilities and liabilities under anti-discrimination, EEO and AA law. At the time, the NSW sex discrimination commissioner was an eloquent lawyer called Steve Mark. His title, and his capacity to bring humour into the case studies he shared about the impact of discrimination in the workplace, meant that the Sydney-based seminar participants were polite and appeared to take Steve seriously.

Similarly, the Queensland sex discrimination commissioner, a woman, soon had a group of senior managers at a seminar I was facilitating in Brisbane, hanging onto her every word. She was not only blonde and beautiful with a sharp intellect; she was also dressed in a black leather mini skirt and a pale pink silk top with two large pink earrings shaped like bows dangling from her ears. When the two women who'd engaged me to run this seminar and I dined together later that evening, we tut-tutted about her dress sense – or rather what we saw as a lack of appropriateness of what she'd worn. We agreed that in our opinion she would have to change how she dressed if she was going to be taken seriously. How wrong were we! Her name was Quentin Bryce – now Dame Quentin Bryce AD, CVO who was Australia's first female governor-general.

I had neither the position power nor the wardrobe to match either Steve Mark or Quentin Bryce. I needed to invent ways to present the quite complex framework of the raft of legislation they'd presented in a way that would hopefully engage and make sense to my seminar participants. I decided to use my nursing background, because I thought that most men would know how to relate to a nurse. I would begin by putting the two headings of 'Curative' and 'Preventative' in large letters on the whiteboard. I would then explain that I began my nursing career as a hospital-based nurse where our job was to care for our patients as they underwent treatment to help them get well – the 'curative approach' to health care. Next, I would explain that after I'd qualified as both a general nurse and midwife, I chose to move into community health nursing. Here our role was to be part of a team of health professionals with the goal of helping clients make changes to their lifestyle to enable them to stay well – the 'preventative approach' to health care.

I would then write the words 'Sex Discrimination Legislation' under the heading of Curative and 'Affirmative Action Legislation' under the heading of Preventative. I would explain that anti-discrimination legislation is complaints-based, while AA legislation is change-based. Under the Curative heading I would list the names of the sex discrimination acts that applied to the participants. I would also list the federal sex discrimination act that applies Australia wide.

Next, I would explain that all legislation taking a curative approach requires an aggrieved person to make a complaint of discrimination or sexual harassment. This would then be investigated, and damages awarded if the complaint was found to fit within the guidelines of the act. Sex discrimination legislation therefore sets up a power imbalance because it requires the less powerful person to complain about the more powerful one in their workplace, who could be, and often was, their boss. This is hard to do, which is why lots of people choose not to complain, but instead to live in fear, or resign from their job.

Under the heading of Preventative at my seminars I would write the Affirmative Action (Equal Employment Opportunity) for Women Act and explain that this legislation shifts the onus of responsibility for change onto those with power – managers, including them. The sanction for non-compliance was being mentioned in parliament. Most seminar participants would titter about what they saw as this 'soft' sanction; but I thought it was clever, given the huge PR and communications budgets that most companies spend annually to ensure that their customers see them as good corporate citizens.

The rest of the one-day seminar would be spent looking at the eight-step program, as well as doing exercises and case studies planned to help the participants to understand what they needed to do. My hope was that this experience would also help to shift the hearts and minds of at least some of them about how the changes they were required to make would be good for their business as well as their women, rather than yet another bureaucratic burden. After all, I would, and still do argue, that it makes good business sense to have a workforce that reflects the communities within which one does business.

The other challenge I had in presenting a whole day seminar was keeping the participants engaged. I searched for ways to show how affirmative action measures are all about putting in place initiatives to help women become competitive (so called 'catch up' measures), and so are not unfair to already competitive men. This was and remains a hard concept for many to grasp. One way I'd tackle it was to invite participants to respond to a True/False quiz with one question being:

There is nothing so unfair as the equal treatment of unequals.
True or False?

Senior managers in corporations have usually got there because of their intellect, the relevant skills for their industry and their political skills, so they tended to be bright enough to quickly unpick this little tongue twister: that treating people who are unequal in the same ways, does not achieve equality of outcome.

Another technique I used was a running race analogy that I hoped would speak to at least the sporty ones. I would draw a long line on the white board and mark this as the starting line for a running race to find the best candidate for an upcoming position. I'd then suggest that there were already several – usually male, almost always white – candidates at the starting post, and that the fastest of these runners would win the race; that is, get the role they were competing for when the starting gun went off.

However, if for example, a woman in the team was interested in the upcoming promotion, and if she had taken two lots of maternity leave in the past five years, she would have missed out on some of the work and training experiences of her male peers. This would mean that, staying with the running race analogy, she would be some distance back from the starting line when the recruiter's 'gun went off'. Providing this woman with some extra training, as well as a mentor perhaps, and the opportunity to get her IT skills up to date, would be three possible special (affirmative action) measures that would enable this woman to be at the starting line and therefore competitive for the promotion. The best candidate would still be selected on merit. Unequal? Well yes, to the extent that the field is now more competitive. But an intervention that would be good for the business? Undoubtedly yes because this could well draw on a better best candidate than before.

I was engaged to facilitate dozens of these EO seminars in Sydney, Melbourne, Adelaide and Perth. Did I influence a shift in attitude of at least some of the participants about the value of improving the status of women in their organisations? I sincerely hope so but the fact that so few women still lead large organisations suggests there must continue to be factors that mean that competing for promotion in Australian organisations can still be an unfair 'running race'.

What more can be done?

To me, Julia Gillard and Ngozi Okonjo-Iweala in their book *Women and leadership* summarise perfectly the challenge ahead in terms of changing hearts and minds to give women a fair go:

*Our world can only eradicate the gender bias in politics and leader-
ship generally, if it is identified, discussed, studied and challenged,
and evidence-based change strategies are implemented.*[173]

These two authors encourage women leaders to think about whether,
how and when they will call sexism out if it happens to them. As well,
I would encourage all leaders to put in place 'evidence-based change
strategies' for the benefit of the women in their organisations.

Conclusions

As I reminisce about the dozens of EO seminars I facilitated and the
hundreds of managers, mostly men, who attended, my conclusion now
is that I'm left feeling both curious and tired. Curious, because I would
love to know whether anything that they heard about, or participated
in during those seminars has stayed with them and has helped them
use their position power to influence change for women in their workplaces. But also tired, because it was hard work standing in front of so
much resistance while having so apparently little impact.

I don't think I understood then, but my conclusion now is about
why the EO managers in the organisations where I was engaged, chose
to use an outsider to facilitate these seminars. At the end of each one,
I could withdraw, reflect on how it went and then move on, whereas
they had to stay and keep doing their best to influence the change that
legislation was requiring of their organisations. I learnt from them first
from the years of my consulting, and later from my coaching practice,
about the many and varied forms of resistance that these women met.
This would range from being allocated an inadequate budget to effect
any real change, to having the EO role situated in middle management – which meant they did not have the positional power to influence
change – or to a lack of leadership support when this was most needed.
I could go on but, in summary, it was a thankless task to be appointed
to the role that was called the EO manager and more recently, the inclusion and diversity manager.

Chapter 6

Affirmative action in action

A s I've explained in the previous chapter, affirmative action for women is about putting in place special measures to ensure that they can be competitive on a level playing field – the best candidate is still chosen on merit but, because the competition is now potentially tougher, there might be a 'better best' candidate, but as I've already written elsewhere in this book, isn't that good for business?

The purpose of this chapter is to explain the subtleties of how affirmative action works with some research to support this.

A wonderful example of affirmative action in action recently came to my attention. A prestigious scientific research centre in Germany was planning to host an international conference in one of their fields of research. The planning committee prepared a list of potential guest speakers. Then one of them pointed out that the list consisted entirely of men. To ensure that there were some women speakers too, they were each asked to nominate a woman in their network who was doing research in their field. Several of these women were then included as guest speakers. I don't think that anyone who was involved in planning this conference called what they did 'affirmative action'. Nonetheless, the outcome of their extra efforts to find some women researchers was twofold: first, the conference participants heard from female scientists as well as male ones; and second, the women themselves had the chance for exposure and networking at an international level that they would otherwise have missed out on.

Research

Dr Noriko Amano-Patiño lectures in the Faculty of Economics at the University of Cambridge. While a PhD candidate at Yale she wrote a piece published on January 12, 2017 called *What are the Effects of Affirmative Action Regulation on Workers' Careers?* Amano assures the reader that there is 'substantive evidence' that AA regulation has played an important role in reducing differences in wage and unemployment rates between white men and women, and between majority and minority workers. She also referred to studies that have found that:

> *Affirmative Action regulation in the labour market has positive effects in equalizing employment rates for women and minorities with respect to white men. There is also evidence that the share of minority employees increases when firms become regulated. More strikingly, there is evidence that firms in the same industry as a regulated one, tend to change their hiring practices in a similar fashion as those that are under the regulation, and that in those firms that are regulated, the share of employees continues to grow even after the firm is deregulated.*[174]

This suggests AA legislation is having a positive impact on both women and other minorities in the US, at least.

Some scientists at the University of Innsbruck have also explored the impact of AA in organisations. Their research was published in *Science* and reported in an article in *Science News* in February, 2012 headed *Scientists show positive effects of affirmative action policies promoting women.*

In a multi-stage experiment, research subjects were randomly assigned into groups of six, each consisting of three men and three women. They were put through a series of tasks that as a non-scientist I'm not going to try to explain. The main results of the experiment were that, without intervention, the number of women willing to compete in the tasks was only half the number of men. With intervention, the frequency of competing women was significantly higher. And as one of the researchers said, 'the most exciting result of the experiment is that … overall performance did not suffer.'[175]

In summary, the researchers' findings were that interventions to support women in the workplace do indeed have a positive effect, and that teamwork was not threatened by the interventions made during the experiment.

What about women in politics? Julia Gillard in *Women and leadership*, co-authored with Ngozi Okonjo-Iweala, tells her readers in her introductory piece that she 'helped establish a Labor women's organisation called Emily's List, with a mission of supporting and fundraising for pro-choice, pro-feminism and pro-equity candidates.'[176] Emily Maguire in her book *This is what a feminist looks like* also refers to Emily's List and tells her readers that, 'In its first 18 years, Emily's List has supported over 540 female candidates' campaigns and seen (sic) more than 235 of them elected to state, territory and federal parliaments.'[177] Labor women comprised 38% of the chamber in the 2022 parliament – the highest ever proportion on record – after 58 women were elected to the lower house, including 10 first-term MPs, suggesting that affirmative action through Emily's List have been successful. Have some prospective male candidates missed out because of the List? Probably, but is the Party the beneficiary? I would argue a resounding 'Yes'.

Interviewees

KB, a senior partner in an international law firm, gave me several excellent examples of AA in action:

> When someone is being put up for partnership, our CEO insists that we have women as well as men go through the training process, and that we must be conscious about whether we have enough women coming up for review and consideration.

As an example, KB explained that she sat on one promotion intake panel where the candidates were initially all men until the CEO insisted that they include some women. In response, the panel members searched for and identified two women from the firm to be included in the interviews. 'They got up by a country mile – the women turned out to be the standout best candidates.' As KB concluded, those women would not have been considered as partners but for the CEO's insistence – AA in action.

Another example KB gave was that her current firm does an assessment of any gender pay gap every year, and if discrepancies are identified, an attempt is made to redress these – quite unlike her earlier years in a different firm where, 'I expect I was paid less back then, but I didn't ever compare my salary with others.'

KB then talked about how client pressure is helping with her firm's gender diversity as well:

> *Clients now insist on us reporting on our gender diversity policies when we pitch to go on panels. One of the major companies within my area (mining) declared about 2 years ago that they're working towards a 50/50 workforce … and now do some reverse discrimination hiring – e.g. they may consider only employing a female electrician because they need more women in the workshop.*

PC has had a long career in health management including as CEO of the Royal Australasian College of Surgeons for many years. There he helped put in place several measures that encouraged women to join the college's training programs; including making the curriculum more flexible, allowing part-time and interrupted training, and allowing two trainees to share a single training post. As he said, 'This not only helped young mothers, but young fathers too.'

A specific program PC told me he was particularly proud of, was in response to the college realising that there was a dire shortage of female urologists in Australia and New Zealand at the time. It came to his notice that Muslim women were suffering from a higher rate of urological problems because, as he discovered, they would not see a male urologist. Under his lead, the college made a special effort to attract more women trainee surgeons into urology – a win for those women surgeons we hope, and for their Muslim female patients.

However, PC stressed to me that it's not enough to attract more women into traditionally male specialities like urology – it is also essential to change the environment in which they train and work. He told me the college put in place five steps for change to ensure that women succeeded:

- *They changed the environment to be more female friendly.*

- *They set up a mentoring program to support all trainees.*
- *All other things being equal [which as he said 'they rarely are'], they would choose the woman to redress the gender imbalance.*
- *They ensured that all their trainees were ready for leadership roles, rather than just selecting them and hoping for the best.*
- *They used a series of learning videos targeted at existing surgeons to try and bring about attitudinal change regarding female colleagues and female patients.*

So, have things improved for women because of affirmative action change programs here in Australia?

JER is now an executive coach having had a long and successful career as an HR practitioner. She told me that things have certainly improved for women compared to some of the things she experienced early in her career. For example, she believes there's much more awareness about issues underlying peoples' unconscious biases. However, she also lamented the fact that the actual numbers of women in senior leadership roles and on boards hasn't changed much at all:

Why? The answer is quite complex but in part it's because of the whole corporate milieu and the nature of competition and hierarchies.

PM, who left a senior health career to enter politics and is now a cattle breeder lamented:

I think for a woman to get there she's got to be a lot better than the men, and unfortunately, I think this is going to continue for a while yet.

When I asked GW, who has had a long career in the IT sector, whether she believes things have improved for women, she said:

OMG yes – unequivocally. Overt sexism is not tolerated anymore and is stomped on very quickly. But I'm the only female director of IT in my region and walking into a room full of men is still daunting.

AS, a former CEO who now serves on several boards, said:

Have things improved? I think they have – the basic stuff has really changed. People know that harassment and discrimination are illegal and all those really obvious things have definitely improved.

In some places bad behaviour has become more subtle and harder to see, but that's usually about bad management.

After a career in the public sector, TT now consults to and coaches senior leaders. In response to my question about whether things have improved for women at work, her impassioned reply was:

No, not really. If you want to use the tired old example of women now being 'allowed' to continue working after marriage, then I guess on the face of that, and other discriminations, there's been an improvement. Mind you, we are far too quick at times, to use such examples followed up with, 'look how far we've come!' It's just rubbish – we haven't come anywhere – we should never have had to fight for our right to be equal – we are equal. Such discriminations should never have been a condition of women's rights, or anyone's rights to work, ever. And where did that nonsense rule (amongst a thousand other nonsense rules) prohibiting women to make work choices even come from? Who made those laws? We all know who… so my question is, why are we continuing to tolerate a particular group (males, perhaps middle aged and afraid) to make so many decisions that negatively influence the real lives of women?

It amazes me we are still in work situations that are less than equitable. Many people who work in the public sector are, for the most part, well educated, and dare I say somewhat privileged. The salaries are good and the conditions generally excellent. With all this advantage, and access to the comforts of work and information, why on earth are we still unsure of creating equity of all people? The salary gap is still very real; the lack of diversity at the decision-making table, blindingly obvious: the go-to language of 'he, him, male', if not that, then 'other' predominates, lack of child care options, men never being asked how they manage being a dad while working full-time; need I go on.

A final point and more in the larger scheme of things; in 1986 sanctions were imposed by several countries against South Africa with the view to essentially ending the system of apartheid. The degree to which the sanctions were responsible for ending apartheid can be a matter for debate but the point I'm making is, where

*there was fierce racial injustice, countries rallied to bring about
humanitarian change. My question is, where in the world have we
ever seen any such sanctions imposed on countries and regimes that
blatantly discriminate in violent ways against women? We always
hear the excuse of 'religious rights' but really? Does that even hold
up at all, make any sense, especially if you're a woman? Or is it that
women are still considered the lesser sex, the 'possessional' object,
the toy of men, the hysterical and disposable ones...the ones rules
need to be made for, especially to control. I'll leave you to decide.*

SA has been an allied health practitioner, an academic and leader in the
higher education sector, and is now the managing director of a small
business that provides information, resources and advice to the allied
health sector. She told me that she believes there are increasing opportunities for women in the higher education sector because of affirmative
action policies:

*Universities are now implementing positive discrimination policies
to ensure there are at least 50% female candidates, so the opportunities are there for women. And if they're not, my suggestion to
younger women is that they ask why not.*

CP has spent her career thus far in increasingly senior roles in health
information systems in the large public hospital setting. She shared with
me her experience earlier in her career of working to a board where
senior women were a feature:

*I was the secretary for a board 20 years ago and we had several
females on that board. They were corporate high-flying females.
That was the first time we'd seen this in health, and it was good. And
this was due to affirmative action in the late '80s and early '90s.*

CP went on to explain that now that there's no longer the legislated
requirement, 'there's the male domination, and it's like we need a second
wave of affirmative action'.

The fact that Australia is being left behind in terms of gender parity
was reinforced by two interviewees.

First, JG who has had a stellar career in HR consulting in both
Australia and South-East Asia. After she'd spent several years in
expatriate roles based in Singapore, she told me how shocked she was

to find on her return to Australia how male-dominated organisations still are here:

> There is diversity throughout the multinationals in Asia – diversity in race, religion, gender, colour etc – and this is just how the world is up there.

And second, LM, who is the legal counsel in a finance company with a US parent supported JG's observations:

> My current workplace is more diverse because it's global. A lot of the leaders are from India, Singapore, the UK and other parts of Europe where the culture is different, and so I'm finding there are more likely to be more women in the leadership group.

KB, who is quoted earlier, enabled me to close this section of my AA chapter on an optimistic note in her reply to my question about whether things have improved for women:

> I think things have changed a lot for three main reasons. First, men now have much more awareness of what they're saying and doing and do now understand what is sexist and discriminatory, so just from that perspective things have changed radically. Second, there's a lot more reporting that forces organisations to behave differently; and third, there are a lot more women around in my sector, which changes the power balance and reduces the likelihood of 'bad' behaviour.

In summary I think it would be fair to say that my interviewees responded both 'yes' and 'no' to my question about positive change for women at work in Australia: 'Yes' because there are now procedures in place, there is a feeder pool of bright young women, and an under-standing about acceptable and unacceptable behaviour at work. But 'no' because underlying these positive shifts are still entrenched attitudes and cultures that serve to maintain the status quo. I plan to unpick some more of this later.

What more can be done?

To continue to improve the status of women in their workforces, I think organisations would do well to adapt PC's five-step change plan that was put in place at the Royal Australasian College of Surgeons. Step five, achieving attitudinal change in senior men, is likely to continue to be the most challenging one to achieve. Why? Because as I've already written in chapter 1, 'to the privileged, equality feels like oppression'.

When asked what more needed to change to achieve gender equity in the workplace, JES, a now retired IT professional, told me:

> *Regrettably, I believe that regulated affirmative action – the oppor-*
> *tunity to be considered for any role – is required for employment.*
> *Note that I mean the opportunity to be considered, not a mandate*
> *for appointment as it is in no one's interest for a woman to 'fail'*
> *because she is not the most suitable candidate for the role. If not*
> *appointed, a fair post-interview appraisal and plans for meeting the*
> *identified 'gap' in capacity are important.*

Conclusions

My first conclusion at the end of this chapter is that just as I gravitated towards community health nursing because I preferred the preventative approach to health care, I also firmly believe that leader-led preventative measures through affirmative action will shift organisations much more quickly towards true gender equity. This will work better than continuing to rely on the complaints-based approach.

My second conclusion is that it's beyond time when leaders can still think that their organisation will achieve gender equity organically, just because of the increased pipeline of available women. Specific change programs are needed, and the data supports this.

The challenge now is to work out how to jolt our leaders' awareness from this complacent position so that they commit to making the necessary change. Whether this gets called affirmative action, or indeed evidence-based change, matters not. Whatever the 'jolt' for each individual leader – whether that be from seeing their own partner, daughter or granddaughter overlooked for promotion, or whether it comes from law and policy – my call to Australian leaders is, just do it – and now.

Chapter 7

We need to talk about quotas

In the previous chapter I've discussed how a change program involving special measures for women (affirmative action) can help them become more competitive with their male colleagues. This chapter sets out to explore the use of quotas to measure the effectiveness of such a change program.

I've never been able to work it out: measures are set for every other change program in organisations to enable an assessment of the effectiveness of changes made. For example, if an engineering business does a recruitment drive at their local university, they would most likely set a target of how many of the new engineering graduates they hope to attract because of their efforts. So, as I've already written earlier in this book, what's the problem with setting a quota when the change program is about improving the status of women in our workplaces? If an organisation invests the time and energy in putting in place some special measures to help their high-potential women progress, surely it makes sense to set a numerical measure to evaluate the effectiveness of their efforts? As a consultant with an accounting background, who's working in the diversity sector said on the ABC program *The Drum* one evening, 'Things with measures get done.'

The argument is often put that, if a quota is set to achieve a pre-determined number of women at a certain level, then women will be promoted over more skilled and qualified men, thus compromising the merit principle. However, as I've explained, if affirmative action measures are implemented correctly, they are about enabling women to become competitive, rather than giving them an extra advantage. The setting of quotas is then a way of assessing if these measures have served to widen the pool of available talent to include more women now eligible for promotion. There is, of course, the danger that, even though a woman is promoted on merit, she feels uncomfortable about having reached the 'starting line' through a special measure. Further to this, her colleagues who missed out, could spread the word that the successful woman was promoted to fulfill the company's, quota. Both these possible outcomes could potentially undermine the success of the newly promoted woman, and this is where strong leadership is essential to reassure one and all that she is indeed the best candidate.

Is there something about the word *quota* itself? Has the fear of any woman running roughshod over her male peers given it such bad press that it's become a poisoned chalice? One of the challenges in Australia is that the US right demonised the concept of quotas back in the 1980s, which I suspect has influenced the conservatives here in the same way. This means that the Australian Labor Party (ALP) sets gender quotas with excellent results (as discussed later in the interviewees section), but that the Coalition continues to resist doing so.

If the word *quota* has too much negative history, then why don't we just change the word – what's wrong with the word *target*, or *goal* instead? Although, as you'll read later in this chapter, one of my inter-viewees eventually conceded that the use of so-called 'softer' words such as targets and goals were not working, and she's now reached the con-clusion that, despite all its bad press, quotas it needs to be.

I feel frustrated by these circular arguments because they feel like a distraction from the real goal of creating a gender diverse workforce. Julia Gillard rightly argues that, given merit is gender blind, any team that is made up of more men than women is likely to be a team of lesser calibre than it could have been. Surely this alone, is an excellent reason for the achievement of gender balanced work teams.

Research

In March 2017 Anne Summers published what she called *The women's manifesto: a blueprint for how to get equality for women in Australia.* Summers proposed that for equality for women to be achieved in Australia, the four key areas where change is most needed are in relation to women's financial self-sufficiency, women's reproductive freedom, women's freedom from violence, and the right of women to participate fully and equally in all areas of public life.[178]

Summers then outlined ways that we can rally to achieve these. In terms of the fourth area named above – women's equality in all areas of public life – she recommended that a gender quota of 50/50 be set for all parliamentarians, all cabinet ministers, all directors of public companies and all government boards.

Summers explained her reasons for this:

> It is clear that increased representation of women in all decision-making organizations of our society is not going to happen organically. If so, it would already have happened. We need affirmative action in the form of quotas to ensure that the best talent available leads these organizations – and that means including the group that makes up 50 per cent of the population.[179]

As already referred to in chapter 1, in September 2018, the global consulting firm Korn Ferry published a report, *Australian women CEOs speak*, summarising research they had conducted in collaboration with the Australian Institute of Company Directors (AICD) with the purpose of exploring why so few women had made it to a CEO role in Australia. One of the researchers' questions was about the women's career objectives, the obstacles to their progression, their motivations and about their experiences on boards. They found that:

> It is clear that exposure to boards is key to developing women in the pipeline for executive and CEO roles. Our interviews revealed that half the women described significant experience with boards before becoming a CEO. This experience helped them gain a holistic view of their organisation's performance and insight into future non-executive director roles.[180]

The report stated that the AICD had called for all boards to set a target that 30% of their directors were to be women by 2018.

At the time of publication of this book, the proportion of women on ASX200 boards had reached 35.7 per cent which is surely an excellent example of the fact that setting targets can work.

While on holiday with my partner in Far North Queensland in the spring of 2018, I was delighted to find a real live example of quotas at work in an article in *The Australian* newspaper. Written by Cliona O'Dowd, the article summarised a speech given by Ann Sherry to the annual Chief Executive Women's dinner. Sherry had been a senior executive at Westpac, next she was a CEO, and she is now a non-executive director on several boards. On the topic of quotas Sherry was reported as telling the 1,300 guests:

> *All of us know that having great people in business is critical to success and a quota is a people target. … I came into Westpac on the back of what was effectively a quota. Bob Joss (then CEO of Westpac) said to everyone on his executive, 'Each of you must hire women.' … And eight of us women magically appeared on the executive ranks at Westpac. So it's possible but it's got to be deliberate, … you've got to want it to happen.*[181]

Julia Gillard and Ngozi Okonjo-Iweala in *Women and leadership* discuss what they call 'twokenism'. This term was used in a study to explain what happens when two women are appointed onto a board: if one woman is seen as tokenism, they appoint two, but the study found that this sets up a scenario where the women are competing on a 'narrower women's track to appointment' – hence 'twokenism'.

It seems that the mining giant BHP is taking a lead in achieving a gender balance in their workforce. An article in the February 5, 2020 issue of *The Sydney Morning Herald* written by Nick Toscano[182] announced that BHP has 'set a target for women to make up half of its 26,000 direct employees by 2025'. At end June, 2022 more than 32.3 per cent of BHP's workforce was female and 38 per cent of the roles that reported to their Executive Leadership Team were held by women, suggesting that good progress towards achieving this goal is being made. Further, the article explains that BHP is also requiring its network of contractors and supply partners – which account for 60% of

BHP's 72,000 workforce – to mirror this 2025 goal by similarly striving for women to make up 50% of their workforces by then.

Given BHP, the so-called 'Big Australian', is investing heavily in achieving a numerically measured gender balance in its workforce in the traditionally male-dominated industry of mining, it's surely time that all other employers saw the business sense in committing to doing likewise.

Interviewees

Many of the interviewees shared insightful responses to my question about the quotas.

JER, formerly an HR professional and now an executive coach, used the example of the Australian ALP, through its Emily's List program, to support her argument that quotas work. Inspired by EMILY's List in the United States, and as outlined in chapter 6, Emily's List Australia is a political network that supports 'progressive' Labor Party women in Australian politics.[183]

DD, a former corporate HR executive, now runs her own international motorcycle adventure soul safari company. She told me:

I'm an advocate of quotas, if that's what it takes to propel us into the 21st century. Everyone needs to see, hear and experience women in senior roles for things to change. Julia Gillard says it well, 'The case for women's leadership is as simple as this, that if you believe that merit is distributed between the sexes equally, then we should, in the ordinary course of things, be seeing half men and half women coming through.' If this is not happening naturally, which it can't in an unconsciously patriarchal system, then we need to encourage the appointment of women in positions of influence so that our society and world can benefit from the capabilities of the total population … until it becomes the natural way of things.

TA, with a background in recruiting, is an executive coach. She shared a close to home example about her daughter who's studying engineering:

Whether we call them quotas or what, we need some system to hold senior corporate people, both male and female, to account. My daughter is aware of pay inequality in engineering and she's already thinking about how she might go about reaching a senior level in what is an industry that's currently highly skewed towards men.

I have no doubt that the organisation that gives TA's daughter this opportunity will not regret it.

GW, a chief information officer, explored the positive and negatives of quotas for women in the tech industry:

> *There are only 18–20% women in IT, so employers are always keen to get their numbers up. But that being said, your gender also hinders you because you're seen as the token female, and so they don't actually believe you've got the skills to do the job – it's just getting the numbers up. So, this means my gender has helped and hindered me. Mind you, I would be extremely foolish to not make use of the diversity numbers to get in, because I can prove it once I'm in there, but getting there is sometimes hard.*

Former CEO and now non-executive board member, AS is a strong advocate for quotas and cites the success of efforts to improve the gender diversity at a board level:

> *The makeup of boards has only changed because a lot of the investor groups have said they don't want boards that all look the same. And suddenly everyone could find women for their boards. … Also, the naming and shaming of the ASX of the companies that have no women has moved things along a bit more.*

AS then went on to explore the use of quotas in the general workforce:

> *Men do this cleverly – they say we'll have incompetent women if we have quotas. My response is always that, when we have as many incompetent women as incompetent men, then we'll have real gender equality.*

> *But it's too slow, and this has become a neat deferral blocking mechanism. So I've just shifted my language – we set hard targets for everything else – for sales, for numbers, for investor relations, for everything except equality in work places. So why when we all say people are our greatest asset, do we not set hard targets around that?*

Finally, and so my readers don't accuse me of being totally biased towards the case for quotas, here is EM, a woman who reached the highest levels of management in the IT sector through her own unique mix of talent, determination and a quirky sense of humour:

> *I don't think quotas are the answer. I think they may lead to unintended and possibly disastrous consequences. For example, a friend of mine is gay and he wonders whether he should reveal this, and then when promoted, he wonders if it was to fulfill a quota rather than on their ability to do the job. I've heard that Barak Obama never ticked the box to say that he was African American on any scholarship form or uni application forms because he never wanted it said that he got into an institution because of a quota.*

Instead, as EM told me, he applied as Barry Obama, and we all know where he ended up.

What more can be done?

KB, a senior legal partner brought her clear legal mind to the topic of quotas:

> *We've been talking about equality for over 20 years and nothing has changed. Why? Because there's been nothing to make it change. …*
> *You've got to have the 'law' to make (some men) accept this.*

KB therefore advocates that the setting of quotas is needed to make the change. She notes that she has only recently come to this position, previously thinking that targets would be sufficient, but the lack of progress suggests to her that quotas are needed. We all understand and respond to rules and measures, so I'm with KB: let's bring compliance into this conversation. However, as she cautioned to me, this needs to be sensibly done – for example, by ensuring that there are capable women in the pool for selection. This might require some affirmative action measures to get them competitive, and then selection must still be done on merit.

In advocating that 'the law' is still needed to make some men change, KB is acknowledging the ongoing importance of sex discrimination and affirmative action laws in Australia but, it's turned out that more is needed. This is borne out by both KB and many others quoted in this book.

Conclusions

In my 35 plus years of experience in consulting in the field of gender diversity and coaching and mentoring women, I have never known of, or been told about, a situation where tokenism has occurred – that is, when a woman has been recruited or promoted into a senior position in an Australian business when there was a more qualified and experienced man in the field of candidates. This has so rarely happened, that I can only conclude that the ongoing resistance to the setting of quotas must come from men's fear of the greater competition that the presence of more women causes.

My conclusion about whether to set quotas therefore remains that some method must be used to measure the effectiveness of all change programs. Whether they're called goals, or targets – or as KB now argues, quotas – I say to the leaders of Australia that whatever you choose to call the means to assess the efficacy of your change programs for women, just get on with it. I can almost guarantee that your business will be the better for it.

Chapter 8

A shoulder to cry on, a brain to pick and someone to give us a kick in the pants

As I've explained in the previous two chapters, affirmative action measures are about opening the way for women to become more competitive at all levels of an organisation. It can be lonely and hard for women to do this on their own. This chapter is about the importance of women establishing supports for themselves, and how to go about this.

Very early in my feminist awakening I read a book that convinced me that we women didn't have to go it alone. First published in 1980 it was written by Natasha Josefowitz and was called *Paths to power: a woman's guide from first job to top executive*. One message I took from this book is the importance of setting up supports for oneself. Josefowitz tells her readers that at various times we all need, 'a shoulder to cry on, a brain to pick and someone to give us a kick in the pants'.[184]

In the tougher times throughout my career, I've often paused and reflected about who I could turn to who could fulfill each of these three needs. For example, when I feel like having one of those 'ain't it awful?' moans about life, I turn to one of my close women friends who will be prepared to share a glass of wine and indulge my need to have a good old whinge. No problem solving; no questions about what I might have done to contribute to the situation; just good old listening and empathy. Conversely, when I've needed and wanted to solve a problem, my thoughts turn to who I know who is a 'subject matter expert' in whatever my dilemma is about.

My late partner Des was the best person I've ever known to turn to when I knew I needed a good 'kick in the pants'. There was no point turning to him to be a 'shoulder to cry on'. As I explained in chapter 4, his approach was about taking personal responsibility – whatever it was that was concerning me, his first question always was, 'So what are you going to do about it, Kate?'

In fact, it was one of those prods from Des that was my primary motivation to first develop my equal opportunity practice and then evolve this into a leadership coaching practice in the early '90s. Another motivation was that the budgets for EO consulting services were slashed in the then economic depression, so my diminishing bank account further spurred me on to make change. Also, having by then seen first-hand the challenges women were facing in what were still patriarchal cultures in corporate Australia, I realised that some of them could well do with a safe 'shoulder to cry on,' a caring 'brain to pick' and indeed someone to, at times, give them a (gentle) 'kick in the pants'. My assumption proved to be correct, and when I put my first proposal – that included words like 'professional loneliness' – to a woman who'd been an EO client, she looked at me and asked, 'How did you know?' 'I've been watching you', was my simple reply.

As outlined earlier, my leadership coaching offer provides clients with regular time for reflective practice in a confidential and pleasant environment close to, but not in, their own office; and that my reason for insisting we meet off-site is so that the rest of the office doesn't know that my client is meeting with me, and to help them separate from the everyday challenges of their working life. Good coffee, tasty biscuits and calming music are also part of the offer.

Together with confidentiality, enshrined in my coaching style is that I provide my clients with an 'advice free zone'. This comes from a belief that my clients' answers lie deep within themselves. It's my job, through asking open-ended questions, to help them gain fresh insights about their issues, and then to decide what they want to do about them. Also enshrined in my practice is a belief that clients need a context for any changes they make. To find this I encourage them to create their vision and purpose for their whole of life, including their professional life, and to write this down. Further, I facilitate them to clarify their core values, and together we ensure that any plans they make for change are congruent with their vision, purpose and values.

As also outlined earlier, my mentoring practice is a pro bono service I now offer in my latter years for women with their own small businesses. With this 'hat' on, my practice almost mirrors my approach to leadership coaching – the only difference being I sometimes include advice, where I sense this might be helpful.

In terms of measuring the effectiveness of my coaching and mentoring services, I ask my clients to complete an evaluation at the end of their contract of support. I forward this to the referrer, and it also acts as a guide to me about ways I can improve my offer. I ask clients to rate my services out of 10, and my typical average from the evaluations each year tends to be about 9.5. Added to this, the fact that I'm still occasionally coaching some women who I first saw as emerging leaders many years ago, I think speaks for itself.

Having learnt the value of setting up a range of supports for myself, I regularly encourage my leadership coaching clients to create a strong network of support for themselves. For example, I ask them who in their organisation they could turn to as a mentor and sponsor from whom they could seek wise counsel about the inner workings of their work environment and culture. Also, who they could look up to as a role model – for example, a more senior woman, either within their organisation or in the wider business world – even if they were to never meet this person. And I ask them. who among their work colleagues and/or wider friendship group could they invite to join them in a network of peer support.

One concrete way I've provided a support network for women is through a Melbourne-based group called the Dolphin Forum. What is the Dolphin Forum, and why such a name?

To answer these questions, I need to go back to when I signed on my first leadership coaching client in early 1990 in Sydney. As my coaching practice slowly grew after that, I looked around for supports for myself. I initially thought I could get this from a Sydney-based women-in-management organisation. However, this group proved to be full of women wearing jackets with large shoulder pads (the larger the better – yes, it was the '90s!), many of whom were also consultants, and most of whom appeared to be competing, rather than collaborating, with each other. This observation led me to a good idea. Through my growing coaching client base of high potential women, I was in the privileged position of spending regular time one on one with some impressive women. My idea was to invite these women to join a more informal networking group than was on offer from the women in management one. And so, the Dolphin Forum was born.

Why the name? I got the idea from a management book published back in the late '80s called *Strategy of the dolphin: scoring a win in a chaotic world*, written by Dudley Lynch and Paul Kordis, who are described on the back cover as 'US based management gurus'. I enjoyed their book, which used the creatures of the sea as metaphors for the various 'players' in organisational life: the 'sharks', the highly competitive people who are on about win/lose; the 'carps', the powerless ones, the so-called 'yes, men'; the 'pseudo-enlightened carps', who pretend to be on about change but actually aren't; and the 'dolphins' who are the leaders of transformational change in organisations.[185]

The analogy that I especially liked from the book was that just as dolphins know when to dive off one wave and onto another, rather than being dumped onto the sand, so too the authors argue, are the dolphins in organisational life smart enough to know when to 'dive' from their current situation onto a new 'wave' that will help them sustain momentum and continue to embrace change for the good.

I set up my first Dolphin Forum in Sydney in the early '90s. Six to eight women used to meet in my tiny Elizabeth Bay apartment once a month. Next, as my coaching practice grew in Melbourne, I set up a Dolphin Forum there too. And when my daughter was a graduate trainee in Canberra, I even had a small Dolphin Forum there for a while.

The Sydney group lasted about two years, and the Canberra one folded when my daughter went back to a job in Adelaide. But I'm proud, and somewhat astonished, to say that the Melbourne group of 20 or so women continue to meet over 35 years later.

Growth in members of the forum was, and still is, the responsibility of the Dolphins themselves. If any current member comes across a woman who they believe has Dolphin qualities (such as openness, authenticity and a commitment to personal and organisational change), they invite them along to the next forum. If they enjoy the experience, they are added to my Dolphin database.

Until the COVID-19 pandemic hit in early 2020, the Melbourne group met for dinner. Over the years we've used a range of pubs and cafes in inner city suburbs for our meetings – our criteria being convenient parking, tasty affordable food, and a quiet enough place to guarantee our privacy. On average, six to eight women attend each forum and the format is that I facilitate the evening starting with some 'show and tell' about what's been happening in our worlds since we last met. This can be the good news (e.g. a promotion), and the not-so-good: at one memorable forum a visibly distressed Dolphin shared her experience about being sexually harassed by a senior manager at a work function. As each Dolphin takes their turn to speak, they relate their stories to the Dolphin purpose and values (see appendix), and share which one or two they've chosen on the night; either because they're currently living by these, or because they're not, yet would like to be.

I then lead a discussion on a topic of their choice. Topics have been wide-ranging: sustaining the work/life juggling act; the so-called 'imposter syndrome' versus self-belief; operating effectively in male cultures; women and ageing; and what was to me a surprisingly hot topic, feminism. I'd assumed that because all the Dolphins are out there in the world making a difference in their own unique ways and juggling their work and their families, that they would automatically call themselves feminists. But several of the younger women said they weren't comfortable with the term because they associated it with the so-called 'men hating/bra burners' of the '70s and '80s. To which I would point out that I was a feminist back then, and never once burnt my bra.

Since the onset of COVID-19, Zoom has become our virtual meeting place. And I'm proud to report that at the time of publication of this book, my next invitation will be to Dolphin Forum #110 and there are 20 women listed on my Dolphin database.

Some of these women have become good friends of mine and each other. I still coach some of them, and I've interviewed some of them as part of my research for this book. I'm a very proud 'Head Dolphin' because when I convened this group back in the early '90s, most of the women who joined were in the early stages of their careers, and most of them now hold senior roles or run their own thriving businesses.

Their ongoing attendance suggests that the Dolphin Forum still adds value to their lives all these years later, a fact that fills me with joy and humility.

The feedback from participating women over the years is that the Dolphin Forum provides a safe place for members to support each other, and to believe in themselves and their worth as managers and leaders, in a continuing male world. Has this meant that they've stretched for more in their careers? I sincerely hope so, and their ongoing attendance suggests that the Dolphin Forum does indeed provide the women who attend with a 'shoulder to cry on, a brain to pick and someone to give them a kick in the pants'.

Research

The Korn Ferry 2018 report *Australian women CEOs speak* already referred to in chapters 1,7 and 11, found that only half of the 21 women CEOs and former CEOs in their research had had mentors, sponsors or coaches, and only a quarter of them said they'd received organisational support through participating in leadership-development programs. Nine of the CEOs talked about the value of a sponsor – 'a person in their organisation who championed them, secured job opportunities for them and offered advice in navigating the organisation'. Only six of the women received coaching, usually at the suggestion of their organisation, but one woman took the initiative herself and found a coach.

I confess I was shocked when I read in the Korn Ferry report how few of these 21 very senior women were being provided with regular support in the form of either mentoring or coaching, and how few had had the chance to participate in some leadership development. This screams of the lack of recognition of how tough it still is for women to navigate and excel in male cultures.[186]

In their book *Women and leadership* Julia Gillard and Nogozi Okonjo-Iweala suggest three kinds of support are needed for aspiring women leaders – role models, mentors and sponsors and define these as:

> *A role model can be any person who is looked up to and whose character traits and achievements are admired ....*

> *Mentoring is a personal relationship between a more-experienced, usually older, person and a less-experienced, usually younger, person. ... The discussions between a mentor and a mentee tend to span giving advice, encouragement and personal support. ...*
>
> *The relationship of sponsorship has more grunt. ... being a sponsor does require the preparedness to utilise your power networks and reputation in service to the other person.*[187]

Further, these two authors stress that we women must champion and support each other, but that this can be difficult because we 'have been pitted against each other since the beginning of time for that one seat at the table.' They also stress that it's important for women to build networks of support, because history teaches us that 'the big advances for women have been made because of collective action.'[188]

Interviewees

To my question about whether they have had supports – be they mentors, role models or a peer network – some of my interviewees, many of whom have been coaching clients of mine, told me that they saw mentoring happening to their male peers in an almost 'unconscious kind of way,' but that they had not been included. However, a number told me about how the support and encouragement they'd received along the way had made a positive difference to the success of their careers.

I've learnt that the difference having a mentor can make to women is both direct and indirect. Some examples of direct support include guidance and advice on what to do in general and specific circumstances; giving a perspective on things because of their additional experience and wisdom; and connections with others through their networks. More indirect support includes women gaining inspiration and role modelling from their mentor as they are 'up ahead', and able to show the way. Mentors inside the workplace are normally in a more senior role. They are therefore able to provide guidance on the workings and nuances of the organisation and decision makers and can act as a sponsor by 'talking you up' in a meeting or discussion at a key time.

KB, the senior partner in an international law firm told me about the 'triumvirate' of three key people who have supported her in her career:

Firstly, my father was my sounding board on every aspect of my career. … He gave me great advice and … a male perspective of how to respond to situations which I found invaluable.

The second person I rely on is my sister. She has been a manager of a large team for the last 20 years and brings a different perspective to problems I sound out with her.

And third I've had a great coach who I thought of as a mentor. She helped me manage my way through so many difficult situations and helped me grow and become a strong leader.

KB concluded that this group had got her through the last 20 years with 'much more grace' than she might otherwise have shown.

KB also talked about people who have 'championed' her at key moments in her career:

In terms of champions, I've had a couple that helped me move into positions that I would not have strived for without their support. In particular, one located a job for me that set me on my way. And another fellow assisted me to become a partner. I don't think I would have done so if he had not championed my capability.

TA, formerly in an accounting placement firm and now an executive coach said:

I did have several mentors during my 17 years within the commercial corporate world from directors at both a local level and also interstate and globally. I was able to take the positive learnings from each one and apply these to my own reality, and I was able to climb the corporate ladder to the level of senior management.

I then experienced a 'glass ceiling' because these internal mentors were unable to provide me with the leadership development I needed to reach the next level. … So I engaged an external leadership coach who was life changing. Her coaching enabled me to realise my full potential and establish strong leadership behaviours which helped me break through the glass ceiling and reach the level of director within the company.

I have continued to be supported by my coach and have had a successful executive coaching business for the past 14 years.

LS, an agriculturist and leader in her region of rural Australia, told me there have been a number of people who've made a significant difference for her at certain stages in her career. For example, her boss at the South Australian Farmers Federation encouraged her to apply for the Australian Rural Leadership Program (ARLP) and she 'would never have applied without his encouragement'. And much more recently, the general manager of the natural resources management board in her region suggested that she apply for a board position and gave her some facilitation work, neither of which she would have done without his encouragement.

In response to my question about what difference these experiences made to her career, LS said:

The real difference my mentors have made is in giving me the confidence to try things I may not have otherwise done (such as applying for the ARLP, applying for board positions, chairing/speaking at/ facilitating meetings and taking on contract work). Just knowing that somebody else believed I could do it, had a significant positive impact for me to give things a go, regardless of what the outcome might be.

MY, a former marketing professional, then equal opportunity coordinator said the only support she ever received in her corporate life was from an external leadership coach that she sought out for herself:

My coaching support helped me in my EEO role [while] working [in] a male-dominated environment, by having someone to talk things through with – a sounding board, someone to give me a reality check and feedback as well as to help me find my own answers, and to trust and follow them.

JER, formerly an HR professional and now an executive coach, told me she's had only one mentor in her very first professional role who had a lasting impact on her career:

It was the male senior manager who was partly responsible for hiring me into the organisation. He took a genuine interest in me as a professional. He had a very broad perspective and was highly progressive in this philosophy and approach. He saw my potential early and expressed a lot of confidence in me.

I think that this was quite formative for me in my career. His role modelling and mentoring made a lasting impression. [Then] as my career progressed, I was able to mentor a number of talented individuals myself, and I found it very rewarding to assist others to fulfill their potential.

JS, a former scientist and now business manager at a university with previous experience as a board member on two boards, talked about the importance of the support she's had from women peers, particularly when more senior women have offered her no support:

In rising up through a [chemicals manufacturing company] it was really important to have strong female co-workers, and we supported each other in a very male-dominated world.

The most amazing support I have had involved a senior manager when I was (in a research organisation). He knew I was being bullied by my boss. He not only reached out, but he actively supported me in getting another job. He is still a very strong supporter, and says he does this for a large number of people particularly where he sees there is inappropriate behaviour.

So, all in all, (except for this one example) I would say I haven't had any overt mentors. Rather it has been a case of having great co-workers support from other females and this has been hugely important.

SA has been an allied health practitioner, an academic and leader in the higher education sector, and is now the managing director of a small business that provides information, resources and advice to the allied health sector. She told me that:

In terms of mentors, yes, they have been pivotal in shaping me and my career. You don't actually realise it at the time, but they are people who come into your life, believe in you, gently point you in another direction and support your journey in that direction.

SA then went on to describe in some detail four mentors who have helped her over the years, ranging from her fifth-grade teacher to the head of a health unit, the CEO of an ambulance service and a quite 'formidable' female professor. As she explained, in each case these people believed in her, showed her new directions, and pushed her forward.

DP, formerly a marketing executive and now a consultant specialising in transformative leadership and organisational change, told me:

> I haven't had any formal mentoring relationships in my time in organisational life. ... My mindset in relation to mentoring is someone, often within the organisation, who plays the role of wiser elder and, ideally, advocate. Informally, I had a boss who later became CEO, who always kept an eye out for me and my career and was a strong supporter. It helped my confidence to know he had my back.

JES, an early IS/IT graduate who went on to have a stellar career in IT in a range of different organisations and sectors, told me:

> I have had some mentors and I am grateful for them. ...

> A significant mentor was the woman who challenged my self-doubt when I said to her that perhaps I should not apply for the role of manager when I had a 3-year-old. (For the record, she pointed out that many male managers had 3-year-olds – and left me to draw my conclusions.) This woman listened well when I had 'situations' to address and always was supportive.

> Another was a female manager, senior in the organisation, who convinced me that I would be among peers if/when I took the executive management course for which she had recommended me. (I had thought this course was for 'other' people). She understood the power of networking, and also supported me in career choices I made outside the organisation.

LM, a law graduate and now legal counsel in an international finance business, talked about the value she gained from an external group:

> I've been part of a group of women outside my workplace who I have met with regularly for over 10 years. Meeting in a supportive environment with women from different fields and different paths to

*me has provided me with a constant source of inspiration and has
often caused me to challenge my own thinking.*

When pressed, LM said, yes, she was referring to the Dolphin Forum,
which put a big smile on my face.

LM then talked about how men are more likely to be sponsored
than women inside organisations, and she shared a specific example of
when this happened:

> *I was at the leadership table when a project I had been working
> on was discussed. A male leader was enthusiastically praising
> a male member of the project team, effectively sponsoring them for
> a promotion as a result. The reality was the individual had actually
> hindered the success of the project. I could not remain silent and
> had to call out the greater contribution of two women on the team.
> Ultimately the male team member was promoted.*

LM concluded by giving me a wry smile and saying, 'They did enjoy
golf together'.

CP, who is amid a stellar career in information systems in the public
health sector and is also a member of the Dolphin Forum, talked about
the wise counsel she got from an older member of that women's network when she was pregnant with her first child:

> *[This woman] told me to make a plan, and to make my plan known.
> And also, to remember that you can change your plan – and this
> was in the days where you didn't have a right to come back to your
> previous job [after maternity leave].*

CP then explored the value of having leadership coaching support
throughout her career. She talked about how this had given her the
confidence to negotiate her salary package at an early stage. She also
said that the 'early vision work' she did in her coaching helped her to
explore her values and what was important to her at work.

Further, CP talked about the importance of also having mentors
inside the organisation for support:

> *I have had mentors along the way and the difference they have
> made is… that they would stretch my thinking. They've [also] been
> supportive in terms of encouraging my development.*

> *And I've had the confidence to seek people out to help me with [difficult] situations, and that includes my boss, if I'm struggling with something.*

Finally, some wise advice from a long-term high achiever to younger women. EM, a now retired CIO interviewee, told me that on International Women's Day in 2019 her then firm asked senior women to provide some advice to the more junior women:

> *My advice was to never volunteer to set up the room, take the minutes or get the coffee for meetings. Just don't do it. I've had women argue with me – if you take the minutes you can control the agenda but NO, you don't take the minutes, you review and approve the minutes. It's about ownership, not doing.*

What more can be done?

On the topic of support, recommendations in the Korn Ferry report included what the researchers called 'takeaways' for both senior women and their organisations. For women:

> *Women should be sure to sharpen their operations and strategic skills with formal training and mentoring.*[189]

For organisations, the researchers recommended setting up coaching and mentoring for their senior women to better equip them in the areas of 'developing talent, directing work, building effective teams, … strategic thinking, decision-making and delegating'. Further they recommended that leadership development programs be tailor-made to meet the unique needs of their senior team, especially their women, and that 'mentoring and sponsorship will be much more effective if the mentors and sponsors themselves are coached on what women need'.

DP, quoted above, made a valuable suggestion about what women need to help them succeed:

> *What women need even more than mentoring is advocacy, and while they are not mutually exclusive, I think women need someone sitting at the exec/senior table actively having you in mind for opportunities and pushing this where appropriate.*

Another name for such a person is a 'sponsor' who, as DP suggests keeps you in mind for opportunities – for example further professional development and/or a promotion – that you, yourself, would otherwise have not known about.

Retired IT professional JES reinforced DP's recommendation suggesting that once a woman is appointed that there be:

> … an overt supportive mentorship program to support the appointee. There is blowback when such programs are introduced, as I have heard men say they feel they are not offered the same opportunities, and justifiably so. It is good HR practice for all new appointees – men as well as women – to have their needs assessed and then the appropriate support provided: training, mentoring, peer support and encouragement of networking opportunities.

When I started leadership coaching, my first challenge was explaining the value of such a service to the market. Leadership and executive coaching are now mainstream services. I agree with JES that internal mentorship programs are an excellent idea and would also recommend to all leaders and aspiring leaders that they seek out the services of a skilled external coach as well. I believe that it's essential to provide leadership development programs to new leaders with one condition, which is that the program includes some one-on-one coaching support for participants, because each new leader's issues are unique to them.

I also remain an advocate for women-only programs in larger organisations. This supports emerging women leaders and helps them name and navigate their way through the male cultures that they are still very likely to experience.

Conclusions

I have certainly heeded the advice of Natasha Josefowitz in her 1980 book by regularly seeking out 'a shoulder to cry on, a brain to pick and someone to give me a kick in the pants' at different times in my career. I also agree with Gillard and Okonjo-Iweala that we women all need the three kinds of support of role models, mentors and sponsors. I continue to encourage my leadership coaching clients to ensure they have these set up for themselves.

The first conclusion I take from my research and interviewees in this chapter is confirmation that a strong network of support is essential for both women and men to help them develop their full potential and thrive. My second conclusion is confirmation that this must be actively sought out by women, because these types of support do not automatically happen for them in the way that seems to occur for most men.

Chapter 9

The career woman/mother juggling act

In the last chapter I discussed the importance for women to set up a range of support mechanisms for themselves. Once a working woman announces the happy news that she's expecting a baby and intends to return to work after taking maternity leave, her need for support multiplies. This chapter covers what I'm choosing to call the 'juggling act' that will be familiar to all working mothers.

Two stories come to my mind as I reflect on this chapter heading. The first is a memory of mine. When my equal opportunity consultancy was slowly growing, I was interviewed by a women's magazine during which I was asked how I was managing to build a business while being a single mum to two teenage children. I clearly remember my reply: 'It's a juggling act. Sometimes I immerse myself in my business too much at the expense of my kids. Then I suffer an attack of maternal guilt and compensate by over-mothering my poor long-suffering daughter and son.'

My second story comes from a young woman who was attending a career development program for women that I was running in Sydney. As part of her introduction, she told the group that she'd recently returned to work after the birth of her second baby. She then paused and added, 'Now, when I arrive at work in the morning – having got myself and my kids fed and dressed and my two littlies off to childcare – instead of greeting me with a 'good morning', I reckon they should all stand up and cheer.'

Research

Much has been written about the topic of the career/mum juggling act. Let's start with a delightful little book with the catchy title of *Who cooked Adam Smith's dinner?* In this book, Swedish author Katrine Marçal tells her readers that Adam Smith, seen as the father of political economy, was able to devote himself to his wise theories because he lived with his mother, who cooked and 'did' for him. Marçal argues that women are still fighting to gain equal access to the world of 'he' whom she calls 'economic man'.

Marçal shares the somewhat depressing statistic that women currently spend over two-thirds of their working day doing unpaid work. She goes on to state that women's work seems to be regarded as a 'natural resource' that doesn't need to be counted in the gross GDP of any country. Marçal also argues that, because we all assume that women's care contributions will always be there, it's seen to be part of 'an invisible, indelible infrastructure.'[190]

Annabel Crabb's book *The wife drought* also provides a rich source of data about the career/mum juggling act. I think her subtitle – *Why women need wives, and men need lives* – says it all really: that working women are still carrying too much of the burden of home duties, while men continue to be expected to put in the long hours. And further, that men's careers are often penalised if they make their new child a priority by taking paternity leave.

The back cover of Crabb's book describes *The wife drought* as the 'thoughtful, engaging catalyst for a conversation that's long overdue.' So, what does this conversation need to be about? I believe that this is about no less than the more equal sharing of the domestic load when both parents work, and the acceptance by organisations that men are parents too and want the flexibility to contribute more fully to both parenting and the domestic load, without this negatively impacting their careers.

In chapter 6 I outlined what Crabb tells her readers – which is that housework doesn't count towards the gross domestic product which, as she points out, is the best-known measure of national productivity in

Australia. On the topic of the domestic load, Crabb's research revealed that, even when they are in full-time work, women do more housework than men and that, even if they don't have a job, men do less housework than women.[191]

On the topic of work/life balance, Crabb points the finger directly at CEOs. If they mouth that work-life balance is important in their organisation yet are at their desk by 7 am and regularly put in 12-hour days, their team is inevitably going to do likewise. Crabb's, and my solution is simple: it's the message to leaders that if they really believe work-life balance is important, they should say that no one must be in the office before nine, and that no meetings will occur after five.[192]

Maternity leave provisions have improved the lot of working parents, especially mothers. These have been gradually introduced in Australia, starting in November 1973 when the Whitlam Labor government awarded Australian public servants 12 weeks paid maternity leave. This, of course, helped female public servants who either needed or wanted to remain in the workforce to do so. Paid maternity leave and then parental leave slowly followed until 2009 when Kevin Rudd introduced a scheme which provided 18 weeks leave at the minimum wage for either mum or dad. However, as Crabb tells us in her book, bureaucrats told a Senate estimate's hearing that in 2013, 10,000 women took paid parental leave each month, whereas just under 20 men took it.[193]

In 2014, the then Sex Discrimination Commissioner Elizabeth Broderick surveyed 1,000 fathers who'd taken dad and partner pay. She found that 27% of these men said they'd experienced pushback from their bosses and their colleagues for taking this leave. This takes us back to Crabb's basic thesis that 'women need a wife and men need a life'.

One of the leaders interviewed by Julia Gillard and Ngozi Okonjo-Iweala in *Women and leadership* was Jacinda Ardern, the then Prime Minister of New Zealand and the mother of a young daughter. On the topics of work/life balance and maternal guilt, I was delighted to read that Ardern challenged the word 'balance':

> *I don't think I particularly balance anything. I just make it work. …*
> *I don't think women should feel as if they have to do it all and make*
> *it look easy, because it's not easy and we shouldn't have to try to do*
> *everything, and I don't. We must not pretend we're superhuman,*

because that sets a false expectation and it also leaves the impression that we shouldn't need support.[194]

Given their sample group were women in public life, Gillard and Okonjo-Iweala spend time exploring the pros and cons of this for women with and without children. In fact, the fifth hypothesis they propose in their book about women leaders worldwide is about this topic, and it consists of two parts. The first part is that:

Having children and being a leader plays out differently for women than it does for men.[195]

As evidence to support this hypothesis, the authors point out that most women who've made it to the top echelons of political leadership either do not have children, or their children are adults at the time of their political career. Further, I would add how unfair this double standard is for women: where they must time their political leadership around their parenting, a male politician with a supportive wife and a young family is seen as stable and ready for greater things.

The second part of Gillard and Okonjo-Iweala's fifth hypothesis is that:

While being childless means a woman leader has not had to face the challenges of combining work and family life, it brings other issues.[196]

Again, this double standard infuriates me: the fact that Julia Gillard was described as 'barren' and was criticised for having an empty fruit bowl on her kitchen table when giving an interview in her home, just skims the surface of the truth of this fifth hypothesis.

On the topic of available and affordable childcare, Anne Summers argues persuasively in her memoir *Unfettered and alive* that this is an economic issue, not a welfare one. Summers managed to shift the focus on both childcare and paid parental leave while advisor on women's issues to PM Paul Keating. In fact, on 10 February, 1993 in a speech (written by Summers) to launch the National Agenda for Women, Keating said:

'*The time is long past, as far as I am concerned, where childcare was tagged as a "women's issue" or a "welfare issue" and only attracted the crumbs from the table where the budget banquet was enjoyed'.*[197]

On the topic of more flexible work practices for women and men alike, Sue Morphet, then president of Chief Executive Women was quoted in the September 17, 2020 issue of *The Sydney Morning Herald* (digital edition) as saying that the COVID-19 pandemic has 'legitimised flexible work arrangements, but they (now) need to be made permanent'.[198]

While it seems that more flexible working arrangements are turning out to be one of the positive outcomes of the COVID-19 pandemic for both women and men, recent data shows that women are now carrying even more of the bulk of unpaid domestic and caring responsibilities. The Australian Bureau of Statistics (ABS) Head of Household Surveys, David Zago, has revealed that the ABS survey conducted from May 14–23, 2021:

> ...*found that 62 percent of women spent five or more hours in the last week on unpaid indoor housework compared with 35 per cent of men.*
>
> *Women also took on more caring responsibilities than men, spending five or more hours in the last week on unpaid caring or supervision of children (38 per cent of women compared with 28 per cent of men), care of adults (16 percent compared with 7 per cent) and cooking and baking (64 per cent compared with 37 per cent.)*[199]

Interviewees

I got an avalanche of responses from my interviewees to my question #5: 'If you are a mother, did you or do you experience maternal guilt as you juggle/or have juggled work and family?'

Before I share some of these responses, let me reflect awhile on what I've learnt from my coaching clients and my own experiences as a working mother, and then much later as a working carer of my partner. I've learnt that the structures, the systems, the expected hours of work and the cultures of organisations – particularly the larger ones – were created by, and continue to be sustained by, men.

What I've also learnt is that women must work out how to make themselves fit into these man-made places as best they can: many, for example, will adopt the skirt or trousers and jacket with a sensible shirt look, to match the blokes. Some women succeed in their efforts to belong in the early years, but for those who choose to have children, meeting this challenge becomes a constant juggling act. A simple yet profound example of this for working mothers is that they must leave work before their kids' childcare closes at 6 pm. If they're doing their best to succeed in a business that has a culture of long working hours, this excludes them from meetings and even the informal networking that often happens later in the day. And as for leaking milk onto her silk shirt while still breastfeeding or staining her skirt on a heavy period day when her body is still adjusting postnatally – every working mum knows how deeply embarrassing this can be.

Then there's maternal guilt. This topic deserves a whole book. Suffice to say in this book, that again, from my own experience and from that of dozens of my coaching clients, the dreaded maternal guilt never goes away. Not when the children are young, and so being away from them during the day means you miss out on some of their development; and not when they are in their teen years, when you can't always get to their sports day or a parent interview. I remember I was running an EO workshop in Darwin when my daughter was sitting one of her year 12 exams, and my feelings of guilt probably affected my performance. She did brilliantly in her HSC despite my absence, but that didn't and doesn't take the guilt away.

As you will read from LM's responses below, the sacrifices you make as a working mother mean that you really have to care deeply about the work you're doing to make it worth the sacrifice. Of course, this is only for the privileged of us who have the luxury of choosing. Those poor mums who must work to balance the family budget have to make this sacrifice, even if they hate the work they're doing.

This juggling act was even more difficult for women a generation or so ago when there was neither maternity leave nor workplace childcare. For example, JKR, who at the time of bearing her children was a teaching and research academic at Macquarie University, told me:

> *It was hard. It was before the provision of either childcare or maternity leave and I birthed and raised both my babies without either. Luckily, the tradition of entry to Macquarie by mature-aged women doing part-time degrees had started. They had already set up an informal association that secured temporary accommodation*

from the university in which to invent a form of childcare to support their studies. I was able to join that group.

Later I was part of a staff and student mothers' group similarly arranging school holiday care for children.

What a great example of the ingenuity of women supporting each other in times of shared need.

RT, a now retired HR/diversity professional talked about her maternal guilt as a working mother:

Yes. I felt it all the time. I only went back to work when my children were a little older for that reason – [thus] sacrificing any personal goals. And there were many times [when I was] working early/late and travelling overseas quite extensively I found that [doing it all] became a huge task.

JES, a now retired IS/IT professional had this to say in response to my question about the career/mother juggling act:

I am a mother of three children. I was fortunate to be able to take maternity leave after each was born. I was troubled about whether to return to work when the first period expired. …. I chose to resume and, dearly as I loved my first child, immediately felt the guilty personal benefit of it.

At times I experienced maternal guilt, particularly during their teenage years when I was often working long hours and travelling, or when they appeared to run wild. I later learnt that most teen-agers, mother in paid employment or not, have their wild moments/ years. I have some regrets (but just a few) and am proud of all three and what they have accomplished.

In response to my question about whether JES believes things have improved for women over the years of her career, she said several things have improved. However, she then went on to answer my question by naming four areas of life where things have not improved for women:

No, because the pyramid still exists with 'untransformed' men at the top – fewer, granted, but they are still there.

No, because some women reach the higher terraces of the pyramid by aping practices of such men.

No, because many women lead conflicted lives in that the demands of their work life and their out-of-work life seem to be unable to be resolved and that can create extraordinary tension.

No, because many workplaces are still not flexible enough for the needs of parents – whether single parents or dual-working parents (with the lesser paid parent often the woman) – thus women have to compromise their professional life.

SA has been an allied health practitioner, an academic and leader in the higher education sector, and is now the managing director of a small business that provides information, resources and advice to the allied health sector. She told me:

Mummy guilt starts as soon as you fall pregnant, and according to my mother, never ends. I remember the pain of taking my two children to childcare when I returned to work. It started off as only a day or two a week and built up to four days. It was awful to leave (my) kids screaming in the arms of nursery staff and calling out for their mummy.

Later in her career, SA explained that when she took a full-time role it was agreed her husband would stay at home with the kids:

As several male and female friends have [also] admitted, this model rarely works well unless you've clearly negotiated the boundaries of what is expected. I was still doing most of the household chores, while my husband did all the fun mummy stuff like going to the parent groups and the library.

JS, a former scientist and now business manager at a university, with previous experience as a board member on two boards, replied to my question # 5 with:

Constantly! We hired a nanny who was fabulous. … I knew my kids were at home and were looked after by a wonderful woman. But because I was worried about taking time off I didn't [for example] attend [my kids'] sports days – ever. So, I sacrificed these things and I regret that now. It's only now [in my current role with my kids grown up] that I'm starting to experiment with working from home on a Friday and I've only done that twice – last week and the week before that.

The fact that JS, after very many years in various sectors of the Australian workplace, is only now experimenting with working from home on Fridays suggests how inflexible work practices seem to be. As stated earlier, the COVID-19 pandemic has legitimised more flexible working arrangements, but it seems there can still be consequences for those who choose to work part-time for a while.

LM, who is a legal counsel in an international finance business, is currently juggling a responsible full-time job and being an adoring mother of two young sons, said in response to my question # 5:

Yes, definitely I did, and continue to feel, maternal guilt juggling work and family. Mostly it makes me feel frustrated if I am spending time away from my children and the things I am doing do not feel important enough or worthwhile in comparison. I feel guilty because my children will be young for such a short time and I could possibly have a bigger impact on their development by spending more time with them in these early years. But at the same time, I want to represent women as equals to them with our own interests and not purely in a nurturing role, and I feel that it is important that they see me work outside the home for this reason. So, I feel like I need to be home for the toddlers, but out working for the future men.

Here, indeed, are the horns of the dilemma for working mothers – wanting to be there for their children, yet also wanting to be role modelling to them about what a professional woman looks like. LM then went on to tell me that:

My husband has taken a lot of time off to share the care of both our sons and he's been put under quite a bit of pressure about this. Even his brother, who works for a large bank, will say to him [that he] won't be up for promotion and won't be taken seriously until [he's there] full-time.

She then paused and went on to say what I'd always suspected too, which is that if 'you hear that said to a man, you think that's what they're thinking about women, even if they're not saying it.'

117

LS, a rural and regional leader's reply was:

> *Definitely, and it probably led to me pulling back quite a lot because it felt like the right thing to do – even though there was a part of me who yearned for the profile and satisfaction of continuing with lots of work. I think after one particular workshop series, ferrying (my #2 child) around in lots of different childcare places and expressing [milk] in public toilets, and sleepless nights, I decided to pull back. So, I still did things but I kept it at a more local level.*

GW, a senior tech professional, told me she suffered what I found a fascinating form of reverse maternal guilt:

> *I had enormous guilt when I went back to work but it may not be the kind of guilt to which you are referring, I was a miserable stay-at-home mum and I hated it! My guilt was about being a bad mother for not wanting to stay at home with my daughter. ... Once I was back at work my husband, our daughter and particularly me, thrived. I did feel guilty about how little guilt I felt – if you can understand that circular statement!*

I guess this confirms Jacinda Ardern's response about maternal guilt – that we women are 'high-guilt creatures', and that we're somehow damned if we do and damned if we don't be a working mum.

I'll close with an optimistic note from SE, an IT contractor and one of my male interviewees. On the topic of women's broken careers because of childbearing, he said:

> *The gig economy is helping to change that – you do the work when it needs to be done, and from where you want to do it, rather than the old work structure of going to a work site and working 9 to 5 hours or more.*

What more can be done?

On the topic of what more can be done, LS, the agricultural leader quoted above, reflected on the fact that, in her experience, having children can change women's priorities. She acknowledged that childbearing does interrupt things in the workplace. However, she went on to say:

Having said that, … if a woman does want a career [I'm sure] companies can pay for playrooms, [nearby] childcare centres etc that can make this work. You can't tell me there isn't money already being spent on things like golf memberships and travel.

The 2018 Korn Ferry report, already referred to, recommended 'strategising the home front' to women at a senior level. This included finding 'multiple forms of household help'. In terms of the 21 women CEOs interviewed:

Some found that home life complemented and balanced their work life – both because of the encouragement and support their partners provided, and the opportunity for conversation and reflection. They valued all the forms of support they got from their partners, not just caretaking for children.[200]

This recommendation to 'strategise the home front' puts the sole responsibility of managing work and families squarely on the shoulders of women themselves. I'm with LS on this one: we know that businesses sponsor things like golf days and off-site conferences in exotic locations as motivational measures, so surely, creating family-friendly workplaces also makes good business sense. The components of this must include flexible work hours; working from home (one positive that's come out of the pandemic is that it's legitimised this for those who can work from home); job sharing at all levels; and first and foremost, childcare – preferably free, but if not, affordable for all, and employee-sponsored where possible.

I nearly forgot, another response to the question 'What more can be done?' is that CEOs can insist that full-time working hours are from 9 am to 5 pm and that they reinforce this by modelling their own work hours accordingly.

A final suggestion about what more can be done to solve the career woman/mother juggling act is that the whole way work is structured could be turned upside down and shaken. This idea comes from my lived experience when for about eight years in the late '70s and early '80s I was a clinic nurse and nurse educator at the South Australian Family Planning Association (FPA). At that time, all the FPA team of doctors, nurses, social workers, educators and office staff were women, and almost all of us had young families. We all worked part-time and it worked wonderfully well: our clients received an excellent service by day and in the evenings six days a week, and we all loved our work, because we could manage it around our parental commitments.

As another response to 'What more can be done?' how about insisting that leaders make policy changes that embed permanent part-time work as a viable option at all levels of their organisations for those workers who would prefer this, for either a particular time in their working lives or throughout their career? The pandemic has thrown the old patriarchal model of work into disarray, so let's ensure that this destabilising time can be used for the good of all workers, especially those juggling parental responsibilities.

Conclusions

One conclusion I've come to, is that while most men – even many of the more enlightened ones – continue to see themselves as 'helping' their wives/partners with the domestic load, we still have a long way to go in terms of fully equalising things on the home front.

Another conclusion is that while men continue to be given a hard time in their workplace when they choose to take time off to care for their kids, we also still have a long way to go. This is in terms of fully equalising things on the work front in relation to couples juggling work and family.

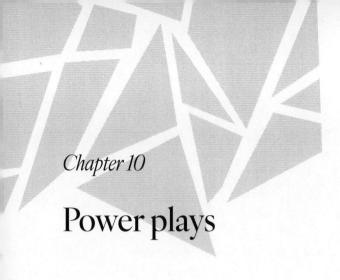

Chapter 10

Power plays

In the previous chapter I explored the multiple challenges faced by working mothers. These include dealing with the unspoken assumption that they won't be fully committed to their job if they have a child to raise. Such an assumption is surely grounds for a woman to complain under either the EO policy in her workplace, or anti-discrimination laws. This chapter explores the ongoing gender power imbalance that usually stops women from doing this.

In chapter 5, I referred to how this power imbalance means many women decide not to lodge a complaint of discrimination against a more senior person in her workplace. For organisations to become truly female friendly, they will need to have a culture of power-shared rather than power-over, and this is going to require a massive shift in the way some people behave and communicate with others in the workplace.

One of the things that continues to perplex me is the ongoing resistance to breaking down barriers to women at work. What's the problem? Surely a fair and equal workplace will benefit all. I remember asking Valerie Pratt, the first director of the Affirmative Action Agency after the AA Act was proclaimed in October 1986, about this resistance. Her reply? 'It's because men fear women's power.'

Research

I was delighted to come across a book written by Mary Beard, one of Britain's best-known classicists. In the inside sleeve of *Women & power: a manifesto* Beard asks the question, 'If women aren't perceived to be within the structures of power, isn't it power that we need to redefine?' And in her Preface, she focuses on how our current culture silences women: 'When it comes to silencing women, Western culture has had thousands of years of practice'.[201]

In the first chapter, *The public voice of women*, Beard turns to Homer's *Odyssey*, written almost 3,000 years ago, as a starting place to make sense of how we women are silenced. She reminds the reader of the story of Penelope, wife of Odysseus who is away being a hero of the Trojan War. One evening during his absence, Penelope enters the great hall of the palace and finds a bard singing about the difficulties the Greek heroes are having. She's not impressed with this gloomy theme, so she asks the bard to sing a happier song. Her son Telemachus intervenes and says: 'Mother, go back up into your quarters, and take up your own work, the loom and the distaff ... speech will be the business of men, all men, and of me most of all; for mine is the power of this household.' And off Penelope goes, back upstairs to her quarters as directed by her son.[202]

Beard concludes from this story that an integral part of growing up as a man is learning to take control of their public voice, and in so doing to silence women.[203] What hope have we got for changing this situation if we are to believe Beard that our conditioning as men and women goes back almost 3,000 years?

Fast forward to the 2020s, and we can soon think of situations where women are still silenced or talked over by men; and maybe even worse than that, of examples where we women silence ourselves.

I've read of two relatively recent examples of women being told to 'shut up' in the public political arena. The first occurred in Australia in 2017, when the then Liberal backbencher Tony Abbott told Ray Hadley on 2GB radio that Kate Jenkins, then Australia's Sex Discrimination Commissioner, should 'pull her head in'.[204] This was after her organisation recommended that contractors to the federal government aim for at least 40% of female employees to help address workplace gender imbalance.

The other example took place in Scotland in 2016. Raheem Kassam, then a UK Independence Party leadership candidate, tweeted about the First Minister of Scotland, Nicola Sturgeon: 'Can't someone just, like, tape Nicola Sturgeon's mouth shut? And her legs, so she can't reproduce?[205]

Hideous stuff, I'm sure you'll agree!

Julia Gillard also suffered from a barrage of insults and put-downs during her time as Australia's prime minister between 2010 and 2013. For example, Tony Abbott, the then leader of the opposition described Gillard's tone of voice as 'shrill and aggressive'. In *The Conversation* on May 10, 2021 two academics in linguistics at Monash University reminded me that while Gillard was regularly criticised for her 'accent and non-standard' English, Bob Hawke was celebrated for his during his prime ministership.[206] Talk about the double standard of one rule for him and another for her!

It seems that, despite all sorts of legislation that outlaws such behaviour, some men still feel entitled to say and do whatever they like when it comes to women. Why? I found David Leser in his 2019 book *Women, men and the whole damn thing* instructive in helping me answer this question. For example, Leser, a self-described privileged hetero male, acknowledges that it is time men made the effort to change their attitude towards women:

> If the twentieth century was about the rise of women, then the 21st century is about the adaption of men to that rise.[207]

Leser reflected on what happened when his sense of privilege was destabilised. As he wrote, 'Once you start seeing the systems and structures that have been in place for centuries, it's impossible not to see them everywhere.'[208]

Leser developed the topic of male privilege by quoting author Tim Winton. Leser writes about an interview Winton had with Andrew Denton, in June 2018. In this interview the author talked about the 'huge amount of unexamined privilege that men go about in the world with'. Winton continued:

> [Men] think that they've got where they've got just because they're good, and a lot of the time they've got where they've got mostly because they're a bloke. They have an enormous tailwind, and if

you're not actually conscious of that, then you don't understand that for so many people, particularly girls and young women, they have a headwind. It's changing, but it's still there, and a bloke who can't see that is a bloke who's just adding to the problem, he's adding to the headwind.[209]

Staying with this theme of male privilege, I shared author and journalist Anne Summers' rage when the Trump administration appointed Judge Kavanaugh to the US Supreme Court in 2018, despite an accusation against him of severe sexual harassment by a female co-student while they were at university. After the hearing of Kavanagh versus Blasey Ford, Summers said she felt flat and immobilised and, to make sense of why she was feeling like this, she wrote an essay she called 'The fragility of feminist progress and why rage is a luxury we can't afford':

This (Kavanaugh's) was a naked display of misogyny. ... My lassitude that day was instructive. Because while anger can be energising, rage has the opposite effect. My rage was, I realised, an expression of impotency. The previous day's hearing had shown me that, despite more than 40 years of feminism, despite the progress we seem to have made, despite our many victories and our reasons for justifiable pride, we women are in fact still utterly powerless in the face of a torrent of raw male power.[210]

So, let's be angry women, but not rendered impotent by rage.

I'll now return to Mary Beard as she explores the tone and pitch of the male versus the female voice. She tells the reader that throughout ancient literature we read about the authority of the deep male voice in contrast to that of the higher pitched female voice. She refers to one ancient scientific treatise that explicitly put it that, 'a low-pitched voice indicated manly courage, a high-pitched voice, female cowardice'. Beard goes on to explore the fact that many women who do succeed in being heard and taken seriously in a public setting adopt what she calls the 'androgyne route'. (Androgyny being a combination of masculine and feminine characteristics that is usually used to describe people who appear to have no specific gender.)[211]

As I watched the movie *The Iron Lady* on a long-haul flight, I was reminded that Margaret Thatcher underwent intensive speech training when she became Prime Minister of Great Britain to lower the tone and pitch of her voice. This was presumably so that she would be heard, and indeed taken seriously, by a mostly male parliament.

I was chuffed to see that Beard includes a *Punch* cartoon in her book, because it's one that I used to regularly use as an overhead projection in my EO seminars for (mostly male) managers as a humorous way to illustrate sexist communication in meetings. The cartoon shows a board table with people sitting around it. There is only one woman at the table. She's sitting to the right of the chair who is saying, 'That's an excellent suggestion, Miss Triggs. Perhaps one of the men here would like to make it.' The male seminar participants would chuckle at this, but any women attending would quietly grimace and, if they were game, would share that this regularly happened to them.

So how can we – both men and women in contemporary society – overcome these deep-bedded conditionings? Beard:

> *We have to focus on the ... fundamental issues of how we have learned to hear the contributions of women or – going back to that Punch cartoon for a moment – on what I'd like to call the 'Miss Trigg's question'. Not just, how does she get a word in edgeways? But how can we make ourselves more aware about the processes and prejudices that make us not listen to her?*[212]

Before we move on – and in case I haven't yet convinced the more sceptical readers about how sexism can play out in communications between men and women – I'll now turn to a series of essays by Rebecca Solnit called *Men explain things to me.*

The first chapter of this book, which also gives it its title, is her essay originally published in 2008. In it, Solnit tells the story of being at a party with a friend. Towards the end of the evening, when most of the guests had left, their host, who she calls Mr Very Important (Mr VI), engages Solnit by asking her what she writes about. She tells him the topic of her latest book, and in response Mr VI launches into a monologue about another excellent book recently published on this same topic with, as Solnit describes it, 'his eyes fixed on the fuzzy far horizon of his own authority'. Solnit's friend tries three times before Mr VI hears that this is in fact her friend Rebecca's book. To which Mr VI pauses, turns ashen, then launches off onto a new topic. It transpired that he hadn't read Solnit's book – merely the review of it in the *New York Times Book Review*.

The 'Men explain things to me' essay went viral when it was first published and caused one of Solnit's readers to invent the word *mansplaining*. This caught on and was included in the *Oxford English Dictionary* in 2014.

There are now more women in powerful positions in Australia than ever before. For example, Anne Summers in *The misogyny* factor lists a number of firsts for women: in 1976 Elizabeth Evatt became the first Chief Judge of the Family Court; in 1979 Deborah Wardley became the first commercial pilot; Susan Ryan became the first female Labor Cabinet minister in 1983; Dame Roma Mitchell became the first governor of an Australian state in 1990; and Carmen Lawrence in Western Australia, and Joan Kirner in Victoria became the first two premiers of a state in Australia. Since then, Julia Gillard has been our first prime minister and Quentin Bryce our first governor general, but progress continues to be slow, particularly at the senior levels of large organisations. For example, in 2022 in the top ASX200 companies only 21 CEOs were women and women held just 19% of board positions in these companies. As a result of the 2022 federal election women make up 38% of the House of Representatives and 57% in the Senate and there are 10 women in the cabinet, 13 women in the ministry and further 19 frontbenchers which includes assistant ministers, and 58% of Labor's caucus is female. This is a record number, in all categories for women's representation – in cabinet, in the ministry and frontbench positions.[213]

When I get really depressed about how slow progress is in terms of the status of women in Australia, I remind myself about what Anne Summers suggested in her talk at an International Women's Day breakfast in Sydney I attended in the early '90s. On the days we get despondent, Summers encouraged us women to compare our lives with our mothers and our grandmothers. Through that lens I, for one, can see massive progress from my mother having to resign as a teacher on marriage, and my maternal grandmother, who'd been a professional dressmaker before her marriage to my grandfather, only sewing for her family after she married.

The struggle to be heard in male-dominated workplaces and in the wider world, was also experienced by women seeking a voice in the world of writing and publishing. Yet another book summarises how women made their voices heard in Australia via the printed word as early as 1888. In her book *This is what a feminist looks like*, Emily Maguire tells the reader that in May, 1888 Louisa Lawson started a monthly newsletter called *The Dawn*. This was published from an office on George Street in Sydney. It was, as Lawson wrote in the first edition:

> *The pioneer paper of its kind in Australia, being edited, printed and published by women … [which aimed] … to give publicity to women's wrongs … fight their battles … repair what evils we can, and give advice to the best of our ability.*[214]

I can't resist including the story that one of my sisters told me, that male printers were so enraged at women working as printers that they tried to destroy *The Dawn*. They even took a room across the street and tried to stop the women compositors from working by flashing mirrors into their eyes. The men claimed the issue was that the women did not belong to their union. Yet they made it a rule of union membership that women were forbidden to join.

Fast forward to the 19th century when, as Maguire reminds the reader, feminist book publishing also became part of the women's liberation movement with bestsellers such as Germaine Greer's *The Female Eunuch* in 1970, and Anne Summers' history book, *Damned Whores and God's Police* first published in 1975.

In 2012 a group of Australian writers, editors and publishers observed that women writers were underrepresented in terms of literary gender equality: they won fewer literary awards, they were the authors of fewer books that received most reviews and media coverage and were fewer authors of books on the school curriculum. In response they launched a 'bold intervention' – a $50,000 literary prize for women. Named after Stella Miles Franklin it's called *The Stella Prize*, and the 2020 winner Jess Hill's book *See what you made me do* is referred to in the introduction of this book.

Now another look at power interplays in the current Australian workplace that makes me feel a wee bit despairing. I have in front of me an article from the *Good Weekend* supplement from *The Sydney Morning Herald* dated February 9, 2019. It summarises a long interview by Jacqueline Maley with Liz Broderick, then Sex Discrimination

Commissioner and founder of the Male Champions of Change group. Maley posed a question to her readers towards the end of the piece: 'How much does an activist engage with the systems of power she is trying to tear down?' She writes:

> It's a question Broderick had already confronted, when she created the Male Champions of Change initiative. … The program was … controversial, some arguing that it elevates men as heroes for doing what they should have done years ago, namely, appointing women to boards and executive positions.[215]

This is, of course true, but how dare those who argued this, to dismiss the courage it must have taken for Broderick to persuade these powerful (and presumably busy) men to meet, and to go public, on how they intended to improve the status of women in their workplaces. And the feeling of despair that this provoked in me is because again it seems that we're damned if we do and we're damned if we don't, as we women do our best to claim equal power at work.

As discussed above the term *mansplaining* was created in response to Solnit's 2008 essay. Fast forward 12 years and it seems that the term still has currency according to Julia Gillard and Ngozi Okonjo-Iweala in *Women and leadership*. They cite research in a biotech company about why highly qualified female scientists talked less in meetings than men did. The findings were, that if women's ideas were not perfect, they would be rejected, whereas if a man put forward a flawed position, the best bits would be salvaged. The study also showed that 'women's ideas tended to be ignored until a man restated the same point' – the Miss Triggs' phenomenon also referred to earlier in this chapter.

The most depressing aspect of this 'daily lived experience' by women, is what came next in this book. These authors found in their interviews of eight women political leaders from all over the world, that being viewed as an outsider, who is 'doubted and doubly scrutinised', continues even when women hold the highest office in their land. Gillard and Okonjo-Iweala write that they both experienced this while holding some of the highest offices in their respective lands. Further, they quote Ellen Johnson Sirleaf, President of Liberia from 2006 to 2018, who told the authors what used to happen to her when she met with other leaders at the African Union meetings. Despite being the President of Liberia, she was:

> ... still treated differently. I would notice that at meetings the men would go off in little groups, and if you tried to get in, they would be very pleasant with you but there was this sense that, 'We know you are president now, but this is our domain'.[216]

I have heard about all the power issues faced by women and discussed in this chapter repeatedly in my coaching and mentoring sessions. I leave it to my interviewees to make those points for themselves in the next section.

Interviewees

Several of my interviewees talked about the need for women to value and step into our power. However, they would then pause and reflect on how hard this can be in male-dominated cultures. As one woman said, 'This takes courage.'

On the topic of silencing, being excluded in a male-dominated work environment is a form of this. KB, then a partner in a national law firm, told me a story that illustrates this:

> I was the only female in the group who wasn't a secretary. Our senior partner took all the blokes to a male-only club for lunch and they didn't come back – there was a long lunch culture at the time. I came back from lunch and found all the boys were gone, including my junior, and that I'd been left with the secretaries.

KB moved firms to become a senior partner in an international law firm. She explained her reason for leaving the previous firm:

> The reason I left there was pretty much the same – it's always been the same – not being treated as a professional and not being treated as someone of worth. .... The fact that I ran the two biggest clients of the office was irrelevant – I needed to keep an older partner in work – I had to feed him work – and it was embarrassing to put him on jobs because he couldn't always do what he needed to do. ... When was it going to be my time, when was I going to be heard?
>
> With the move to this new firm – I at last have positional power, and at last my voice is heard!

AS, former CEO and now non-executive board director argues that the assertion of power is often used to mask poor people management:

> There are a lot of people who are pretty poor managers for whom power is their exercise of authority, not relationships, not getting the best out of people. ... I think this exercise of power is endemic in large corporations because people aren't trained well enough, they haven't got the capability to bring the best out in the people who work for them, so power is their default [position]. ... [This also happens in] group behaviour where people reinforce each other's poor behaviour – you hear when there's only one woman in a room or in a team, that the dominant cultural norms have a covert sexism attached to them – 'this is the way we are and if you want to be part of the gang this is what we do.'

AN, with a background in communications/marketing and sustainability and now consulting online from Australia for a UK-based personal development group, reinforced AS's observations above, about the double standards in relation to men, women and power:

> When I returned to work after maternity leave, the newly appointed leader was an older white male with very scarce emotional intelligence or leadership skills. He joined as the head of a team of four strong women, all leaders in our own right. He's been on performance-management but it was said that 'we were a very hard team to manage'. I was flabbergasted because I knew that if it had been four strong men, this would not have been said. In fact, we were a collaborative, supportive, self-managing group of passionate female leaders – the easiest team [to manage] unless you like control.

Getting noticed as a woman can be a two-edged sword. When you're firing along it's great to be in a spotlight. As LS, a leader in the agricultural sector, said about when, at a young age, she took a leadership role in one of the state offices of the Farmers' Federation:

> I think maybe being a young woman [in a blokey organisation] I probably stood out more, and if you're visible and competent and do a good job, then people remember you.

However, if you muck up, everyone notices, and if Mary Beard is to be believed, women are treated much more harshly than men when they do make a mistake. Some women dress like their male peers and even model their behaviour on them to avoid the spotlight. This rarely works well, and SA, former academic and leader in the higher education sector and now managing director of a small business made a different suggestion:

> One thing I tell younger women is that you need to differentiate yourself and it's not necessarily your professional credentials that do it.

For example, she suggests that they use the advantage we women have to be able to choose whatever style and colour suits us best. Once they've made their choice, SA suggests to younger women that they then consistently wear this style and colour as their brand and differentiator.

JG, a now semi-retired leadership consultant, told me about her version of the Miss Triggs' moments:

> In meetings when I'm often the only woman, this happens all the time. The men dominate, they interrupt and talk over me and repeat ideas that I've contributed that then get attributed to them. It's to do with their style of communication and has an indirect impact on me – I find it's hard to feel welcome and to contribute ideas.
>
> Also there continues to be a hierarchy in which I see smarter women in subordinate roles to less able pale, stale males.

JER, a former HR professional and now executive coach, told me about the challenge of working with women who adopt the dominant cultural style of power over others:

> I've worked with some supportive men, and I've worked with men who were aggressive, bullying types. I've also worked with a few women who've adopted male behaviours, to survive and thrive in that environment, which I found disappointing because I'd expected better from them.

PM, former politician and now board member and cattle breeder, told me about how challenging it has been as the only woman on a board in the livestock industry. She described behaviours to me that as she said, 'in the real world would have been described as bullying'.

But she then smiled and finished on a more positive note:

> *The smart men can cope with me and do not discriminate. … And I guess the happiest relationships are the more equal ones in which everyone benefits.*

I asked my male interviewees whether they thought men feared women's power. To which PS, an agriculturalist, said:

> *I believe this fear is there for sure and is directly related to the insecurity of men and the programming of men who were brought up in the 1950s to believe they were the head of the house. … If a male is afraid of an assertive, yet reasonable female, I would suggest that the problem lies with him.*

JES, retired IT professional, has had a Miss Triggs' moment too:

> *At various times I certainly encountered the, 'that's an excellent suggestion, perhaps one of the men here would like to make it' situation.*

JES also told me how she used to deal with the 'come on' scenarios:

> *There have been times when I thought I perhaps was being propositioned, however, I rebuffed the suggestion so they went no further. I can do a good line in saintliness, though occasionally there was payback further down the line.*

She then paused and shared with me a scenario that a colleague had told her about. She did tell me that this had happened about 30 years ago but as she told me with a wry smile, 'recent events have brought it back to my mind':

> *I had one female colleague recount to me, with incredulity, that some powerful men develop apparent amnesia with respect to their actions whilst 'socialising with a few drinks'. Strangely, they were sufficiently aware to only impose their attentions on the less powerful women around them. Also strangely, they denied their actions once sober, accusing her of making too much of 'friendliness'. It took a set-up situation at another corporate event, in which she signalled*

to others when a particular offender sidelined her from her professional colleagues, for witnesses to document his behaviour.

JES also shared a delightful example of when she pushed back to a member of an all-male interview panel:

I recall one interview when it seemed 'the girl' wasn't a viable choice for one of the interviewers on an all-male panel. When I stepped up to that person's challenge the others seemed to enjoy it.

JS, a former scientist and now business manager at a university with previous experience as a board member, talked about how the current leaders in corporate Australia (mostly men) tend to be motivated by achieving position power. She said she fears her career will stall sometime soon because:

The three factors that determine your trajectory to leadership are power, affiliation and achievement. My profile has always been off the chart on achievement, moderate affiliation and very low on power. ... When you get into higher roles the pressure of the politics is something that I don't feel that I would cope with as well as those who enjoy power politics.

JS concluded that for things to change, there needs to be an 'overt conversation' with women about how the power dynamic works and that, 'If they aspire to a senior role, how are they going to play the politics and the power game?'

Finally, AH, a leadership and organisation development consultant and researcher, got me thinking more deeply about the yin/yang makeup of men and women:

Most leadership and organisational research demonstrate that both masculine and feminine energies need to co-exist in balance for a workplace to function effectively. I'm not talking about men and women. Masculine and feminine energies exist in both men and women: for example, the potential for reflection/action, task/people, confidence/humility, power/vulnerability.

In practice, in many large organisational and political settings the masculine paradigm persists and is implicitly valued over the feminine.

I believe the power is within the collective. We can and should require men to change, but we need women to collectively step up and take up their personal power and authority skilfully. By skilfully I mean women who do not simply replicate the masculine paradigm with its emphasis on power and status. We need both men and women who can operate from an orientation to empowerment and 'power with' versus 'power over' others.

What more can be done?

First, I'll attempt to answer Mary Beard's questions earlier in this chapter. Referring to Miss Triggs in a Punch cartoon she asked how does Miss Triggs get a word in edgeways, and how can we make ourselves more aware about the processes and prejudices that make us not listen to her?

I believe these two questions go to the very core of the challenge I'm exploring in this book – how do we achieve truly gender-equal conversations that will help us reach the higher goal of achieving gender equal workplaces?

As I've written elsewhere in this book, retirement is proving helpful as more and more of the 'old school tie' men with hardcore beliefs about where women belong (and don't belong) put their business suits in mothballs and get out their golf clubs and fishing lines. KB said to me:

The guys who are retiring now [began their careers] when hardly any women studied law. We've got to let them retire and leave before things will really change.

In parallel to this, I believe it behoves us all to critically examine our values and beliefs about women's rightful place in the world and challenge ourselves if we find we're hanging onto some outdated prejudices. Further, I believe that we must all have the courage to name it if we find ourselves in a 'Miss Triggs' situation.

As DD, a former senior corporate HR executive who now runs her own international motorcycle adventure soul safari company, said:

We need to stop accepting the unacceptable and we all, female and male alike, need to call out these behaviours that have become the norm. But this takes awareness and it takes courage. We need to be alert to words and actions that are disrespectful of ourselves and others … and then when we hear and see them, we need to find new ways of responding. We need to find new language. So many of us, for so long, myself included, have let things slide, smiled politely, ignored, we've felt uncomfortable but have pretended things were okay that were not. Sometimes these are seemingly small things, looks, innuendo, 'jokes' and sometimes they are more blatant expressions of disrespect. It is the role of each of us to not accept the unacceptable in our homes, with our families and friends, our work-places, our sports clubs, our communities, our leaders. Together we are gaining strength from each other and we are effecting change.

Ann Sherry, former CEO and now non-executive board director, makes a practical suggestion about one change to help move organisations towards true gender equality: that is to shift what she calls the 'power conversation'. Sherry, who is chair of the Male Champions of Change group in the STEM sectors (science, technology, engineering and mathematics), told me:

Women spend a lot of time talking to each other, and often we don't talk to the men whose views we need to change because we can't get access to them. So, there's a dynamic in all of this which is about shifting the power conversation from women talking to each other, to women and men talking together, and supportive men talking to other men. Because this will accelerate it [the change], and I've seen how quickly you can accelerate change, and this makes me feel optimistic.

What Sherry is suggesting is that women seek out supportive men and encourage them to spread the word to other men about what needs to change.

Finally, back to AS's point that she 'sees some men use the assertion of power to mask their poor people management skills'. What's needed to change this are leadership development initiatives in both group and one-on-one settings to teach all emerging leaders effective people management skills through honing their emotional intelligence (EI). (Based on the work of Daniel Goleman, EI consists of the four quadrants of self-awareness, self-management, social-awareness and relationship-management.)[217]

What's also needed is the expansion of the merit principle to ensure that people with high EI are promoted rather than the 'do as I say, not as I do' types. I'm delighted when I can provide leadership coaching to men as well as women to support them as they first find, and then practise using, their EI to complement their IQ and proven technical skills.

Conclusions

This has been a hard chapter to write, because I admit I can still feel intimidated by powerful men, and I still find that being in the presence of women in positions of power makes me go all shy and over-awed. I can see the apparent contradiction in this confession, given I make my living supporting many highly impressive women, and helping them deal with such feelings in themselves. Mary Beard has helped me understand how deeply entrenched the conditioning about power is within us all, and how much this differs between women and men. One obvious conclusion I have reached, or rather confirmed for myself by researching and then writing this book, is that there continues to be a gender power imbalance in Australian workplaces.

Over the years that this book has taken me to write, I have been reminded of many difficult memories from both my own experiences, as well as from the sometimes quite traumatic experiences that many of my female leadership coaching clients have shared with me over the past three decades.

Two examples come to mind. The first is a personal memory that I've already mentioned in an earlier chapter, which was when a workshop participant tried to 'physical' me, such was his rage about having to comply with EEO/AA legislation, and his apparent sense of entitlement to attack me, the mere messenger of this information. Then there was the experience of a Melbourne client who'd been recently promoted to what had formerly been an all-male team. At her next coaching session, she told me that soon after she joined the team one of the blokes told a disgusting joke to his male peers in her hearing. They all laughed raucously, and she was so shocked that she said and did nothing. By the time she met with me she was feeling furious with herself for not speaking up, and this was dragging down her confidence, and therefore her resources to deal with the situation. We spent the session exploring her options and building up her confidence and sense of entitlement, and she left with a plan to confront the bloke concerned in an assertive manner, and if needs be, to also seek support from their mutual manager.

I have chosen to allow my interviewees, many of whom I've coached over the years, to speak for themselves, and to relate their experiences of how they've managed to deal with the inappropriate behaviour of male colleagues. And turning back to the gender power imbalance that is the topic of this chapter, one conclusion I've come to is how productivity will rise when women don't have to invest such an inordinate amount of time and energy asserting their right to be taken seriously at work.

A second conclusion I've reached is that a redistribution of power in our workplaces and our society is at the core of how gender equity will be achieved. How will this be done and by whom? It will require no less than enlightened leaders who fully embrace the benefits of a gender equal workplace, who create the policies and implement the systems that support this to happen, and who model this in everything they do and say on every single day.

Chapter 11

So can women lead?

Having explored the challenges women face in finding their voice and their personal power in the last chapter, in this chapter I focus on women as leaders. The immediate answer to the question posed above is, of course they can. Then the question that springs to my mind is, well why aren't there lots more women leaders? Given that at the time of publication there were still only 21 women CEOs in the ASX200 companies, what's going on? In this chapter I explore the similarities and differences in the ways women and men lead, and the value brought to organisations, up to and including the executive suite, from a more gender-balanced style of leadership.

Research

As with all the themes of this book, my research for this chapter began with what I've heard from my women clients over the years. They tell me about the problems they've met in first reaching and then working in senior management, and, for those who resigned, their reasons for leaving a senior position. A complaint I often hear is about the double standards that seem to apply in how they are assessed as leaders, versus how their male colleagues are assessed: for example, he is seen as strong, she as aggressive; he as decisive, she as controlling; and he as strategic and she as too 'big picture'.

My research about male versus female styles of leadership took me back to Mary Beard's book, *Women and power*. Beard encourages us to think about how we might re-design the notion of power so that it includes all women as well as men and, to challenge the current idea of leadership as a mostly male construct.[218]

Next, I'll turn to the research undertaken by Korn Ferry in association with the Australian Institute of Company Directors that has already been referred to in several earlier chapters. The findings of this study were released in a report in September 2018 called *Australian women CEOs speak*. On page 20 of the report the authors ask, 'What's needed to put more women in the leadership pipeline?' The report's authors refer to a 2017 analysis of Korn Ferry's database of assessment scores which found that:

> Women who become CEO are … likely to score highly on six specific competencies, and that these differentiating skills are what women must master as they move from manager to senior executive.

The six competencies are:

- *Engages and inspires*
- *Develops talent*
- *Builds effective teams*
- *Directs work*
- *Courage*
- *Manages ambiguity.*[219]

So, over to all you mentors, coaches and professional developers to skill emerging women leaders in these six competencies.

My research led me once more to David Leser's book, *Women, men and the whole damn thing*. Leser encourages his readers to first look at the economic sense in creating a gender diverse workplace. He refers to the 2015 report by the McKinsey Global Institute that I referenced in chapter 1: the report concludes that 'US$28 trillion would be added to annual global GDP by 2025 if women's participation in the economy was equal to men's'. US$28 trillion!!!

Leser shares the work of Canadian-born, London-based consultant Avivah Wittenberg-Cox, who told him that she works a lot in Australia where she says we need to be more 'gender bilingual'. She tells him that in Australia she sees that the problems are always framed as women's issues:

> It's about women's networks, women's coaching, women's mentoring, women's empowering ... We need to be more gender bilingual. We need to talk about customers, talk about talent, talk about managers, talk about opportunity, not keep talking about women.[220]

In response to his question about why we need to strive towards more gender-balanced workplaces, Wittenberg-Cox tells him that they:

> Tend to be more feeling workplaces that end up being less competitive, more flexible, more output than input driven, much less ready to put up with self-marketing bullshitters who talk about themselves. But this only comes by design. ... It's an enlightened, proactive decision to adapt and shift to a more gender-balanced system. It takes a lot of work and leadership and intention, and it's a huge issue that bumps up against entrenched power systems.[221]

In case we need more convincing, Leser also quotes Tomas Chamorro-Premuzic, professor of business psychology at University College London and Columbia University, from his article in the *Harvard Business Review* in 2013:

> When it comes to leadership, the only advantage that men have over women ... is that manifestations of hubris – often masked as charisma or charm – are commonly mistaken for leadership potential, and that these occur much more frequently in men than in women. The truth of the matter is that pretty much anywhere in the world, men tend to <u>think</u> that they are much smarter than women. Yet arrogance and overconfidence are inversely related to leadership talent – the ability to build and maintain high-performing teams, and to inspire followers to set aside their selfish agendas in order to work for the common interest of the group.[222]

Chamorro-Premuzic poses the question, 'Why encourage women to adopt dysfunctional leadership traits when it is flexibility, creativity, modesty, vision – the very qualities of a transformative leader – that is required?' Why indeed?

I believe that an excellent example of an Australian transformative leader is Elizabeth Broderick, former Sex Discrimination Commissioner, women's right campaigner and UN rapporteur. In an interview with Jacqueline Maley in the Good Weekend in the February 19, 2019 edition of the *Sydney Morning Herald*, Broderick said that her vision is a 'World where men and women are paid equally, where domestic work is shared, where there is no violence or harassment … where all human beings are valued and treated equally.' A Utopian vision? Here's hoping not.

Broderick also told Maley that she believes her main skills are her so called 'soft' ones, 'Her ability to listen sympathetically and without judgement. Her knack for bringing together people with wild differences. Her skill for getting people to find common ground.' In my opinion these are the skills of a transformative leader and that the sooner they're no longer described as 'soft' the better.[223]

Now back to *Women and leadership* by Julia Gillard and Ngozi Okonjo-Iweala for their take on women as leaders:

> *This book has not been premised on the idea that there are inherent, biologically determined differences between how men and women lead. Instead, we believe that to the extent there are variations, they arise because, at every stage of life, men and women are socialised and stereotyped differently.*[224]

The authors have named their first hypothesis 'You go girl' to unpick some of the differing socialisations and stereotyping experienced by their eight women leaders during their upbringings. Gillard and Okonjo-Iweala found that all eight of them had had an upbringing that included the conditioning that they could do whatever they wanted to in their lives. The authors stress to their readers that: 'What a girl is told as she grows up matters.'[225]

Christine Lagarde, the first woman to lead the International Monetary Fund from 2011–19, told the authors what she did to prove herself in the role:

> *I worked like a dog! I literally ate and digested files. That's what I did, and what women always do. We over-prepare, overwork, we*

are over-briefed. Where a man would flip pages and look at the headlines, we look at every single paragraph and read thoroughly.[226]

Gillard and Okonjo-Iweala finish the chapter with a message to the parents and relatives of young girls: 'A family that creates the kind of free-from-gender-limits environment our women leaders grew up in will be empowering her to be a leader.'[227]

In their examination of their third hypothesis, 'Shrill or soft – the style conundrum', the authors suggest that advocates for a gender-diverse workplace argue about the benefits that come from having the more team- and people-oriented approach that women typically bring. They refer to a 2011 meta-study that reviewed much of the then research into women's versus men's leadership styles. This study concluded that there had been a broadening of views about the qualities required for leadership. Traits more associated with women, like sensitivity, warmth and understanding, were now cited as well as traditional leadership traits, such as being forceful and competitive. The 2011 study also looked at transformational versus transactional leadership styles and concluded that women are better at the former:

> ... *transformational leadership means the ability to set goals, develop plans to achieve them, innovate, and mentor and empower team members. Transactional leadership was seen as a more narrowly defined approach in which specific objectives for subordinates are set and the leader monitors compliance with the tasks, rewarding or correcting subordinates as necessary.*[228]

The study concluded that men still fit better into people's sense of leadership, especially at the more senior levels. As depressing as I find this conclusion, it is, I suppose, at the nub of why there are still so few women in the executive suites of Australia's large organisations.

Surely with all this both quantitative and qualitative data, the time is ripe for the achievement of gender diverse workplaces here in Australia.

Interviewees

I set out to discover from my interviewees if they believed women have a different leadership style from men, and whether this was being valued in the organisations in which they've worked or continue to work in.

143

JER, former HR professional and now an executive coach, told me:

Things have definitely changed. The sort of things that I experienced earlier in my career – the innuendo etc, have certainly changed in the industries I've worked in. … In professional services you can't get away with that, so from that point of view things have improved. However, the actual numbers of women in leadership roles and on boards hasn't changed significantly. Why? The answer is quite complex – in part it's the nature of the corporate culture and the focus on short-term profit, and partly the overt and covert competition for fewer roles as you progress up the hierarchy.… A lot of women I know have found in the end that working in these kinds of environments doesn't work for them anymore – that certainly happened for me quite a while ago.

GW, a chief information officer in the higher education sector talked about how difficult it is being in a spotlight as the only woman at a meeting:

In Queensland I'm the only female director of IT and walking into that room full of men is daunting. They've known each other for years, they've hung out together for years, whether in current roles or in the past, and I'm walking in from scratch and I find this so challenging. I'll do it because I have to, but oh I find it hard. I often make a mental note to look around the room and count and it's rare that there are more than two women at a meeting at the senior levels of IT – and there'll be 20 men.

AS, former CEO and now non-executive director told me:

Basic stuff has really changed: people know that harassment is illegal and discrimination is illegal and all those obvious things – I'm sure in smaller organisations people still do it but in bigger ones there's [now] a different benchmark around that. In some places bad behaviour has become a lot more subtle, or it's about terrible management.

Confirming my belief that it's up to the leader to influence change in their organisation, AS described to me how a relatively newly appointed CEO has turned his business around:

The CEO in a business where I'm on the board has got a completely different frame of reference about the way the organisation should be led, and that goes to everything from hiring really good women into his team and into the 'meatiest' parts of the business. He's shifted the organisation – the expectations of people have gone up, different people are in, and it's [become] a very different place quite quickly – now you have to deliver outcomes in the right way.

And finally, from my interviewees, KB listed the good news she's now observing after over 30 years at the senior levels of several law firms:

- *Men now do understand when what they say is sexist or discriminatory because they have much more awareness of what they're saying and doing.*
- *There's a lot more corporate reporting that goes on that forces organisations to behave differently.*
- *There are a lot more women around.*
- *The guys who are retiring now [studied] when hardly any women did law. We've got to let them retire and leave before things will really change.*
- *Clients now insist on us reporting on our gender diversity policies and statistics when we pitch to panels.*

What more can be done?

One of the current 'hats' former Prime Minister Julia Gillard now wears is Chair of the Global Institute for Women's Leadership, which is linked to both Kings College in London and the ANU in Australia. In 2020 she cited the three biggest issues still facing women in leadership; the first, that there are still not the structures in place to support family life; the second that there continue to be sexist stereotypes and unconscious biases driving decisions; and the third, is the narrow interpretation of merit, particularly at a senior level.

SA, who spent time in a leadership role in the higher education sector and is now the managing director of a small business that provides information, resources and advice to the allied health sector, gave me six practical suggestions to improve the status of women:

- *Include the topic of gender equity in the sciences.*

- *Appoint leaders who 'walk their talk' in relation to valuing women as leaders.*
- *Teach women the skills, and instil in them the confidence, to negotiate for fair and equal reimbursement.*
- *Encourage women leaders to seek support from their male colleagues when they are, for example, talked over in meetings or frowned on for having to leave work early to pick up their children.*

Back to Ann Sherry, former CEO, who now sits on several boards and chairs the STEM Male Champions of Change board. She told 1,300 guests in a speech at the 2018 Chief Executive Women annual dinner that when some of the STEM organisations introduced blind short-listing to their recruitment by removing the name and gender from job applications, the ratio of men to women being shortlisted jumped from 1 in 10 to 50-50.

Sherry urged her audience that:

> We must have the courage to stand up when others hide. We all need to be change-makers to achieve gender equality, cultural diversity, indigenous recognition and inclusion. It's time to stand up and speak out. … Gender equity, fairness and diversity are our way forward. They matter.[229]

Conclusions

I've provided hundreds of women with leadership coaching support, and continue to coach and mentor women in this, my eighth decade. One of the qualities that I've endlessly admired in these women is their courage – courage to achieve and succeed despite having to work in what continues to be mostly male-dominated cultures. My plea to women is to continue to be brave, to continue to be strong, to continue to believe in yourself, and to name it loudly and clearly when you believe another's behaviour is not appropriate, or that your employer is treating you unfairly.

Two examples of women being courageous come to mind: the first is that I read that Virginia Trioli (journalist, author and radio and TV presenter) excused herself and left the lunch she was having with a male politician when he made a sexist remark. The other was my interviewee GW who left a coffee meeting with a colleague after he'd apologised once for being sexist, then did it again. Go women!

But, as much as I cheer every time I hear about a woman speaking up, I also despair that they still have to. One conclusion that has strengthened in me by doing the research and the interviews for this chapter is that it's beyond time that leaders step up so that women can stop having to carry the burden for change in relation to gender equity in the Australian workplace.

Another conclusion is a resounding 'Yes!' to the question, 'So can women lead?' And that, with research now pouring in about the benefits of a more female leadership style, surely it's time for the leaders of this land to break down the remaining barriers to women's success in their organisations, and surely it's time to have in place safe, confidential processes for people to complain if needs be, and to step aside for a more suitable appointment if they know in their hearts that they do not have what it takes to model this so called 'softer' leadership style day by day.

Chapter 12

Power over at work – the issue of sexual harassment

In the last chapter I presented the case that women can lead just as effectively as men in cultures that embrace a gender complementary leadership style. In this chapter I outline the ongoing insidious threat of sexual harassment and bullying in the Australian workplace, that continues to undermine the success of the very many women, and some men, who are targeted.

In my work as a consultant specialising in equal employment opportunity and affirmative action in the late '80s and early '90s, I informed dozens and dozens of managers about their responsibilities under both law and policy to create a safe and harassment-free workplace. I trained dozens and dozens of employees in how to be an effective sexual harassment contact officer – that safe person who people can talk to if they're being harassed or bullied at work. I also trained dozens and dozens of women in self-esteem and assertiveness skills to help them speak up if they're uncomfortable about anything that's happening to them in the workplace. And I have coached, and continue to coach and mentor women, many of whom trusted me enough to be the first person they'd ever talked to about damaging behaviours that were sometimes still happening to them, but that often had happened many years ago.

Ever the optimist, I was hoping that all these training, coaching and mentoring initiatives, facilitated by many others as well as me, would by now have meant that the issue of sexual harassment at work was a less common occurrence. In March 2020, I therefore read with alarm that the *Respect@Work Report* by the Australian Human Rights Commission (AHRC) found that 39% of women had experienced sexual harassment at work in the past five years. This is although there have been laws in place – both federal and state – outlawing this for well over 30 years, as well as all that investment in training described above.

Then in June 2020, news broke that an investigation initiated by the Chief Justice of the High Court of Australia, Susan Kiefel, had found that Dyson Heydon, a retired High Court judge, had sexually harassed six of his women judge's associates. Further, it was reported that Heydon's behaviour was an 'open secret', and that at least two of these women left the law because of the damage they suffered while working for him.

What on earth is going on? How is it possible that even in the highest court in the land, a powerful man can think such behaviour is acceptable? The statistics and this example both point to the fact that the current complaints-based nature of anti-discrimination law that puts the onus on the aggrieved to make a complaint is not working. Why? Because it fails to consider the power imbalance that is always part of intimidating behaviour – particularly in situations such as the High Court – where people's careers are entirely in the hands of their superiors.

The news of the day shifted from the law to corporate Australia on August 24, 2020 when it was announced that David Murray, AMP chairman, had resigned and that a man called Boe Pahari, who had recently been promoted to the role of AMP Capital CEO, had been demoted. Why? Because a hushed-up settlement of sexual harassment against this man had come to light. It seems that the case was also an 'open secret', and when Pahari's promotion was announced, both the staff at AMP and some of the company's institutional shareholders were outraged. The complainant against Pahari is long gone; she's now furthering her career in the US. Despite Pahari having to pay a $500K penalty, she says he did not apologise to her, and so she was threatening to disclose her documentation to uphold her reputation.

What a mess! And what a cost – both human, financial and reputational to the High Court and AMP. If I'd invented such case studies to be used in sexual harassment awareness workshops, participants would have said this wouldn't ever happen in Australia.

Research

One source of research for this book are the examples shared with me by many of my women coaching clients. As I've mentioned above, I was sometimes the first person a woman trusted to 'confess' her long-held secret that she'd been sexually harassed by her boss or another senior manager, sometimes many years earlier. And why the word 'confess?' Because the tragic truth is that many of these women carry a sense of shame and guilt about their secret. My clients would explore with me what they'd done wrong that meant this had happened, and what they could have done differently that might have prevented it from happening. I always reassured my clients that what happened was not their fault, and that it was important that they stop blaming themselves. But because of the depth of their wounding, this was often easier said than done, and on occasions I would encourage a woman to consider some counselling with a skilled person to help them make sense of this deep wounding, and how to heal it.

When my client still worked with the perpetrator, one topic we'd explore is whether she ought to make a formal complaint about him to either his manager or the Sex Discrimination Commission. As above, despite making sexual harassment unlawful, sex discrimination legislation requires the victim of harassment to complain before any change can happen. Given the obvious power imbalance between a woman and her boss, this is very hard to do. I remember well the ugly and very public case of a woman who had her life and health ruined for a time, and her career forever, by the backlash she received by going public with her complaint. With this memory still sharp in my mind, I admit I err on the cautious as I help any client of mine who's been sexually harassed to explore her options. If she seeks my opinion, I'll share this story as my reason for discouraging her from making a public complaint because of the possible cost to her both emotionally, and in terms of her career. Another option is that she could withdraw, by either resigning or asking for a different role, but this still leaves the onus of responsibility for change squarely on her shoulders. This is another glaring reason why I believe that many more preventative measures for creating a gender diverse workplace are urgently needed.

As outlined in chapters 3, 4 and 12, the *Respect@Work Report* summarises the findings of the 2018 National Inquiry into Sexual Harassment in Australian Workplaces conducted by the then Sex Discrimination Commissioner Kate Jenkins and her team. The report was tabled in Parliament in March 2020 and revealed that there are high levels of sexual harassment in our workplaces. For example, two in five women and just over one in four men had experienced sexual harassment in the workplace in the previous five years. Further it found that Aboriginal and Torres Strait Islander peoples were more likely to have experienced workplace harassment than people who are non-Indigenous (53% and 32% respectively). In the information, media and telecommunications industries, for example, 81% reported experiencing sexual harassment in the last five years.

In relation to the costs involved, Deloitte Access Economics estimated for the report that workplace sexual harassment cost the Australian economy $3.8 billion in 2018: 70% of this was attributed to lost productivity by employers; 23% was borne by government losing tax revenue; and 7% was borne by individuals losing income.

As Kate Jenkins wrote in her foreword to the report:

> *Sexual harassment is not a women's issue: it is a societal issue, which every Australian, and every Australian workplace, can contribute to addressing. … Ultimately, a safe and harassment-free workplace is also a productive workplace.*[230]

In her keynote speech to The Beijing Platform for Action, 25 years on: Progress, Retreat and the Future of Women's Rights conference on December 3, 2020 Kate Jenkins said:

> *[Our report] identified that sexual harassment is a form of violence against women, is widespread and pervasive, and is driven by gender inequality. … As we know, women's rights are first and foremost a question of justice. But achieving gender equality also makes good sense for everyone. Progressing gender equality not only*

promotes the rights of women, it also increases the efficiency and productivity of our businesses, economy and community. And in turn, the absence of women from the paid economy acts as a thorny roadblock to the healthy and robust economy for which almost every country strives.[231]

Karen O'Connell, Associate Professor, Faculty of Law at the University of Technology, Sydney, wrote in *The Conversation* on June 26, 2020 that the current complaints-based focus of sexual harassment law is 'set up to fail'. She also revealed more data from the AHRC report: 72% of Australians over 15 have experienced sexual harassment in their lifetimes, and that in the previous 12 months, 23% of women and 16% of men said they had been harassed at work, but that only 17% of people who experienced sexual harassment at work in the past five years made a formal report or complaint. Even fewer were brought as formal complaints to the AHRC, and of those that were, only a tiny number of cases went to court or tribunal each year. O'Connell:

> *We are refusing to acknowledge the truth: Australia has a sexual harassment system that is set up to fail at the very thing it is intended to do – eradicate sexual harassment. … Our sexual harassment system is designed to look as if we are addressing the problem. … It requires the harassment to have already happened and it requires the person who has been hurt to take responsibility for making a complaint. … But making a complaint often means more distress, more unwanted focus on the person's sexuality and further risk to their career. It is a passive, backward-looking system that potentially amplifies the very harm the person has already experienced.*[232]

Bri Lee, a former judge's associate and at publication, was doing a PhD in Law and lecturing at the University of Sydney in Media Law, addresses the question of how it's possible that sexual harassment remains an 'open secret' within the legal profession, given its role is to oversee the law. In an article in *The Saturday Paper* on June 27, 2020, Lee explains:

> *The legal industry is built on strict and rigid hierarchies. The roles of judge and associate are perhaps one of the most extreme examples – a judge is an absolute gatekeeper and arbiter of a young graduate's professional trajectory. … An associate is both a personal*

and professional assistant: they can be asked to research and proof-read judgements, or to collect their judge's dry-cleaning or his car from the mechanic. The pair often travel together too. ... This kind of working relationship presents privileges that the system simply hopes won't be abused.[233]

It seems such hopes are sometimes not being realised.

David Leser's book, *Women, men and the whole damn thing* attributes the recent #MeToo movement for why people who would otherwise have remained silent are speaking up about their experiences of harassment. For example, Leser tells us that in response to the #MeToo movement Tracy Spicer (former journalist and contributor to the Fairfax Media) sent a tweet to her nearly 50,000 followers asking about sexual harassment in the media and entertainment industries in Australia. Thousands of women contacted Spicer about direct experiences of rape, harassment and assault.

Leser continues:

But, of course, it's not only sexual harassment. It's discrimination, conscious or unconscious, barefaced or subtle, conducted in plain sight or undercover, that continues to affect half the population. You're pregnant so you lose your job. You've had a child, but you can't get back into the workforce. You're denied a raise in salary, even though your male counterparts are earning more and performing less. You're doing double the work, but he's getting the praise. You're on the receiving end of sexual slurs or putdowns and discriminatory remarks – all the smaller aggressions that undermine your sense of safety and belonging.[234]

I found these insights on current gender inequalities impressive from Leser, who, as I've already noted, describes himself as a white, middle aged, heterosexual, privileged male.

Inevitably I suppose, there was a male backlash to the #MeToo movement. Anne Summers wrote about this in a long essay on Twitter in October 2018 titled *The fragility of feminist progress and why rage is a luxury we can't afford*:

Men are being cast as victims ... their lives destroyed by vengeful women. The #MeToo hashtag now has its male counterpart: #HimToo. As described by Wired magazine: 'The hashtag #HimToo identifies accused men as victims, using the same power-in-numbers technique that made #MeToo a force to recast the movement as a widespread feminist witch hunt, forcing men to walk on eggshells.'

Summers' response?

So #MeToo is being recast as Jezebel behaviour: evil predatory women intent on destroying good men. Sound familiar?[235]

Although Summers says, 'rage is a luxury we can't afford', I was left feeling pretty despairing about this #HimToo backlash until I read the following take on #MeToo from two women I admire. First, Liz Broderick, former Sex Discrimination Commissioner, in her interview with Jacqueline Maley expressed her delight about the #MeToo movement and what Maley called 'the global flowering of feminism that brought it forth.' And second, Ann Sherry, former CEO and now on several boards, gave me a healthy reframe about this male backlash:

Every change starts with a radical reaction … because we never get to the middle ground if we start too soft. And things the #MeToo movement have called out are egregious… so let's not get caught up in the anxiety about men not wanting to be on their own with women; well if their behaviour is that bad, they shouldn't be. … And there's a generation of women coming through who've got different tools as well, such as social media … where previously we could only complain to our manager or HR. So now there's a different platform for women, and I think that's good.

My research has also unearthed a more subtle form of sexual harassment – what Julia Baird, author and journalist calls 'above the neck' harassment. In a piece in *The Sydney Morning Herald* on January 12, 2018 she described this more subtle form of harassment as:

The moments when you get demoralised as a woman in a room when you feel that you are circumvented and that you are not seen or heard, and the boss only thinks it's a good idea if a guy presents it.

Baird then goes on to say that 'above the neck' harassment also:

Includes another specific kind of behaviour: bullying by powerful men who reach out to younger, usually female colleagues, declare

> *they will champion and mentor them, then overstep boundaries. When the objects of their attention demur, they grow angry. Some 'mentors' wreak revenge, some try to destroy confidence by telling their protégés they are talentless, or tell them to work elsewhere.*[236]

Baird shared with her readers her own example of 'above the neck' harassment. It occurred when she was an 'excited, determined' junior journalist who was also 'very harsh' on her own work. A senior powerful colleague appointed himself as her mentor and repeatedly asked her to lunch. Once when she refused his invitation, he sent a long and furious email telling her, among a lot of other demeaning things, 'how little ability' she really had. This understandably further undermined Baird's confidence in her writing.

Researchers Emma Tseris and Nicole Moulding, from the universities of Sydney and South Australia respectively, wrote in *The Conversation* on March 9, 2021 about the impact of sexual harassment, sexual assault and gendered violence on some women.

> *Research, including our own findings, reveals many women survivors demonstrate resilience after violence and abuse. However, others report struggling with mental health and seek support for feelings of shame, fear, sadness, flashbacks, panic attacks, low self-worth and other painful experiences.*

> *The mental distress associated with gendered violence is often made worse by disappointing system responses, victim-blaming, and other negative social impacts such as difficulties gaining and maintaining employment.*[237]

Interviewees

I remain shocked and amazed by the stories I've heard, in both my work as a leadership coach and from my interviewees for this book, about the number of experienced and highly skilled professional women who've had to field covert and at times obvious unwelcome advances from (mostly) more senior men in their places of work.

The most blatant story I was told was from JG, a now retired leadership consultant, when she was a training manager in the transport industry, admittedly a long time ago:

I was facilitating a session on equal employment opportunity and affirmative action to an all-male group of managers who had been truck drivers. In a break one of them had drawn a pair of tits on the flip chart. When I turned up a new page of the flip chart – there they were. They all laughed, and I blushed and said something like 'that's not appropriate' and moved on with the session. I didn't report it and I felt dreadful.

Then there was PM's example from when she was in a senior role in the health sector:

One evening after a dinner which he'd hosted and I'd attended, the owner of the company and I were walking along the footpath together when he slung his arm around me. I attempted to get away from him by walking faster, but he would then speed up and do it again. This was all in the presence of other men from the same workplace. Then of course the stories that went about were that I only got promoted because I had a sexual relationship with the owner, although I couldn't stand the man.

LM, now a legal counsel in an international finance firm, shared with me one example of many from when she was working in a law firm and tried to help some younger lawyers:

A graduate came to me and said she worked for someone who was so notorious that we all kept a file on him. She was on a traineeship and he was the only person she'd worked for. She told me that he'd said that if she didn't sleep with him, he'd be giving her a bad performance review, which would mean she would not be hired.

LM told me that she brought this matter up with the leadership, but that they did nothing except give the young graduate a role in another department. LM:

I have so many situations like this … and in my experience this is usually to the detriment of the woman, not to the person who was alleged to have harassed them.

A stark example of a power imbalance in action happened to GW, now a chief information officer, back in 2005 when she was working at a financial institution that had a very old boys' club culture. She was presenting a new-look customer counter to the board:

> *I had a dummy counter to show them what was going to be in the branches. I was the only woman in the room. There would have been 20 men and one of the board members said, 'All we need now is topless tellers.' I just said, 'Excuse me?'. Some of the men were chuckling, others were grimacing – oh what a horrible situation. I just had to wear it.*

EM began her career in IT when it was a very new industry and ended her career many years later in a senior leadership role:

> *I've certainly experienced men making passes persistently to the extent that when you eventually get through to them that the answer's NO, you then become invisible.*

RT, now retired but formerly a senior HR professional in the tech sector told me:

> *Sexual harassment? Yes, several times personally. I was propositioned by a senior executive quite extensively when I was at a relatively junior level. I was able to deal with it directly; but [otherwise] I would have had to report it and it would have been very difficult given his position. [There were] several other times too, from people less junior. I was able to deal with them; but it was extremely uncomfortable each time.*

JES, who also held several senior roles in the tech sector before retiring, shared examples that even included her compromising her career because of what she perceived as potentially unsafe work environments:

> *I suppose bullying of women fits into this category. My first manager made it his objective to have every woman who worked for him cry, at which point he would offer a folded white handkerchief 'that you can keep'. As if! It was washed and ironed, and placed on his desk the following morning, and never referred to again. His power exercised, he did not feel the need to make me (or the others) cry a second time. Nevertheless, I watched and learnt.*

> *I have observed discrimination and harassment happen to women (and some gay men) around me, so have been hyper-alert to*

the possibility. I have chosen at times, to consequently avoid career options.

And these power dynamics are not just occurring in industry, but academia as well. SA, who reached a leadership role in a university, told me:

I worked with a number of men and I would say they pushed the boundaries of appropriateness … in particular there were two of them who pushed those boundaries to see how I'd respond, and it's a test. I'm not sure what it's a test of. But if you pass the test and don't bite, you're in, but if you respond with an accusation of sexual harassment, you're out.

Back on the topic of so-called 'above the neck' harassment, AH, a leadership and organisation development consultant and researcher, told me that:

On a number of occasions at X hospital, I got support from men until I challenged them and then I would get shut off.

AH then went on to tell me:

Julia Baird's article about 'above the neck' harassment spoke to me and my experience. My observation is that these sort of men generally surround themselves with young attractive females that I suspect feeds their ego, and as long as you're on side and not a threat at all, you're OK, but they're pretty brutal if you cross them.

So, it seems that whether in the transport or tech industries, health, the law, financial services or academia, women are still having to navigate their way through the power imbalance of hierarchical and patriarchal cultures.

What more can be done?

In response to this long-term destructive and expensive situation, the recommendations of the *Respect@Work Report* put the onus of responsibility for change where it belongs – with employers – given 'prevention is better than cure'. It seems to me that if employers make the changes that mean people are not harassed at work, both they and their organisations benefit. More about this later.

The *Respect@Work Report* (available on the AHRC's website) makes 55 recommendations, two of which stand out:

> *That sexual harassment laws be amended to explicitly make the creation or facilitation of a 'hostile environment' at work unlawful: this can include belittling and sexual comments, not necessarily directed at one individual.*

> *The creation of a 'positive duty' on employers to take 'reasonable and proportionate measures' to eliminate sexual harassment from their workplaces. And that a 'positive duty' means there is a clear responsibility for employers to create the kind of workplace systems and structures that will prevent sexual harassment occurring.*[238]

Vivienne Thom, the investigator who found that six women had been sexually harassed by former High Court judge Dyson Heydon, made several recommendations for change in the High Court which I believe could be easily applied in other sectors:

- *Develop an HR policy for associates and provide them with a supervisor to make clear that the confidentiality requirements for associates relate only to the work of the court.*
- *Make it clear to associates that their duties do not extend to an obligation to attend social functions.*[239]

But as Julia Baird pointed out in *The Sydney Morning Herald* on June 27, 2020 about these recommendations:

> *What was missing were instructions that should be blindingly obvious to judges – just don't harass, be creepy or assault women, or you will be out.*

> *Perhaps the time is at last right for the onus of responsibility to achieve a harassment free workplace [to be] on those most able to effect change – management. Perhaps too there will be consequences to perpetrators that will mean there are no longer 'open secrets' about serial offenders, in any organisation in Australia.*[240]

In the 15 July 2020 edition of *The Conversation* Julian Webb, Professor of Law at the University of Melbourne, reported that a round table hosted by the Law Council of Australia committed to 'developing a national model sexual harassment policy and guidelines and enhancing professional training.' However, Webb argues that these alone are likely to be 'insufficient to transform an endemic cultural problem', and recommends that more profound change is needed including two further reforms:

- *Regulation could impose a positive obligation on legal practitioners who are aware of harassment to report it confidentially to the regulatory authority.*
- *The use of non-disclosure agreements to enforce a victim's silence as part of any settlement is also a key part of the law firm's arsenal. This should be outlawed.*[241]

These proposed changes specifically relate to the legal system. However ,they could be adapted and implemented in other organisations.

After the AMP story broke in August 2020, Lisa Heap, an adjunct professor at the Australian Catholic University reported in *The Conversation* that organisations need to take the recommendations of the Australian Human Rights Commission seriously by shifting the management of sexual harassment to being a work health and safety issue. She went on to explain that it is the employer's 'positive duty' to keep workers safe and they are required to identify risks to the health of employees and to eliminate these. Heap concludes:

> *AMP's self-inflicted wounds demonstrate the need for such an overhaul. A board treating sexual harassment as a matter of health and safety would have to eliminate or manage the risk of it.*[242]

In summary, what is urgently needed is leader-led culture change. How? In essence, an organisation's culture is about 'the way we do things around here'. So, of primary importance if real change is to be achieved, is for leaders to change the values, structures and systems that are still supporting dysfunctional and at times criminal behaviours in the Australian workplace.

If this sounds like a massive challenge – and it is – there are any number of quite practical steps towards achieving the change. For example, ensure:

- that all policies and procedures stress up front that the organisation strives to be a safe and harassment free work environment
- that these policies and procedures are included in the induction process for new employees

- that a complaints-based process be set up where people can safely and confidentially make complaints and be believed
- that leaders walk their talk by not tolerating inappropriate behaviours in their workplace and demonstrating by their actions that there will be consequences for transgressors – even if they are a senior member of the organisation
- that the Sex Discrimination Act be strengthened to include a positive duty on employers to prevent harassment and bullying
- increased budgetary support for change programs in organisations, not for profits, government agencies etc
- enactment of all 55 of the recommendations of the *Respect@Work Report.*

What about how to assess the effectiveness of all this change? To measure this, former prime minister Julia Gillard proposes that Australia set a national goal that by 2030 we be rated in the top 10 countries by the World Economic Forum Global Gender Gap Report (we are currently ranked 50th).

Conclusions

I have wept with dozens of my female leadership coaching clients over the years as they've poured out to me what they saw as their shameful secret about an embarrassing experience of a sexual nature that they've had to tolerate from a more senior male colleague or boss.

I am writing this conclusion in the winter of 2022 so I can map the progress of the government's response to the *Respect@Work Report* that had been tabled in Parliament 15 months earlier and had languished on the former Attorney-General Christian Porter's desk until then.

First, in mid-April, 2021 then Prime Minister Morrison announced in a press conference a plan, entitled *A Roadmap for Respect: Preventing and Addressing Sexual Harassment in Australian Workplace.* This plan expressed agreement (either in full, in part or in principle) or 'notes' all 55 recommendations in the *Respect@Work Report.*

Then, in early September, 2021 the then government passed aspects of the *Respect@Work Report* into law. However, of the 12 proposed legislative measures from the total of 55 recommendations, only six were enacted including:

- harassment, defined as 'unwelcome and demeaning conduct that could reasonably be anticipated to offend, humiliate or intimate' becomes a sackable offence
- increasing the time to make a harassment complaint from six months to two years
- introducing compassionate leave for miscarriages
- extending harassment laws to parliamentary staff, the judiciary and all levels of government.

For the first time in my many years as an equal opportunity consultant and then as a leadership coach, I was feeling hopeful. My hopes were dashed again on the very next day when I heard Kate Jenkins say on ABC radio that, although she was pleased the government had finally responded to her report, she was disappointed that what she believes is the primary recommendation – that the onus of responsibility for change be shifted to employers – has so far not been included in these legislative changes.

Jenkins had said that she intended to continue pressing the government on the six unimplemented measures; especially regarding the onus of responsibility for change being moved to employers who have the power to create safe workplaces for their women rather than the onus of responsibility for change remaining with the victim to complain. And the good news is that in January, 2023 legislation was passed requiring employers to take reasonable measures to eliminate certain forms of sex discrimination and sexual harassment.

Given that on March 15, 2021 tens of thousands of both women and men Australia wide marched in the March4Justice rally demanding change for women, and that commentators including Julia Gillard are making 'not a plea but a demand' for change, and given the obvious skill and determination of former Commissioner Kate Jenkins, and given the recently elected Labor government promising to improve the status of women in Australia, I'm concluding this chapter by letting myself hold a glimmer of hope. I hope that we are in both a #MeToo and a March4Justice moment in Australia's history of the gender wars, and that there is currently the kind of momentum that could mean real change might at last be possible.

Chapter 13

What on earth is going on?

H aving covered in some detail the issue of sexual harassment in the last chapter – a somewhat overt form of sex discrimination – in this chapter I look at the more covert ways that women (and others) can be discriminated against through what is being called 'unconscious bias'.

Throughout the late '80s I worked tirelessly running EO/AA awareness raising programs for managers and leaders around Australia, truly believing that these were having an impact on the attitudes of at least some of the participants regarding women in their workplaces. One of the concepts I used to raise with them was the idea of homosocial reproduction – that unconscious tendency to choose to be among people like oneself. Participants would either blanche, or chuckle in an uncomfortable way because of my use of the word 'homo'. But as for my convincing any of them that they might indeed be 'homo-socially reproducing' their own kind, and thus blinding their ability to assess women's skills and strengths on merit, I now fear I was a dismal failure.

The challenge in naming unconscious biases is the fact that decisions about recruitment and promotion are often made by managers based on their norms and beliefs, most of which are at an unconscious level. For example, without bringing it to the spoken word, a manager might think, 'she's expressed some self-doubts, so I don't think she's quite ready for that big promotion' or 'she's just got married, it's maybe best that we don't promote her in case she's planning to have a baby sometime soon.' Should this manager be helped to see the impact of excluding a woman based on their own conditioning, rather than for reasons related to the requirements of the job, they would likely be shocked to discover that they were in fact indirectly discriminating against her based on her gender.

Back in the early '90s, it became fashionable for organisations to change the names of their equal employment opportunity and affirmative action programs to diversity programs (and later still, to inclusion and diversity programs). The idea was, and continues to be, that people be helped to understand the value of a diverse workforce because it makes good business sense to have a team of people who reflect the community within which they do business or provide services – be that in terms of the number of women, Indigenous Australians or other racial and ethnic groups, LGBTQIA+ people and people with disabilities.

By then I was pretty burnt out from doing my best to help change the hearts and minds of the leaders in corporate Australia, regarding the status of their women. When HR people began asking me to provide awareness raising sessions about gender diversity, my intuition was to refuse. Throughout the late '80s I'd experienced firsthand how hard it was to convince senior people about why it was good for their business to commit to removing the barriers to women in their workforce. Occasionally, in an EO seminar, there would be a hint of insight when, for example, one chap described the dreadful sense of not belonging when he walked into a gay bar by mistake. I encouraged those attending to consider the possibility that women in predominantly male cultures might feel like that every day.

Now the brief we consultants were being given was to devise exercises that would enable the mostly male participants to challenge their core values about the place of women and diverse groups, in their workplaces. I knew in my bones that this was a task beyond my capacity because what would be needed were experiential exercises to help people recognise and understand their unconscious biases. In my burnt-out state, I knew I didn't have the bandwidth to develop such programs, so chose to transition to offering leadership coaching services to some of my women EO clients.

So, what is this thing called an unconscious bias? According to the Australian National University's definition:

> *Unconscious bias or 'hidden bias' is created and reinforced by our background, cultural environment and personal experiences. It is often interpreted as the first impression and intuitions we have when interacting with other people. Unconscious bias is deeply ingrained into our thinking and emotions and is outside of our control.*[243]

The stories I continue to hear from the women I coach and mentor illustrate that there are still subtle and not so subtle ways that women continue to experience sexism in the workplace. This has the effect of reducing their ability to fully contribute. I sat down one afternoon and wrote down all the double standards I could think of that I'd either experienced myself or had heard about from my coaching clients – all of which are possibly, even probably, sourced from unconscious biases on the part of both men and us women. Here's my list:

- He's strong and decisive; she's aggressive and combative.
- He's across the issues and tough but fair; she's bossy, controlling and has favourites.
- He's a good strategic thinker; her head is in the clouds half the time.
- He's good at prioritising and makes the tough decisions; she's indecisive and argues for the soft/equity issues.
- He's a good delegator; she either micromanages or leaves people to flounder.
- He's a good family man, so is ready for the top job; she puts her family first, so is not ready for the top job.
- He's well built; she's gained weight.

I could go on – perhaps you can think of some more?

Now for a couple of specific examples of unconscious biases in action before I move onto my research:

First, I'll turn to my colleague Lesley's story. Her mother had chosen a gender-neutral name for her and she's always been grateful for this. She graduated with a law degree and is now pursuing an impressive career, currently as the legal counsel at the Australian head office of an international company.

Her career progression has not been without its bumps. For example, soon after graduation she was applying for roles as a junior solicitor in a range of law firms. In one firm, when she was called from the waiting room for her interview the interviewer said, 'You're not the person I'm meant to be interviewing next. I'm meant to be interviewing Lesley.' 'I am Lesley,' she replied. 'But I can't interview you, I've prepared questions for a male candidate.' Needless to say, Lesley was not offered a job at that firm, and I doubt that she would have accepted, even had she been given an offer.

Lesley is currently juggling the joys and challenges of returning to work after giving birth to her second bonny, bouncing boy. She told me that should she have a daughter at some later stage, she's determined to give her a gender-neutral name like hers.

And then there's my colleague Christine. Her gender was obviously quite clear when she was applying for roles in accountancy firms, having recently graduated with a Bachelor of Commerce degree. The man interviewing her in one such firm was well armed with his questions for female applicants: he asked Christine whether she had a boyfriend and whether she was planning to get married and have children. Christine asked the relevance of that question, and whatever her interviewer's answer, she did not accept the role she was offered at that firm.

Admittedly these examples happened a while ago: one in the late '80s, and the other in the early '90s. I doubt that either that senior lawyer or senior accountant would now be so blatant in their recruiting techniques, yet I fear they might still have unconscious thoughts lurking within them about their female applicants.

I've written a large part of this book during the first two years of the COVID-19 global pandemic. As 2021 was ending, state borders were opening in Australia and we were moving towards what was being called a new 'COVID-normal' world. We had fingers crossed that there wouldn't be a third, or indeed a fourth wave of infection here in Australia, before a vaccination was available to us all. I'm finishing the book in mid-2023 when most Australians are triple-vaxxed and yet, Australia is still nowhere near the hoped for 'new COVID-normal' and the world is yet to be declared 'COVID-stable'.

As researchers and commentators are telling us, the challenges involved in the economic downturn caused by lockdowns in every state and territory have fallen disproportionately heavily on women. I've reflected long and hard about where this research needed to be included in my book. I decided the topic belonged in this chapter, because I sense that unconscious bias on the part of politicians, employers and economists alike, has played a part in this extra burden women continue to bear.

Research

I'll begin my research in this chapter by referring once again to Mary Beard from her 2017 book *Women and power* in which she invites us to turn to the ancient Greeks to help us understand the cultural norms that continue to disempower women. Beard tells us that in Athens 'respectable, elite married women were rarely seen outside the home', and that Medea, Clytemnestra and Antigone were 'portrayed as abusers rather than users of power … in a way that leads to chaos, to the fracture of the state, to death and destruction'. Beard concludes that 'it is the unquestionable mess that women make of power in Greek myth that justifies their exclusion from it in real life, and justifies the rule of men.'[244]

In the closing pages of her manifesto, Beard stresses that we can't blame the Greeks and Romans for everything we think and do. However, she does suggest that researching deeper into the history of Greece and Rome enables us to examine our culture in ways which will help us to further grasp where we've come from.[245]

As for the effectiveness of diversity training programs, an article in *The Conversation* by Victor Sojo, and Melissa A Wheeler, both from the University of Melbourne, stated that 'an evaluation of 40 years of research has found that such programs have only a small effect in reducing bias against members of minority groups.' They also found that the impact on behaviour change fades over time.[246]

The 2020 *Quarterly Essay # 78* has given me the best explanation I've yet found about why it's hard to change peoples' minds about their deeply held beliefs. Called *The coal curse: resources, climate and Australia's future*, the essay was written by Judith Brett. Brett cites focus groups with climate sceptics undertaken by two Swedish social scientists.

With one exception, the focus group participants were aging white men, and the researchers concluded that their scepticism was 'linked to their fears about the disappearance of the masculine-dominated industrial modernity in which they had enjoyed power and success'. Brett used the word 'identity' to explain why these men were challenged:

> *When a political opinion is embedded in the core of a person's identity, it is hard to reach with evidence and arguments, no matter how compelling. It is also resistant to the bargaining and compromise that successful political outcomes depend on.*[247]

Of course, that's it I thought, as I underlined Brett's writing on this topic. It seems that expecting mostly ageing white men who continue to lead most of Australia's larger organisations to welcome women as peers in their executive suites, seems just too hard for their identity to embrace.

Next I'll turn once again to Annabel Crabb who, in her 2014 book *The wife drought*, brings her unique humour to some extremely serious topics.

For example, she refers to the work of a Queensland researcher called Terrance Fitzsimmons who interviewed dozens of Australian CEOs and company directors for his 2011 doctoral thesis on gender differences in leadership. In this research he found many women 'swan-dived away to virtually nothing when plotted against seniority in the Australian workplace'. He called this phenomenon the 'Stupid Curve'. Of special interest to Fitzsimmons was the exact process by which corporate leaders achieved advancement. He concluded that, 'when no formal process exists, people fall back on stereotypes and personal biases in decision-making, which results in homo-social reproduction' – what Crabb calls 'people promoting people who remind them of themselves.'[248]

Crabb also refers to the then Sex Discrimination Commissioner Elizabeth Broderick's work in her Male Champions of Change campaign. Broderick worked with dozens of Australia's most senior CEOs, chairmen and bureaucrats to 'help them recognise the subterranean assumptions within their organisations. ... Many of them were stunned – after learning about unconscious bias – to discover the implicit attitudes they never knew they had.'[249]

Now to my research about the impact on working women because of the COVID-19 lockdowns in Australia. Chris Wallace, Associate

Professor, Faculty of Business Government & Law, University of Canberra wrote a piece for *The Conversation* on September 24, 2020 called 'It's a man's (pandemic) world: how policies compound the pain for women in the age of COVID-19'. Wallace stated that 'the pandemic's gendered impact has been especially stark. Under pressure, dynamics many people thought were in deep retreat visibly sprang back into action.' Wallace highlighted that:

> *Because women are more likely to occupy low-paid, precarious jobs than men, women suffered first and disproportionately from pandemic job losses.*

> *Domestic violence – mostly committed by men against women – has spiked, and is even more difficult to escape than usual.*

> *Women perform the vast share of lockdown-driven home schooling, compounding their pre-pandemic burden of an unfairly large share of domestic labour generally.*

> *The free childcare early in the emergency … was snatched away again in the government's first act of pandemic policy rollback. This doubly impacted on women as workers as well as parents, given the overwhelming bulk of childcare employees are female.*

> *The (then) Morrison government's positive job initiatives, such as they are, favour men, with job-creation plans focused on male-dominated industries.*[250]

As Wallace observes, this last government initiative reinforces the idea of men as primary breadwinners – a stark example of unconscious bias in action as far as I'm concerned. In summary Wallace argues:

> *The (then) Morrison government (was) not just indifferent to the gendered impact of COVID-19. The pattern of its pandemic policy decision-making suggests an active if not explicit 'men first, women and children second' approach.*[251]

Journalist George Megalogenis provided an update on the impact of gender during COVID-19 in his article 'Women may yet be the PM's downfall' in the March 13/14, 2021 edition of the *Sydney Morning Herald*:

> *Women, as is well known, bore the brunt of retrenchments during the lockdown. They accounted for 55% of the almost 880,000 jobs lost across the country between February and May last year. By January, the economy had restored around 815,000 of those jobs. Of the 65,000 jobs still to be recovered, almost 9 in 10, or 55,000 belong to women.*[252]

Further, the Grattan Institute released a report in mid-March, 2021 about the then Morrison government's response to the COVID-19-induced recession. Mike Seccombe wrote about this in his article in the March 13, 2021 edition of *The Saturday Paper*:

> *(Women) were saddled with more unpaid work, including supervising children learning remotely. They were less likely to get government support, because JobKeeper excluded short-term casuals, who in the hardest-hit industries are mostly women. Yet the government directed substantial support to sectors, such as construction, that were little affected. It pumped more resources into apprenticeships, which historically are 70 percent male, and ignored tertiary education, which is heavily female.*[253]

In their 2020 book *Women and leadership*, Julia Gilliard and Ngozi Okonjo-Iweala ask their readers what would happen if we cried to the heavens, 'What on earth is going on?' They believe that the heavens could well respond that 'unconscious bias still exists and impacts how people perceive women in leadership positions.' In their prologue they write that they yearn for 'a world in which leaders are selected or elected based on fair evaluations of their wisdom and capacity'.[254]

I've always been fond of using the term homo-social reproduction to describe unconscious bias because of, as above, the shock value it often engendered. I found another name for this phenomenon in the September 17, 2020 *Sydney Morning Herald* (digital edition), written by Charlotte Grieve. Grieve quoted Sue Morphet, the CEO of Chief Executive Women (CEW) regarding the annual census of women leaders in Australia by CEW. The audit found that the number of female CEOs was at its lowest level since the count began – there were 10 women CEOs among ASX200 companies in 2020 compared to 11 in 2017. Morphet attributed this to what she called the 'merit trap', which she said is about 'confusing merit with the person who looks like, sounds like, and has the same experience as the person who is making the hiring decision'.[255]

Interviewees

In response to my question about unconscious bias, the 'elephant in the room' that tends not to get talked about, JKR, who has been an academic and a feminist bureaucrat, offered:

> It's the way the 'elephant' fills the room with a loud voice. If there are a number of men present, their voices rise, their voices insist, and it's hard for women to be heard. Men need to learn to listen to women, and they might just learn some really good things. Of course, as many women have reported, sometimes they do, without acknowledgement, and later make the same suggestion as if it was their own.

I probed JKR a bit deeper about whether she believed things had improved for women over the past few decades in which she's been a feminist activist. She said:

> I'd draw a U-curve: things were very active in my early years in management – the 1980s with real achievements thanks to the cunning, sophisticated, strategic thinking of we [sic] women. For example, the AA legislation was strategically thought through and that went with the opportunities of UN level conventions in support of women. This was seen by strategists as a three-fold opportunity – the value of the legislation itself, consequent international kudos (for Australia) and also getting Australia involved with bringing the international pressures back into Australia. So, these were busy, exciting, productive years.
>
> From 1995, however, the then Howard government's 'white picket fence' view of women systematically whittled things away, and I think we're now [in the Morrison era] at a very low point.

GW, the chief information officer at a university, admits to her own internal biases that hold her back:

> *My mum was very sexist against women – to her, men were superior and must be looked up to, and I find myself thinking I'm not as good as a man in the same role – so I'm assuming that within myself. It's that whole thing about women not putting themselves forward unless they're 120% ready for the role, but a man will be 80% ready and jump in. So, for me it's about pushing myself when I'm 95% ready. To me, men are calmer, men are more relaxed, men are better at this – all my own biases!!!!*

In GW's personal life she and her husband used to raise cattle and, because she grew up on a farm, she was the one with rural experience:

> *It's still a man's world. For example, when we were buying cattle, they'd look to my husband and he knows nothing about cattle. I was the one who did the negotiations, and you could see how the men had to change the way they were dealing with me when they realised I wasn't just a dumb wife.*

LM, a career lawyer, shared examples experienced by both she and her sister when they missed out on a promotion. It's a long quote but I found her story 'pure gold' in terms of explaining how unconscious biases work in a way that no amount of analysis by me could do:

> *I applied for a promotion and didn't get it so I sought feedback. First, I was told I was too young for the role, and I pointed out that there were some men at that level [who were] 2 years younger than me. Then I was told that I'd be ready in 2 years' time. Next, I was told that I hadn't managed staff before, to which I said that I had, and this was in my resume. Then [I was told] I was too passionate for the role, and so it went on like this for a while. I felt very much like the person giving me feedback was searching for reasons, and he finally said the fact that I was arguing back told him I wasn't ready for the role.*

> *I shared this experience with my sister and she told me she'd also applied for a promotion but didn't get it either. The feedback to her was that she didn't put her hand up for enough things, to which she said she'd put her hand up for A, B, C, D and E. She was then given the feedback that she hadn't managed enough staff, to which she*

responded that the role she was applying for had 3 reports and that she currently had 6 reports. By then the manager was a bit flustered and said, 'I think we've got this wrong. I just assumed that you didn't put your hand up for things, and that you didn't have management skill.' He was very open, and finally admitted that she had not been given the role 'based on assumptions that weren't true'.

DD, a former senior corporate HR executive who now runs her own international motorcycle adventure soul safari company, challenges the stereotypical assumptions of both men and women:

My own experience demonstrates that unconscious biases are woven into the fabric of our living – for both men and women. For example, leading motorcycle tours globally, for more than 15 years, the most common question I am asked is 'do you ride?'. I used to bristle (feel insulted and a tad defensive) each time I was asked this question – after all not only do I ride, while I am riding, I lead the entire tour! My job has included me leading a male-only group of 24, 3-week tour, to the Indian Himalaya's highest motorable road in the world, and someone is asking me 'do I ride'?

But now I realise people are surprised that (a) I'm a woman and I ride a motorcycle, that (b) I'm a woman and I ride that motorcycle around the world, that (c) I'm a woman and I lead motorcycle tours, and that (d) as a (sometimes) well-presented woman I don't look like a motorcyclist … whatever that is for them. There are a range of implicit biases at play here. I am asked this question by a lot more men than women. Experience has taught me to embrace this situation, be myself, do a great job, and in doing so show what women are capable of, make the unconscious bias more conscious and hopefully inspire both women and men to be all of who they are.

To my question about whether the 'elephant in the room' is peoples' unconscious biases, KB, a senior legal partner, had some insightful things to say about men's fear of women's increasing power:

I think that the elephant in the room is that men recognise that if women gain power, then they're losing power and they don't want to give it up. I've now heard it said several times that 'she is going to get that because she's a woman', or that 'I'm less likely to get promoted because I'm a man'. And whenever I hear that my response is to diffuse the gender issue and point out that promotions will be awarded if there is a business case for it [sic]. So, I now think that there's a feeling amongst men that there are winners and losers and they're on the losing side in this gender debate and they're fighting against it in quite unsubtle ways.… Unconscious bias is there without a doubt and I think this (men's fear of missing out) is becoming a problem now.

AS, a former CEO and now a non-executive director on several high-powered boards, no longer has anything to prove to herself or anyone else:

On the topic of homo-social reproduction – when I joined a major board, I looked at some recent hires and I wondered why they'd chosen someone just like the person they're replacing, and then realised that this is obviously why they all look the same.

On the topic of unconscious biases AS told me:

I have a hard line on unconscious biases – to me bias is bias – it's almost like we're giving people an excuse now. Whether it's unconscious or not, I think you run out of excuses as you get senior in organisations, and you should be more aware of the things that you do that impact differently on one group from another. … You can't just look around and go, gee they're pretty much all middle-aged white middle-class men and think that's natural, because it's not! … I just don't think unconscious bias is a good enough excuse because it means you don't read about anything or think about anything, and if that's the case you shouldn't be in a position of power.

SE, one of the men I interviewed who is a manager in the tech industry, blames the 'shock jocks', and world leaders such as former US president Donald Trump, who make it OK for people to think and say racist and sexist things:

This comes from the absence of the capacity for critical thought and unconscious bias is born of this stuff. The Trumps of this world are playing into a divide and conquer campaign and normalising an unviable agenda.

EM, who was a senior manager in the tech world before her retirement, said on the topic:

> I've lost count of the number of times that the assumption was that I take the minutes because I'm a woman. I quickly learnt to say, 'I'm not real good at that, so I think we should choose someone who's better at it.'

PS, an agriculturalist and another one of the men I interviewed for this book, shared with me that:

> [I believe that] unconscious bias is [at] the root of most problems, so there is a need to continually work on your awareness and your assertive and respectful communication, and the interdependence of your relationships at work and at home. We can't challenge the fact that women have babies. However, an interdependent approach will assist in the elimination of discrimination.

On the topic of recruitment at a senior level RT, a retired HR professional, told me:

> When I was in the workplace, merit-based selection and development was very hard when the people making the decisions (typically male) had the narrowest of views of success – and their natural instinct was to replicate their model of success which was also male.

And to my question about the 'elephant in the room' RT concluded on a forceful note:

> Everything I've already told you was due to unconscious biases. Historically, this was understandable. In the enlightened era it is not. Even if it has had to be forced upon men to listen, due to the foresight of AA legislation etc, anything less is unacceptable.

LS, a female agriculturalist and leader in her rural region, said in response to my question about unconscious bias:

> It's definitely there, coming from both men and women too about what men and women should do – although less so in the younger ones.

> [In terms of awareness raising] all you can do is start that awareness process for people; and we all have to be willing to be aware of what our biases might be. And even if we don't catch them at

that moment, we can reflect and learn and try to capture it sooner when it appears again. In a way it's human nature – we're always comparing ourselves with those around us. Like so much, I think it's about awareness and thinking and working on ourselves, which it's really easy not to do!

On the topic of the 'elephant in the room' JES, a retired IT professional, said:

> I agree that some men have unconscious bias – this is not a case of 'seeing is believing' but 'believing is seeing'. They are convinced there is no bias so cannot see it. How do you shake 'the level playing field' conviction of so many? Sometimes it takes (bitter) personal experience.

I'm ending this section from my interviewees about unconscious biases on an optimistic note by quoting PC, another man interviewed whose management career has spanned leadership in the health and higher education sectors:

> Let's assume there is unconscious bias, so where does it come from? If it's unconscious it has derived from somewhere else and has become part of someone's subliminal brain function and I suppose it comes from their deep dark past where things were very different, and it's lingered. … So, knowing the origins of unconscious bias is the secret to knowing how to deal with it. But these days the patriarchal prejudice is called out, so you can no longer get away with it.

I do hope you're right, PC.

What more can be done?

I'll repeat my hope that retirement is helping to remove what PC has called 'patriarchal prejudice', as the last cohort of men who spent most of their careers in a man's world, are hanging up their suits, business shirts and ties and getting out their golf clubs and fishing rods.

I've read that when some symphony orchestras are recruiting new musicians, they ask the candidates to play behind a thin curtain so that the recruiters select on technical skill only. This could also be done in workplaces by removing the names and addresses of job applicants to prevent recruiters from bringing any of their unconscious biases into the short-listing process. As well as removing the possibility of gender bias, this may also eliminate any racial or religious bias.

In terms of what to do about the gender inequities revealed by the COVID-19 pandemic in Australia, I'll leave the last word to Kate Jenkins, from her opening address to The Beijing Platform for Action, 25 years on conference on 3 December, 2020:

> *In a post-COVID world, where the focus for many nations will be on economic recovery, we need to ensure that the case for including gender equality as a necessary step towards national productivity is loud and clear.*[256]

Conclusions

One of my core beliefs is that 'people are by nature good'. I'm not so naïve that I don't know that there is evil in the world, and that there are evil people. But to me these are an ugly aberration from the true nature of humanity. As I reflect on the various examples of unfairness to women that I've included in this chapter, to stay true to my belief that 'people are by nature good', I can only conclude that each of these acts of indirect discrimination was done unconsciously. Were this pointed out to the unaware discriminator, my hope is that they would be both shocked and keen to make amends.

That said, I've learnt over the years from my own life and from my many consulting and coaching clients, that we humans don't like change, and that we need a compelling reason to make us change. For most of us, a positive inducement is more likely to persuade us to change than a negative one, when this is asked of us. However, when change proves resilient, a less pleasant inducement in the form of a sanction is sometimes needed for change to be achieved. For example, since getting a hefty fine in the early '90s, I no longer drive through red lights, even if there's not another car in sight.

If I were to pause and show some empathy towards those – mostly men – who currently inhabit the executive suites of corporate Australia, by putting my feet into their shoes I too would probably feel proud that I'd reached such heady heights in my career, and that I too would likely resent any changes being made to the current status quo that had helped to get me there. So in concluding this chapter, if I sound frustrated, I want to stress that it's not men I'm frustrated with – rather it's the patriarchal culture which, as is explored in other parts of this book, still lurks insidiously in far too many organisations.

I love it when my current reading includes something relevant to a topic that I'm also writing about at the time. An example of such a synchronicity occurred when I was reviewing this chapter and wondering yet again why apparently honourable people can so doggedly resist change for the good. In this instance I'm referring to the many leaders in this land who still do not 'get it' that their workplaces are at best unfriendly, and at worst hostile, to women. I was reading *Sapiens: A brief history of humankind* by Yuval Noah Harari for the second time. And there the synchronicity was. In his chapter called 'Building pyramids', Harari explains that for any aspect of the cultural norms of a society – what he calls the current 'imagined order' – to change, a shift in consciousness is needed by the leaders of that society. Harari then explains that for this change of consciousness to occur, leaders will first need to believe in an alternate way of viewing the world – a new 'imagined order'. At last, thanks to Harari, I have an explanation for what has perplexed me over all my years of feminist activism: that is, that many of our current leaders are yet to make that conscious shift towards a new 'imagined order' which involves a belief in the value that women can contribute throughout their workplaces. [257]

It's been clear to me over the years of my consulting and coaching life that the sanctions involved in both anti-discrimination and affirmative action laws are blunt as well as inefficient instruments. With Harari's help I can now but conclude there's only one way to convince the senior leaders of Australia that it is in their best interest to remove the barriers to women's full participation in their organisations. This is by convincing them of the value of what he calls a new 'imagined order,' and of the benefits to be achieved in their organisations when they choose to make this shift.

My hope is that the research and stories contained in this book will make a positive contribution to this project.

Chapter 14

How much are you paid?

Having done my best to thoroughly unpick the mysteries of unconscious bias in the previous chapter, it's time to look at the issue of the lingering gender pay gap in Australia. This must surely be the product of unconscious beliefs about the value of women's work versus men's work in the minds of those setting remunerations.

Talking about what you earned was a taboo subject in my middle-class upbringing. I certainly never knew how much my father earned and I strongly suspect nor did my mother. When it came time for me to be applying for jobs, I just gratefully accepted whatever I was told my salary would be. It wasn't until many years later that I worked out that one of the reasons there's still a gender pay gap is that, like me, most women gratefully accept the salary offered, whereas most men negotiate.

Another contributing factor to the pay gap is the continuing sex segregation in the Australian workforce. For example, nurses (mostly women) earn less then doctors (mostly men) and engineers (mostly men) are paid lots more than childcare workers (mostly women). An example of this happened in my own family: I, who'd done just as well at school as my brother, chose to train as a nurse while he trained as a doctor, with neither of us ever thinking about our remuneration on graduation. I'm proud of my 20-year career as a general nurse, midwife and community health nurse, but I sure as hell never earned what my brother could as a doctor.

My conditioning that money is a taboo subject and therefore not nice for respectable women to talk about has also worked against me during my years of self-employment. First, as an equal opportunity consultant and then as a leadership coach, I always hated the dreaded question, 'how much will this cost?' The invention of email was a god-send because I can now say to prospective clients, 'let me get back to you with a proposal about what you've asked me to do, and the costs involved'. Nonetheless, I strongly suspect that I've almost always charged less than my peers in the consulting world because I've never felt comfortable asking any of them what they charge.

It's now over 50 years since the Whitlam government intervened to help secure an industrial court judgement awarding women equal pay for work of equal value. Yet, as you will read in more detail in the research section below, Michelle Grattan wrote in *The Conversation* on June 27, 2022 that the 2022 report from The Workplace Gender Equality Agency, using data from the ABS, found that there was still a gender pay gap in all age groups and that the overall average pay gap was 13.8%.[258]

Research

One source of research for this book is from the data I've gathered from my over 30 years of consulting and coaching experiences. An example related to one of my coaching clients comes to mind that demonstrates the danger of the privacy that seems to still enshrine private sector pay scales. The public sector has pay grades that are well known – although, as an aside, I've heard anecdotally that public service men are often remunerated on the highest band, while their women colleagues are paid on the lowest band of that grade.

I coached a woman for several years after she was recruited into a senior role in the HR department of a nationally listed manufacturing business. She was offered a salary on entry that she accepted. It was only years later that she worked out that a male peer, who was recruited at the same time into a similar role as she was, negotiated his salary on entry, and so started on a higher salary than she did. On every subsequent pay rise, both their salaries rose commensurate to their starting salary, so his was always that much higher than hers. This is an example of what is called the gender pay gap.

Anne Summers in her 2013 book *The misogyny factor* tells readers that it was in the 1972 Equal Pay Case, that the Conciliation and Arbitration Commission granted women 'equal pay for work of equal value.'[259]

But then in her chapter called 'Scorecard' Summers explores examples of ongoing gender pay gaps. She quotes a study that looked at earning differences between male and female graduates from the same university school:

A report released in October 2012 showed that a 25-year-old woman with post-graduate qualifications would, over her lifetime, earn $2.49 million. The 25-year-old man who sat beside her in class would, by contrast, accumulate $3.78 million.[260]

And of course, as Summers then explains, one outcome of a lifetime of working less because of things like breaks on maternity leave, and of earning less than men throughout their working lives, is that women have far less superannuation on retirement.

Next, I turn to journalist and author Annabel Crabb in her 2014 book, *The wife drought*. On the topic of the gender pay gap she writes in her inimitable style:

When researchers … dig down and compare male and female workers with comparable levels of experience and qualification, there remains a stubborn 60 per cent or so of the gender pay gap which cannot be explained by anything apart from the presence or absence of certain dangly bits.[261]

How has this ongoing gender pay gap happened? Leonora Risse, a lecturer in economics at RMIT University, wrote in *The Conversation* on June 19, 2019, that we can blame 'decisions dating back a century… to the unequal wage patterns we still see today, with female-dominated jobs clustered at the lower end of the pay spectrum'.[262]

On August 16, 2019 Kristine Ziwica reported in the *The Age* the launch of the report *Closing the Gender Pay Gap* by the Chifley Research Centre and PwC. This study was timed to mark the 50th anniversary of

Australia's equal pay case back in 1969. The report describes the continued existence of the gender pay gap 50 years on as 'a failure of both public policy and public will'. It concludes that the biggest driver of the pay gap was gender discrimination. And the report further states that at the current rate that the pay gap is closing, it will take another 50 years for parity to be achieved. Fifty (that is five-oh) years![263]

Soon after, a report by KPMG for the Diversity Council of Australia and Workplace Gender Equality Agency was released in late August, 2019 and was reported by Emma Williamson of Monash University in *The Conversation* on 23 August. This report showed that the gender pay gap had declined from $3.05 an hour in 2014 to $2.43 an hour in 2017, accrediting two-thirds of this decline to 'diminishing industrial occupational segregation.' However, as the report concluded, 'proving harder to erode is gender discrimination and the impact for women of career interruptions.'[264]

In *The Conversation* on April 21, 2020 Lyn Craig, Professor of Sociology and Social Policy, University of Melbourne wrote an article called 'COVID-19 has laid bare how much we value women's work, and how little we pay for it'. As the title suggests, Craig argued that the pandemic revealed how little we pay for so-called women's work:

> *Australia has very low gender equality when it comes to remuneration, ranking 49th on the World Economic Forum Gender Participation and Opportunity Index 2020 that measures workforce participation, remuneration and advancement.*[265]

Craig explained that, because paid women's work tends to be concentrated in the caring and service industries, it is more likely to be low paid, casual and part-time. Added to this, Australian women do more unpaid domestic work and care. As well, most Australian women move in and out of the paid workforce, or limit their paid work hours, to care for children and/or other family members. As Craig rightly points out – this unpaid caring work supports our society but is taken for granted and its value is discounted.

Craig then looked at the areas of work deemed 'essential services' during the pandemic and observes that 'it is striking how many jobs that are now seen as essential involve care, and how many of them are female dominated.' She identified childcare workers, aged care and disability workers as providing essential services, all of whom are among the lowest paid workers in this country. Add to this list the nurses and teachers who also earn less than equivalently or less qualified professionals in similar occupations. For example, 32% of police and 27% of ambulance officers earn more than $2,000 per week, compared to 10% of nurses and 12% of teachers.

Craig concluded with a plea to pay essential workers well:

> *The coronavirus has made brutally clear that care work, both paid and unpaid, is fundamental to our economic and social survival. We should not continue to undervalue it, or to free-ride on those that do the most. We should pay our care workers properly for the skilled and expert work they do. And for both employers and governments alike, I would argue that this will involve the challenging of deeply held assumptions about the value of so-called women's work – both paid and unpaid.*[266]

In late winter 2021 some more data about the gender pay gap came to light. On August 31, Patty Kinnersly, CEO of *Our Watch* revealed that the disproportionate impact of the COVID-19 pandemic on industries dominated by women workers had resulted in the gender pay gap in Australia growing to 14.2%, an increase of 0.8% in the previous six months. Further, according to the Workplace Gender Equality Agency, this increase in the gender pay gap represented a drop in wages of $261.50/week for full-time women workers, compared to the average full-time male wage in the same six months.[267]

In her book, *Who cooked Adam Smith's dinner*, author Katrine Marçal explores the conundrum associated with the fact that a high proportion of workers in the care sector are women, just like Adam Smith's mum. Marçal argues that this then leads to economic inequality, and she suggests a proposition that care work is poorly remunerated because of a 'dichotomy between love and money.'[268]

On further research, I was horrified to read about some world-first data in *The Conversation* on 31 March, 2021 regarding one outcome when women earn more than their male partners. In an article Robert Breunig and Yinjunjie Zhang, both from the Australian National University, reported that 'Domestic violence committed on female partners in heterosexual couples occurs significantly more frequently when the woman earns more than the man – according to our findings about 35% more often'.[269] I can't find the right words to unpick why this should be, nor indeed any words to express how this 'shocking statistical fact' makes me feel.

The *Bridging the gap?* report by King's College London and the Australian National University, published in the 21 October, 2021 edition of *The Sydney Morning Herald*, revealed some more alarming research about the gender pay gap in Australia. This report looked at gender reporting in Australia, the UK, France, South Africa, Spain and Sweden, and it ranked Australia equal last with the United Kingdom. It found that women in Australia 'have to work an extra 61 days to earn the same as the average man.' Further Dr Miriam Glennie, one of the authors, cautioned that 'Australia's current reporting framework ... tends to capture only relatively privileged women ... in full-time corporate roles.' This is because only employers with 100 or more employees are required to report to the Workplace Gender Equality Agency. Glennie argues that, to achieve widespread improvement in the gender pay gap in Australia, the reporting structure needs to be simplified to include smaller employers.[270]

In terms of up-to-date statistics about the average gender pay gap in all age groups in March, 2022 it was 13.8% according to the Australian Bureau of Statistics. Then in mid-June, 2022 the Workplace Gender Equality Agency (a federal government body) released the results of their latest *Wages and Ages: Mapping the Gender Pay Gap by Age* data series. As above, using data collected from private sector employers with 100 or more employees, the agency found that there continues to be a gender pay gap in all age ranges, the highest being 46% in the 55+ years. What I found alarming in this data is that less than 50% of working women are employed full-time. Given it's almost exclusively full-time workers who get promoted into management roles, this explains the huge gender pay gap in the 55 + age group.[271]

Interviewees

KB, a senior partner in an international law firm, told me:

> *I expect I was paid differently (less) in my earlier years, but I didn't ever compare my salary with others.*

Just as an aside, the gender pay gap is something we [her firm] assess every year and, to the extent we identify any discrepancies, attempt to address it.

Corporate lawyer LM experienced what happens to whistle-blowers about pay inequities:

In around 2006 when I was working at a large private law firm, I found out that my charge-out rate (the amount clients were charged for my time) was less than for my male peers. I alerted other females at the same level ... and was censured by my superiors for sharing the information. I believe that the charge-out rates were later made the same for lawyers at the same level.

JKR, retired academic and bureaucrat, shared with me some of the subtleties of pay inequity despite the equal pay decision of 1969:

Earning equity does not only relate to basic pay levels. Increments of salary at the discretion of superiors are also relevant and so are opportunities to progress up a professional and salary ladder, particularly in organisations as hierarchical as my two workplaces.

For example, JKR told me the following story:

After working away in the tutor ranks for several years, I saw an opportunity to apply for a move up to be a lecturer. However, a man (married with three children) was selected for the academically mainstream ... course and I (married with two children) would be appointed to teach a new course on the history of women. It was effectively an intention to move me sideways. The man with three children would get the appointment that was the straightforward step towards a safe academic career, I would be given the course that had sat on the books at the school for a number of years because they couldn't find anyone 'suitable' to teach it. That actually meant anyone who would risk their career to take it. Now, I couldn't see all that at the time. I was pretty overwhelmed with unexpected pleasure to have the chance of a lectureship role at all.

As it turned out, the 'backhander' course was not only one of the most stimulating and rewarding experiences of my working life but so successful that it attracted higher student numbers (not only women) than all but one of the mainstream courses. It also proved to be an important career path opportunity when I entered my second professional career as a public servant working on policy for women.

JKR's womanly gratefulness is obvious here, as is her appointment that fits the definition of the 'glass cliff' that I've recently learnt about – which is the appointment of a woman to a risky position that could fail.

JKR concluded:

It was not until well after I'd left the university that I worked out about discretionary decisions to deny me the annual increments in salary taken for granted by my (male) colleagues. If challenged, their excuse would have been that (because of my two young children) I had not kept up with the 'publish or perish' expectations of an academic career.

In response to my question about the gender pay gap GW, the only female chief information officer (CIO) in her sector, told me:

I am currently the lowest paid CIO in the sector. There are two factors at play here, the size of my organisation (it's one of the smallest in the sector) and gender inequality. I have put the latter into the hands of my boss to resolve. It will be interesting to see what happens. (By the way), this is the first time in my career that the salary ranges equivalent to my role have been put into a review, so this is the only time I've been aware of it.

I followed up with GW about the outcome of her requested salary review with her boss. Her reply? All salaries have been frozen because of the challenges to the higher education sector because of the global pandemic.

In terms of pay inequity, EM, the recently retired CIO in my research, told me:

I was aware of it but did nothing because there's not a lot you can do. I think I got better at negotiating my salary over time to the point that in my most recent position … my male manager was paid less than me. How come? Because he wasn't as good at negotiating as

I was. That said, I did spend most of my career making 30% less than my male peers, so learning to negotiate was crucial.

JS has had a diverse career, first as a scientist, and now as a business manager at a university, with previous experience as a board member on two boards. She told me:

On the topic of remuneration, I don't think we females are very good at benchmarking – if I had my time over again, I would ask about my offered remuneration as a benchmark against males. I've never done that.

LS, an agriculturalist and rural leader, drew on the experience of one of her close city-based friends on the topic of pay inequity:

My friend A is almost a partner in her accounting firm. She's been given the role of HR in her firm as well as her client work, but without being paid anything extra. Because she wants to be seen as being really good at her job, she hasn't complained about this.

I confess that this example really raises my hackles because it brings to light not only obvious pay inequity relative to A's peers, but also gender discrimination. I can almost hear her leader's thoughts along the lines of, 'there's not much to do in HR and I'm sure A won't mind at all fitting this in as well as her client work'. Added to this is to me, the glaring unconscious bias on the part of the partners in her firm that 'HR is women's work.'

SE, one of my male interviewees told me he would love to work fewer hours. However, he's paid a lot more in the IT sector than his wife is paid in the services sector, so he's the one that must head out the door and/or turn on the computer in his home office, every weekday.

Finally, from my interviewees, SA, who has been an allied health practitioner, an academic and leader in the higher education sector, and is now the managing director of a small business that provides information, resources and advice to the allied health sector, has an excellent tip for younger women to ensure they achieve pay equity:

Negotiate your salary – the blokes do it all the time. And get some coaching to help to do this if you think it's too hard.

What more can be done?

In terms of what can be done to close the gender pay gap sooner than the predicted 50 years hence, the Chifley Research Centre's report, *Closing the gender pay gap* recommends that a 'suite of strong actions' will be needed to 'force adequate, timely closing of the pay gap'. The report recommended that this suite include:

> *Transparent reporting of gender pay statistics for all employers with more than 100 staff.*
>
> *A 'use it or lose it' policy on Paid Parental Leave (to encourage 'second carers' to take their entitlement, which could allow mothers to return to work sooner).*
>
> *Pay increases in female dominated sectors to bring them more into line with male-dominated professions.*[272]

Further, five female academics at the Australian National University published an article in *The Conversation* on 1 October, 2021, called 'Australia has ranked last in an international gender pay gap study – here are 3 ways to do better'. The three ways they suggest are:

1. *Publish pay data for individual organisations*
2. *Set a new minimum standard that matters*
3. *Make use of sanctions.*[273]

I would add one more action, which is that organisations conduct an annual salary assessment of all employees to bring to light any gender pay gaps. The federal parliament has passed a bill to address the gender pay gap which is outlined below in my Conclusions.

Conclusions

Writing this chapter has brought up many memories of the stories I've been told by women I've coached over the years who've discovered, well into their careers, that they were being paid less than their male colleagues. One of the problems, in corporate life anyway, is that peoples' salaries typically remain a secret unless they choose to compare notes with their peers.

What can I conclude from all that I've learnt from my clients over the years, as well as from the research and interviewees in this chapter about the existence of, and the reasons for, the ongoing gender pay gap in Australia?

Once again, while holding close to my heart my belief that 'people are by nature good', I simply won't let myself think that the heads of remuneration in corporate Australia and the public service are bad people who actively set out to pay women less. Sadly, my conclusion, therefore, is that the ongoing and oh so stubborn gender pay gap in Australia is the result of deep cultural norms which mean that we women are conditioned to graciously accept the remuneration offered, while men have been conditioned to feel entitled to negotiate.

Two interventions to change this are – to first convince women that they too are entitled to negotiate their salary; and second to train them in negotiation skills to enable them to do this. However, let's not yet again put the onus of responsibility for change on women's shoulders only. What's essential right now is that all organisations develop fair and transparent remuneration policies, systems and processes that include a total upheaval of the current gendered status of essential, mainly caring, work.

Of course, as we now know, the electorate lost patience with the previous government and elected a new federal Labor government in May, 2022. And the good news is that the *Workplace Gender Equality Amendment (Closing the Gender Pay Gap) Bill 2023* has now been passed by federal parliament. This means that from early 2024, the gender pay gaps of employers with 100 or more workers will be published.

Chapter 15

When will they find me out?

I n the last chapter I've encouraged women to negotiate for a higher salary than is first offered to them. However, this requires them to believe that they're deserving of more money than they've been offered. In this chapter I'm exploring a phenomenon that gets in the way of women feeling deserving.

I've learnt from both my own journey through the bumps and twists of life, and from many hundreds of women I've had the privilege of coaching over the years, that one way self-doubt manifests in us women is that we feel like a fraud and therefore fear that we don't belong in the rarefied atmosphere of a senior role in an organisation. This gets called the 'imposter syndrome' – that phenomenon in which we don't believe that we're good enough to be in the position we're in, and that we're going to be found out as a fraud some time very soon.

I remember well a woman I was coaching in Sydney many years ago. She was the only woman in the senior executive team in her large corporation but was battling her own negative thinking about whether she was good enough to be a peer of her male colleagues. She was already better qualified than any of them, yet when we first started meeting, she told me that to prove that she was good enough, she'd decided to embark on some further study. I strongly discouraged her from doing this; indeed I pointed out that, aside from the time and energy this would involve, she was also likely to alienate herself from her male peers if she gained even more qualifications, because she would be seen by them as a threat.

Instead, we spent time using a simple model from my coaching toolkit called the Slipped DISC, which is based on the principles of cognitive behavioural therapy (CBT). This model is designed to help people increase their self-confidence. It involves working through four simple steps: first, identifying, and second, challenging negative thoughts; third, replacing negative thoughts with positive self-messages; and the final, fourth step is setting an action plan for change. With the help of this simple model, I'm happy to report that, by the time this woman had completed her coaching contract with me, she was standing tall with a strong sense of entitlement and belonging in her senior executive team.

As this story illustrates, the impact of the imposter syndrome on women is that our self-limiting messages mean we tend to undersell ourselves and not take risks in our careers. And of course, as a result, the impact on organisations is that they fail to tap us women's full potential.

Before I move onto my research on the imposter syndrome, I've decided to share a very personal story about how my self-doubt stopped me stepping up as a leader right back in my school days. In my all-girls school in suburban Adelaide, each class selected a class captain at the start of each of the three terms of the school year. I was typically selected class captain in the first term of each year. Then I was chosen by the staff and headmistress as a probationary prefect in year 10 and a prefect in year 11. Towards the end of year 11 the headmistress – a rather daunting, yet awe-inspiring, English woman called Miss Gertrude Monica Millington – told me she would like me to be the head prefect in the following year. I blushed and thanked her and said I would think about it. Then what did I do? I chose to leave school a year earlier than I might have, to avoid being put in the spotlight and potentially being found out as not good enough, and therefore a fraud, as head prefect.

The older, wiser Kate would so love to be able to talk to this young woman who clearly demonstrated leadership qualities throughout her school years. Given the opportunity, I would have encouraged her to think deeply about her decision, and to offer her support if she did change her mind and choose to accept this leadership role. Miss Millington obviously thought I had the potential. I still wonder how different my career might have turned out had I been the head prefect of my school by attending that final optional year that I chose to avoid by leaving. Of course, I will never know, but I do know how proud I was when my daughter was selected head girl in her final year of school. I'm also totally delighted that all five of my granddaughters have been selected for leadership roles at their schools.

Fast forward to now, when on every day that I've researched, written and edited this book, the wretched voices of self-doubt have kept yabbering at me about why I think I'm capable of writing about such a huge and complex topic as gender equity. In response, I take a deep breath, sit up taller and tell them to butt out.

Research

As referred to several times already in this book, Korn Ferry, in association with the Australian Institute of Company Directors, released a report in 2018 called *Australian women CEOs speak*.

In this chapter, I'm focusing on the parts of the report that deal with the imposter syndrome. Under the heading of 'Transcending self-doubt', the report identified that more than one-third of the women interviewed talked about periods of painful self-doubt. Even as they were performing well, they talked about 'feeling like a fraud,' with one noting specifically that she'd suffered from the imposter syndrome:

> *I was appointed, and I thought, this is great, this is what I wanted. And then I thought, my God, I'm a complete fraud, they are going to realise that I actually don't know how to lead a division, and this is just going to be a disaster.*[274]

In the 'Takeaways' section for women in the report was:

> *When women doubt themselves regarding leadership positions, they should re-evaluate, recognising that it is not necessary to have 100% of the desired experience and qualifications. If other people express confidence in their abilities, women should take those evaluations seriously and own them.*

And under the takeaways for organisations the report recommends:

> *Organisations should highlight the success of women who are already in leadership. This conveys to younger women that it is absolutely possible to make it to the top as a woman.*[275]

In a February 2019 edition of the *Good Weekend* supplement in *The Sydney Morning Herald* written by Jacqueline Maley, I was shocked to read that even a woman as smart, savvy and successful as Elizabeth Broderick has been a self-confessed sufferer of the imposter syndrome.

At the end of her term as Sex Discrimination Commissioner when Broderick applied for the position as a rapporteur to the UN, she told Maley that she 'came down with a bad case of imposter syndrome' when writing her application: 'I thought that there's no chance I would get this role. I'm not qualified enough.' When she was interviewed by a panel of men – Broderick again, 'You've got to love that, for women's rights!' – she told her husband she'd performed poorly and had no chance of success. To her surprise and delight she was offered the role. Even as she was boarding her flight to Geneva to be inducted as a UN rapporteur, she said to herself, 'Oh my god, what have I done? Am I going to have the skills necessary to do the job well?' History has proven she does.[276]

Julia Baird, journalist, historian and regular columnist in *The Sydney Morning Herald* writes well on women's self-doubt. In a piece in the *Herald* in August 2016 she cited research published in the *British Journal of Psychology*. This study was conducted in 12 countries, and it found that men think they are more intelligent than women in every country they researched. The researchers found 'male hubris and female humility in self-estimates in intelligence were not affected by differences in actual cognitive ability. In every country, men considered themselves smarter than women.'[277]

Further, in the publication *ABC News*, also in August 2016, Baird tells us that a Hewlett Packard study found that women only applied for jobs when they thought they had 100% of the job requirements, while men applied when they thought they had just 60%.

Former political leaders, Australia's Julia Gillard and Nigeria's Ngozi Okonjo-Iweala in their 2020 book *Women and leadership*, also discuss what I'm calling the imposter syndrome and what they call 'the confidence effect'. On the topic of the data that shows that women are less likely to apply for a position if they don't meet all the stated criteria, they cite a study of over 1,000 professionals in America in which women more often failed to apply for a role because they believed they weren't well enough qualified.[278]

These authors then turned to data from 610 million LinkedIn users to describe the 'confidence effect'. This data showed that, even though men and women browse for new work opportunities in a similar way, women are 16 per cent less likely to apply for a job than men, and that women apply for 20 per cent fewer jobs.[279]

I'll leave the last word in my research into why women suffer from the imposter syndrome to Virginia Woolf. In the September 24, 2020 edition of *The Conversation* Jessica Gildersleeve, in a piece headed 'Guide to the classics: A Room of One's Own, Virginia Woolf's feminist call to arms', Gildersleeve quotes Woolf asserting that 'Women have served all these centuries as looking-glasses possessing the magic and delicious power of reflecting the figure of man at twice their natural size.'[280]

Interviewees

When I began interviewing women for this book, I didn't include a question on the imposter syndrome. However, once I'd found the research described above, I realised this was an important topic, and added a question that I asked subsequent interviewees. I also went back to my earlier interviewees to pose the question to them as well. And to my surprise, several replies landed within days of my email.

A few women told me that they'd heard of the imposter syndrome, but that they hadn't ever felt like a fraud. Two reasons given for this were a 'healthy level of self-confidence' by one woman, and another who said, 'I have always had a fair amount of confidence in my ability, knowledge and capacity to deal with challenging people and problems.'

However, most of my interviewees told me they had suffered from some degree of self-doubt at certain times in their careers. For example, KB, a senior legal partner, wrote:

I've spent my entire career dealing with the imposter syndrome —
both in myself and with my female friends and (women) I mentor.

The best manifestation of the imposter syndrome was on the day
I first became a partner. I happened to be on leave overseas with

my mother. She made a fuss and ensured we had a great meal to celebrate my promotion. During dinner I said, without thinking, 'I hope I have a job when I get home and nothing has blown up.' My mother couldn't believe that I was expecting to lose my job [because I was no good], when I had just been endorsed by my firm.

KB did end her email response to me on a positive note:

I've never allowed the imposter syndrome to limit me, as I regularly put myself in positions that make me feel uncomfortable [because I think I'm not good enough]. So, although I might be throwing up with fear that I will stuff up because I am useless, I do not let that fear stop me.

GW, a CIO in the higher education sector, told me:

I have had a severe case of imposter syndrome for the better part of my life. It's only now after coaching with my leadership coach that it's finally disappearing. Every woman I have worked with has had the syndrome to a certain extent. It takes quite a bit of support and acknowledgement to overcome!

SN, who has been an allied health practitioner, an academic and leader in the higher education sector, and is now the managing director of a small business, also admitted to suffering from the imposter syndrome:

Yes, to the imposter syndrome – I don't know many women … who don't suffer from it, to be honest. I still experience it, but because I know it's there, I'm better at calling it out. I also have a little internal voice that goes, 'hang on – you know this is wrong', but it is still restricting, because you're never sure what you are unconsciously not doing as a result of not believing in yourself.

JS, a former scientist and now business manager at a university, with previous experience as a board member on two boards, said in response to my question about the imposter syndrome:

I have felt this fear when I have been promoted or landed a very senior position. … As a female it's hard to ask for support because you don't want to look like you don't know what you're doing. So, the level of difficulty in getting up to speed is doubly high. The other difficulty is that you feel like you don't have a supportive network to help you learn the ropes, and when you do make mistakes, it feels like these are very public.

JS then told me how she's learnt to build up her self-confidence:

I've done a lot of work in the area of self-confidence and call the negative voice in my head 'Edna'. She comes out when I've done something wrong, when I'm not feeling confident and when I'm tired. I've also learnt that your brain sends out random thoughts – good, bad, irrelevant, constructive etc. As a scientist I had always thought you should listen to your thoughts and it was only when I was sick and started seeing a psychologist that I was introduced to cognitive behavioural therapy (CBT) and understood my thoughts are not always helpful. This has been one of the biggest learnings in my life. I continue to struggle with self-confidence but am better off when I'm able to label these sorts of thoughts as 'Edna' mouthing off, being wrong, or making something worse than it really is.

I think CBT is an important tool that has strong merit in women's leadership training.

RT, a now retired HR/diversity professional, talked about the challenge of staying confident while lacking an available qualification in her field. She was working as an EEO/diversity change agent in a large corporation at a time when higher education institutions were yet to provide relevant research and courses in this field:

I did worry about this (the imposter syndrome) – particularly because my role was running ahead faster than my educational background. So, I was running on instinct and felt vulnerable at times that my time would be up sometime soon, when I would be found out, given I was surrounded by exceptionally well-educated people. I had to build a belief in myself, which was hard to find some days if I was getting push-back on a lot of things.

But after years of retirement and the opportunity to look back on these days more candidly, I know now that I completely trusted my very good instincts: observation skills, life's experiences, and vigilance to back up my (growing) skills and knowledge – and that was more than enough strength and preparedness to deal with the unknowns we faced each day.

It was an outstanding opportunity to create the future as we went, and I know that my insecurities actually turned into great insights, which I was able to use to help many others who felt overwhelmed or under-prepared for a world of change where they [women and minority groups] could be included and contribute equally and even more so – exceptionally – with their well-earned education and skills.

DP, who's been a marketing executive in a large corporate and is now a consultant specialising in transformational leadership and organisational change, said in response to my question about the imposter syndrome:

Yes, I definitely experienced a version of this in my 30s. As I recall, my thinking was not so much that I'd be found out as a fraud, it was more a crippling lack of self-confidence/self-esteem. At a low point, I remember a work colleague and good mate coming into my office and I looked up startled from budget papers that made no sense and he said, 'Jeez Deb, you look like a scared rabbit.'

And that's exactly what I was, sick with anxiety and self-loathing. This propelled me into counselling for the first time for which I am extremely grateful. I had been experiencing self-doubt for quite some time, with this vignette being the low point. During this time, I was getting recognition from my boss, I got a company car for the first time and I got promoted, and yet none of this external recognition meant a jot. It was my own lack of love for self that was at the root cause.

I'll give JES, another early achiever in the IT sector, the final word from my interviewees about the imposter syndrome:

When I applied for a management role, I was my own doubter – so common in women – by asking myself, could I apply and perform this role with a three-year-old?

What more can be done?

Before we all start slashing our wrists in despair about all of this, at least two writers have given us women some practical tips to bolster our belief in ourselves.

Julia Baird makes a couple of good suggestions in a piece in the online publication *ABC News* on August 15, 2016 headed 'Why you should carry yourself with the confidence of a mediocre white man'. First that '… it is often uncertainty and not mediocrity that holds women back, and that we should all shun self-doubt and embrace a little white man confidence'. And second, she recommends that we women do this by '… splashing a dab of white-man-confidence-cologne on our wrists before heading out to work each morning'.[281]

In a piece in the *Harvard Business Review* Associate Professor Zoe Kinias recommends 'a simple exercise whereby women reflect on their own core personal values'. Kinias has found that this 'will boost self-worth and close gender gaps in performance'.[282]

The Korn Ferry study discussed earlier also suggests three useful tips for women when they find they're doubting their worth:

- *Normalise such feelings: By being authentic and open with others about their periods of self-doubt, women found they could get through them.*

- *Reflect on achievements: Taking stock of past successes, moments when they bounced back, and the confidence others placed in them helped women believe in themselves.*

- *Reject fear: Interestingly, even though these women had self-doubt, they recognised that they also had tremendous courage. By using that – confronting issues head-on, saying what needed to be said, or taking a big risk – they could get past self-doubt.*[283]

If all these tips sound just too difficult for you to put into practice – especially if you're one of those who is currently consumed with doubt about your legitimacy – another very sensible action would be to get yourself a coach or a mentor.

Conclusions

It's been both reassuring, yet disappointing that I'm not alone as a chronic sufferer of the imposter syndrome. One conclusion at the end of this chapter is that patriarchy sure has taken a toll on the conditioning of us women about where we belong and, more especially, where we don't belong.

When I was passionately pursuing my work as an EO/AA consultant in the late '80s and early '90s, I genuinely believed that a combination of law, policy and management commitment would have meant that the barriers to women's advancement in the Australian workforce would have been totally broken down by the year 2000. Given that the most recent gender stats show that most women workers are still in the bottom pay ranges in organisations, and there are only 21 women CEOs in the ASX200 companies, there's still a long way to go before we achieve gender parity. My optimism failed to consider not only the resistance to change by the then culture holders/leaders, but also the depth of the conditioning within us women.

I recently led a workshop for women in a finance company. It was called Maximising Your Potential and included a session on the imposter syndrome. One of the women in a management role expressed surprise and relief that this was 'a thing' and that it wasn't just her who often felt like she didn't belong and was going to be found out as a fraud any time soon. I applaud the board and the executive team of this company for sponsoring this program which enabled their high potential women to meet and learn. This leads me to conclude that the hearts and minds of at least some of our current leaders are changing and that they do now want to welcome women throughout their organisations, and to convince them to fully step into their personal power and achieve their full potential.

Chapter 16

The F word – to be or not to be?

Having unpicked in the previous chapter, the phenomenon of the imposter syndrome that holds many women back from stepping into their full power, in this chapter I'm exploring a revolution that gave us women permission to believe in ourselves. Its name is Feminism.

My feminist awakening began in my 30s in the mid-1970s with the help of Germaine Greer's book, *The Female Eunuch*, and my older sister – an already well and truly out there feminist by then – who would regularly give me novels as birthday and Christmas gifts that told the story of bold and brave women. I well remember one Christmas when our mother threw the book I'd just unwrapped from my sister across the table as she muttered, 'More feminist propaganda I see.' On reflection, Mum's fear was well founded. My sister had already ended her respectable marriage, and Mum probably feared that I was going to take a similar path in ending my marriage too because of my developing feminism (rightly as it turned out).

Since this gradual awakening over 40 years ago I've been proud to call myself a feminist. Although that said, I've not always felt inclined, or maybe even brave enough, to share this fact with others up front for fear of what they might think of me. For example, it's not been my habit to say to either my clients, prospective lovers or indeed my kids' friends, 'Hi, I'm Kate and I'm a feminist.'

How do I define feminism? To me it's the actions taken, and the attitudes held by anyone, be they female or male, that contribute to achieving gender equality in all areas of life.

Most literature about feminism uses the metaphor of the 'waves' of feminism from the struggles of the suffragettes until now, when so much has been achieved, yet still so much more needs to be done. I had always identified with the 'waves' metaphor until my historian sister Janet persuaded me to adopt a different metaphor: that of a persistent underground stream. She explained her metaphor in a long email to me that I've chosen to include in full because it challenges the 'wave' metaphor so compellingly.

> *The most persistent and familiar image used to describe the historical eras of feminism is that of a series of waves. Often the feminism of the fight for women's suffrage (although it fought for many other things as well) is referred to as 'first wave feminism, and the feminism of the Women's Liberation era, starting in the late 1960s, is described as the second wave. Subsequent actions have sometimes been referred to as 'post-feminism' and more recent ones as 'third wave feminism'.*
>
> *I am uncomfortable with the 'wave' descriptors for a number of reasons.*
>
> *The first is that feminism – whether English, European, Western society, Australian or worldwide feminism – did not start, as a first wave during the nineteenth and early twentieth century suffrage etc struggles. As just one example, expressions of feminism can be found in English writing during the Middle Ages, and in every century following. The same can be said for French, German, Russian and so on feminism. Indeed, if one looks hard enough, Ancient Greek and Roman feminist expressions can be found. And those are just the evidences of feminism recorded in the written word. So, objection number one is that a two-wave image beginning in the nineteenth century is a demeaning and distorting picture of feminism and its history. Feminism has existed and always exists wherever, and*

whenever, women identify their then and continuing disadvantages as women and proceed to challenge them.

My other objections are about the implications suggested by 'wave' imagery. Two things in particular trouble me here. First, if what we are picturing is the movement of waves far out in the ocean, then my problem is that a wave image consists of peaks and troughs: it implies an activism that rises and then falls away and disappears before rising again. On the other hand, if the image is of the shore arrival of waves, it is even worse, because that means that the political impulse does not just wallow but instead crashes and dies. Another of my objections is that wave imagery suggests, at the same time and somewhat confusingly, a process of ever moving progress, as ocean waves lift and fall but appear to move ever onwards.

My historical understanding of feminism supports none of these images: neither the excessively negative ones nor the excessively positive.

To start with the rising and then wallowing or the crashing on the beach images, I contest the presumption that the feminist impulse ever dies away. Just to consider the first half of the twentieth century in Australia, to see the supposed trough between the securing of women's rights to vote, state by state and federally – that process not complete until 1908 – and the supposed upward thrust of feminism in the late 1960s as a 'death' or disappearance of feminism, is to deny the ongoing commitment and work of splendid feminist activists throughout that period. The denial of feminist activism in this period would ignore, for example, campaigns for women's rights to custody of their children after widowhood or divorce; the work of women via trade unions and the labour movement for improvement in working conditions and pay for women; the activism of women in the international peace movement; campaigning for government financial support for mothers – what turned out to be child endowment and maternal benefits before, at and after childbirth; continuing activism to control male violence towards women through the restriction of access to alcohol; the active participation of women in every political party, some of which resulted in the achievement of the first women members of each parliament; participation by feminist activists (for example Jessie Street) in the Aboriginal organisations that eventually achieved referendum establishment of Aboriginal people as effective citizens of Australia; influence on the crafting of the United Nations including ensuring inclusion of the Commission on the Status of Women (Jessie Street again); and the lived feminism of women's participation in both World Wars, overseas and at home, in many cases smashing established constraints on possible areas of women's employment. And that is just what I can come up with off the top of my head.

To turn to the wave image presumption that feminism is a process of steady ever-moving progress, I find that implication equally historically false. Feminism is not, and has never been, an easy onwards and upwards ride. It is, rather, a continuous battle against power bases and attitudes that work just as persistently to interrupt and reverse whatever we achieve. As just one example, in the area of work to protect women from male violence in the home, and over the period of my own involvement in this issue, we have seen laws directed specifically towards domestic violence diluted into general violence response laws; government information materials shifting the message of responsibility from male perpetrators to 'the family'; and in a recent case, the NSW State Government setting up a tender for services to address domestic violence and appointing representatives of male violence sufferers but not women's organisations, arguing that the latter would be a 'conflict of interest'. (The services concerned intended to support all or either of the above.)

Feminist activism is far more a struggle to keep and often to regain territory achieved and then lost than a cheerful ever-onwards progress.

My own preferred image for feminist history is not of waves but rather of a persistent underground stream, ever present and taking opportunities as they arise to burst forth in splendid, publicly recognisable activism, but too often later beaten down, dammed and driven back underground. The strategic use nineteenth-century women made of the human rights arguments of the anti-slavery movement to turn them to demands for women's rights including suffrage is one example of such an opportunity. The new economic opportunities for women in the prosperity of the 1960s, followed by the educational and policy reforms offered by the Whitlam government, is another. The #MeToo movement is a further such, using the internet to turn the courageous revelations of complaints against Harvey Weinstein into a worldwide movement. But just watch the fight back getting under way. How long will it take, if ever, to have it accepted in courts of law – and FBI enquiries – that there is never 'corroborating evidence' in a matter of sexual assault.

As both an historian of women and as a feminist activist, I will always prefer imagery that acknowledges embattled realities and the brave feminist struggle that meets them, to the glib ease of those misleading waves.[284]

Research

One of the more strident feminists I had the pleasure of knowing back in Adelaide in the mid- to late '80s was fond of saying, 'They used to call us witches – and they burnt them at the stake.' I was curious, therefore, to read in David Leser's book *Women, men and the whole damn thing* that in his exploration of feminism, he drew on the history of accusing women of witchcraft and murdering them *en masse* throughout Europe from the late 14th to the late 17th centuries. Leser:

The figures are still debated, but possibly millions were hanged, beheaded or burnt at the stake – healers, herbalists, poetesses, midwives and anyone displaying signs of sexual independence.[285]

Robert Jensen, in his 2017 book *The end of patriarchy* believes that feminism is the end of 'patriarchy's gender-as hierarchy system,' which is why patriarchal forces attempt to eliminate or marginalize feminist ideas.[286]

Katrine Marçal in her 2012 book *Who cooked Adam Smith's dinner* argues that feminism is about much more than social justice. She writes that as well as the obvious equality for all argument, solutions will also be found for challenges such as global warming, population overcrowding, and our ageing societies if seen through a feminist lens.[287]

Next, I'll address the question, can men be feminists? António Guterres, the UN Secretary-General, describes himself as a 'proud feminist' with a belief that if women are excluded, everyone pays the price, and that when women are included, the whole world wins.

So yes, if we define a feminist as anyone who actively supports the status of women in our society, of course men can be feminists. And indeed, we need more and more men to join in this gender revolution by declaring themselves feminists – especially those men, like the UN Secretary-General, who have the positional power to effect change for women.

Jane Caro in her 2019 book *Accidental feminists* defines the feminist project as 'nothing less than a redistribution of political, social and financial power more equally between men and women'.[288]

I also like Emily Maguire's definition in her 2019 book *This is what a feminist looks like*:

> *The definition of feminist I'm working with is a broad one: someone who works to correct the injustices and inequalities that stem from sexism and misogyny.*[289]

At the end of her book Maguire asks the question, so 'what does a feminist look like?' and then answers her own question:

> *A feminist looks like a person taking whatever action they can to counter sexism and misogyny and end the injustices they produce. A feminist looks, I hope, like you.*[290]

Jess Hill writes in *Quarterly Essay # 84*, 'The reckoning – how #MeToo is changing Australia', that 'we need to accept that feminism is a political movement, and one that needs structure and representation.'[291] Hill quotes Moira Donegan in the May 11, 2018 edition of *The Guardian* where she explores whether we will achieve the 'feminist project' through either women's individual empowerment, or through a form of collective liberation?'

Given my fondness for living life through a philosophy of and/both, I would suggest that both women's empowerment <u>and</u> collective action are required.

Interviewees

To further understand the word 'feminism', I asked my interviewees whether they call themselves a feminist, and what this term means to them. Here are some of their replies:

- *I'm a feminist because I want women to be taken seriously.*

- *Yes, I call myself a feminist because to me this is about redressing the imbalance of power and opportunities for women.*

- *I define a feminist as someone who cares about there being a feminine and masculine balance. I don't love the word but will continue to call myself a feminist while there is still an imbalance in our world. If in our lifetime I didn't have to be a feminist anymore because the world is balanced, then I'd love that.*

- *Feminism has become an emotive word – it's become tied to burning bras and all that sort of history. However, I believe that feminism is about strong women standing in their power and, yes, I am one such woman.*

- *My 2019 definition is that feminism is about creating environments in a world where women and men are treated equally. Men can be feminists too and I think more of them should be. [From a male interviewee.]*

- *[Feminism is] expecting things to be equal – but not the same – regardless of your gender.*

- *Feminism is a loaded word. It is deeply political. It confers difference. I believe this expresses its true purpose and usefulness – where there is unjust difference, most conspicuously for women, there needs to be special attention to opportunity.*

LS, an agriculturalist and leader in her industry, told me during her interview:

Yes, I certainly would say I'm a feminist but, interestingly, I don't tend to say it publicly because, for whatever reasons, the word has developed some connotations that can make people defensive,

209

which is a pity. So, I don't often use the word – depending on the company – especially to older fellows in the country. But would those same men want their granddaughters to have an equal go? Of course they would!

KB, a senior law firm partner, has done a redefinition:

I think the word 'feminist' got hijacked and is now used in a pejorative sense and it's hard to go back on that. So, I'm an 'equalist' – I support and encourage younger women and other women. And that's across everything, not just the gender divide.

I was cheered to note that all my male interviewees said they regarded themselves as feminists with PS, an agriculturalist, saying:

From a male point of view, I see feminism as interdependence – women being emotionally and financially independent coming to a relationship and sharing common goals.

I'll leave it to EM, a retired CIO, to have the final word with her definition of feminism. It includes the recognition that for equality of outcomes to be achieved, people will at times need to be treated differently, because we are not all the same:

To me it means having the freedom to be the person you want to be in the society that we live in. So, it's not having others' expectations imposed on you. It's being able to step outside that and fully be yourself. I'm being careful not to use the word 'equality', because I think in some cases we should argue beyond equity.

Conclusions

To be or not to be a feminist? My conclusion at the end of this chapter in answer to the question posed in the title, is that it's a choice for each of us to make at a conscious level. For those of us, like KB who think it's a term that has lost its original intent, the descriptor of 'equalist' serves equally well. However, I also support EM's caution about the use of the word 'equal' because we humans don't get born on an equal footing, and what feminism is striving for is an equality of outcomes for all.

I strongly agree with my historian sister Janet's challenging of the 'waves' analogy to describe the history of feminism and support hers about feminism being like a 'persistent underground stream' that comes to the surface when the political climate is conducive to change.

I am recalling the 2021 March4Justice rallies Australia-wide where thousands of women and lots of men marched to the slogan 'enough is enough', and I am asking myself, is this another example of the surfacing of feminism's 'persistent underground stream'? I wish I could conclude that it is, but only history will tell.

As for me, I'm now in my eighth decade of life and have reached the conclusion that I'm at that wonderful stage where I no longer care what 'they' think of me – whoever 'they' may be. I'm now proud to stand tall and shout to the world that 'I am a feminist!'

Chapter 17

Patriarchy can be hard on men too

I n the last chapter I described feminism as the revolution the world has needed, to ensure that women can overcome the constraints of patriarchy. In this chapter we look at how patriarchy can, and does, put constraints on men too.

As a woman and a feminist, I've been conditioned into thinking that patriarchy is the 'bad guy', and that it's only we members of the 'fairer sex' who are the victims of the subtle control that patriarchy holds over the society I grew up in, and in which it still lurks today. Once I'd become the proud mother of a son, I could see that, even as a little boy, there were constraints put on him to conform to masculine stereotypes – such as needing to be tough, not tender, and strong, not vulnerable. In fact, a fond memory of my wee boy is when he was in grade one at our local primary school: one day he came home and told me that, 'Gail and me are super tough.' Go Gail – here's hoping you kept breaking through the constraints of patriarchy into your adult life. But on reflection I feel sad that my beautiful boy had already got the message from somewhere that, even at such a young age, he needed to be not just tough but 'super tough'.

Research

In keeping with the theme throughout this book that the data I've gathered from my many years as a EO consultant and coach to women qualifies as research, I'll begin this chapter with an example of what I've learnt about how patriarchy can be hard on men too.

The situation that's coming to my mind takes me back to the aftermath of the recession we had in Australia in the early 1990s. In response to tough economic times, most large organisations did what was called a 'restructure' of their workforce. This, in effect, was a process of identifying where the so-called 'head count' could be reduced, so another word that was commonly used in those times was 'downsizing'. A lot of men, including some very senior ones, lost their jobs at this time.

I began to hear about the impact of this, because my women clients were telling me that they'd become the primary, or in fact sole, breadwinner in their family. They would share with me the shame that their male partners were feeling about this. They would then give me a smile that was almost a grimace, as they told me about the effort they were needing to constantly make in order to boost their partner's confidence – and not rub it in – that they, the woman, was now the sole earner. This suggested to me that for each of these men, their role as the primary breadwinner for their family, was inextricably bound up with their identity of who they were. I regarded this as a cruel biproduct of the influence of patriarchy on these men.

Robert Jensen's 2017 book *The end of patriarchy* has been informative in helping me understand the constraints of patriarchy on men as well as women, and the positive contribution that feminism has made to helping break some of these down:

> *I came to understand that the fear and isolation I felt, and many men feel, was the result of a conception of masculinity in patriarchy. And through feminism, I came to understand that the way I was used as a child by other boys and adults wasn't the result of my weakness or failure but was the product of patriarchy's brutal sex/ gender system that sexualizes domination and subordination. ... The patriarchal sex/gender system has proved resilient, and everywhere institutionalized male dominance continues to structure our lives and influence our understanding of ourselves.*[292]

Jensen is however optimistic that what he calls the 'feminist project' will continue to challenge the patriarchy because it no longer serves men as well as women with its links to hierarchy and racism.

Jensen also helped me understand why there is often such resistance to change programs to improve the status of women in the workplace. It's because feminism is still intertwined with all social justice programs and that this poses a threat to the patriarchal status quo.

In his conclusion, Jensen explains that feminism gave him a way to understand why he'd never felt like he was 'man enough':

> *The dominant conception of masculinity … asserts that men are naturally competitive and aggressive, and being a 'real man' is therefore marked by the struggle for control, conquest, and domination. … Feminism [gave me] the tools to stop trying to be the man I had never really wanted to be, to reject the rules for a toxic masculinity that I had been socialized into but never felt comfortable with and often felt threatened by.*[293]

Instead, Jensen has been helped by feminism to 'reject the quest for patriarchal control and embrace the struggle to be fully human'.[294]

Let's now turn to Annabel Crabb's 2014 book *The wife drought* to find out how she thinks men are going within the constraints of patriarchy. Her closing paragraph in chapter 2, 'Looking at things the wrong way up' is instructive:

> *For all the changes that the last five decades have held for women, the changes for men have been scandalously narrow. Men continue to be over-represented at work, and under-represented at home. Viewed one way, this is an unforgivable and continuing annexation of money, power and influence. Viewed the other way up, it's a continuing tragedy for children and for men, bound tight into a web of expectations no one even asked them if they wanted.*[295]

Crabb uses the example of a man she interviewed to support her title statement that men still 'need a life'. She tells us that this man was regularly chastised for coming in late to work because he'd dropped his kids off at school first. His boss acknowledged his performance was excellent but would then say that he preferred for all his team to 'work the same hours'. In response to which Crabb's interviewee told her:

Despite … all the right words about work-life balance and look-ing after oneself and the family – my experience is that it remains lip-service when it comes down to it. … The expectation on [us men] is (still) to conform to the stereotype of male success.[296]

In his 2019 book, *Women, men and the whole damn thing*, David Leser writes about how what he calls 'rampaging male aggression' dominates women and girls. He also explores its damaging effect on men who are different from the strong macho stereotype – less strong men, men with a well-developed feminine side, gay men, transgender men, in fact any man who is in some way or another different from this macho norm.

Leser laments the denial of the feminine that is drummed into boys at a young age:

Many boys are taught early that to avoid the bullies they have to side with them. They join the gang in order to look tough. … This denial of the feminine is deeply imbued in men and it's learnt first in the school yard, then burnished bright with posture, swagger, flexed biceps and curled lip in sporting clubs, universities, the military and corporate boardrooms. The message is often unspoken, but it's loud and clear: Join us, or suffer the consequences of derision.[297]

Leser argues that what needs to happen to help men free themselves from the limits of patriarchy is for them to 'turn in, not out', because he believes that men will only become liberated when they achieve the 'integration and inner union' of both their masculine and feminine selves. He ends on a hopeful note:

I'd like to believe that there's a legion of us men who know that our own liberation is joined to the liberation of women, who recognise that the triumphs and achievements of the other, and that the next part of the women's movement is a men's movement that rejects so many of the old definitions of masculinity. … By doing so, hopefully we will be helping a whole new generation of boys grow up in a more integrated way, where both their masculine and feminine qualities are celebrated, and where ideas around consent, mutuality, healthy communication and respect are first and second nature.[298]

This theme was also discussed by three women – Michelle Stratemeyer, Adriana Vargas Saenz and Elise Holland – from the School of

Psychological Sciences at the University of Melbourne in the March 28, 2019 edition of *The Conversation*. In their article, 'How challenging masculine stereotypes is good for men', they reported that to improve men's health and wellbeing, the American Psychological Association recently released guidelines for psychologists working with boys and men. The guidelines aim to challenge some aspects of traditional masculinity that might cause problems in men's lives.

> *Traditional masculinity encompasses a set of norms, ideas and beliefs about what it means to be a man. Such beliefs include identifying men as self-reliant, emotionally reticent, focused on work over family, and oversexed. When these beliefs are taken to an extreme level, they can result in poor outcomes for men, such as being dissatisfied in romantic relationships, having mental health problems, and engaging in more risky behaviours.* [299]

I would add something else to this list of poor outcomes for both men and women, which is driven from the beliefs underlying traditional masculinity: that is, the perpetuation of the command/control style of leadership in Australian organisations.

The authors include three of the 10 recommendations made in the APA guidelines. These are outlined in the final section of this chapter.

On the topic of whether patriarchy is hard on boys and men as well as girls and women, I found further information in an article in *The Conversation* on December 8, 2020. With the long title, 'Who is a real man? Most Australians believe outdated ideals of masculinity are holding men back,' the author, Michael Flood, an associate professor at the Queensland University of Technology, reported on a national survey that was commissioned by the Victorian Health Promotion Foundation to gauge people's attitudes towards men and masculinity. The sample of 1,619 respondents was representative of the Australian population by age, state and gender. Within the sample most people agreed on a few basic principles:

- *Traditional gender stereotypes are limiting and harmful for boys and men.*
- *There is pressure on men to live up to traditional stereotypes.*
- *Masculine expectations or outdated ideas of masculinity prevent men from living full lives.*

- *Boys need both women and men as role models, rather than only men.*[300]

Somewhat depressingly, the survey shows that men are less supportive of gender equality, less likely to recognise sexism, and more likely to approve of men being dominant in both their relationships and their families. The survey also found that young men have generally more progressive attitudes than older men, and that young women's attitudes are the most progressive of all respondents. There was also agreement that men and boys are influenced by social forces just as much as they are by their biology.

The key recommendations of this survey to community and health providers to better engage with men were to:

- *focus on progressive ideas that will appeal to the vast majority of people, rather than pandering to men with traditionally masculine language or focusing on myth busting*
- *emphasise the need to free men from outdated masculine stereotypes*
- *focus less on the problem, and more on the solution.*[301]

Michael Flood, concluded with the optimistic summary that:

> *There is a wealth of evidence that conformity to traditional masculine stereotypes is limiting for men and boys and harmful to those around them. [And that] most Australians agree that it is time to foster positive alternatives, to improve health and wellbeing for everyone.*[302]

All of which makes me hopeful that over time these findings will infiltrate the still patriarchal cultures of many Australian workplaces.

I'm referring back to Crabb from *The wife drought* to end the research section of this chapter. In her conclusion she makes a plea to men to pick up the reigns and do their bit to achieve the work versus home duties dilemma that research tells us is still carried by women in a depressing number of households:

> *Perhaps it's men's turn now to change. ... For years, we have argued about quotas and affirmative action and all the ancillary techniques to move women up through leadership ranks, but we've taken our*

eyes off the other half of the equation. In focusing so hard on encouraging women to lean in, we've neglected to convince men of their entitlement to lean out once in a while. The men who already do – who have the confidence to stare down the expectations of them that lace invisibly but unmistakeably through the world of work – will perhaps be the advance riders of change.[303]

Interviewees

To my question about patriarchy SE, one of my male interviewees, reflected on earlier times versus now:

> *My lived experience is not so focused around patriarchy. I can understand the oldest male getting the land when strength was needed, but it no longer is.*

> *I don't cry as much as G [his wife] and other women around me. Why is that? Neither my mum nor dad sat me down and said don't cry – the school yard? Don't know.*

And to my question about whether he's felt the constraints of patriarchy he told me:

> *I'm the primary breadwinner – but don't feel this as a pressure.*

PS, agriculturalist and another of the men I interviewed, talked to me about how his father assumed that he would automatically become the fifth generation who had farmed the same land. However, his mother made sure he had other options by encouraging him to travel and study and do other things. He has now moved back to the family farm on his own terms:

> *I've seen lots of examples where other guys have conformed to the patriarchy and thought they had no options – but it then all blowing up.*

What more can be done?

To break free of the shackles of patriarchy, Robert Jensen argues that this will require 'not only new ways of organizing ourselves socially, politically, and economically, but a different way of understanding what it means to be human'.[304]

And how might these changes be achieved in practical terms? I'm aware of two programs in my region of the northern rivers of NSW that are designed for adolescent boys. The first is the Uncle Program, which is a mentoring service for boys who lack a positive or present male role model in their lives. The second is a Rites of Passage Program in which fathers and sons are led through the kinds of rituals that will aid the safe transition of adolescent boys into the adult world.

I'm also aware of the rising number of men's support groups. As I understand, these are aimed to provide men with a safe and supportive place to share, among other things, how they're coping with the constraints put upon them by the patriarchy. In fact, one of my neighbours is both a volunteer in the Uncle Program and regularly attends a local men's group.

The guidelines by the American Psychological Association, referred to above, include the following two recommendations for psychologists working with boys and men, that I believe could well have a wider application by general practitioners with their male patients, and by the coaches and mentors of male executives:

- *Stressing the importance of encouraging men's positive involvement in families.*
- *Shifting the beliefs around self-reliance so men feel more comfortable looking after themselves and seeking professional help and services needed.*[305]

Conclusions

In relation to the pervasiveness of culture, a wise man I once knew used to say that 'when you go in the water, you can't help getting wet'. Summarising my research and interviews on the topic of patriarchy being hard on men too has reminded me of this saying because it seems that we are all quite unconsciously 'swimming around in the water' of patriarchy. So, one conclusion I've reached is that it's not only difficult for us women to free ourselves from the bonds of patriarchy – it's tough on lots of men too.

To help me reflect on that last sentence, I'm taking myself back to when, at aged just 21, I was a blushing young bride. Just as growing up in the '50s and '60s I was conditioned to believe that 'women's place is in the home', so too was the young man I was marrying conditioned to believe he would have to be the one to go out to work as our breadwinner. Despite being two well-educated young people, these unconscious beliefs that were bound up in our patriarchal culture, had influenced us to make choices that suited neither of us. Our marriage didn't stand a chance.

Likewise, many of the current leaders – the so-called 'culture holders' in large organisations – have been similarly imbued with some old-fashioned conditioning, which means they quite unconsciously create a culture that is congruent with this conditioning. As a consultant I used to move in and out of organisations, and I could readily sense the many and varied sub-cultures that had developed in each place – little things like the type of notes in the tearoom, how people dressed, and whether it was open plan or peppered with cubicles. New employees probably notice these things too, but then soon join their colleagues in becoming so enculturated that they're not aware of the unique aspects of the 'water' they are each immersed in.

It's not long ago that bosses were all male, and secretaries, 'typing girls' and 'tea ladies' were all female. Digitisation has put paid to typing pools and indeed deliverers of tea, but the patriarchy still lurks – be that in the language of business, the hours of work and the way work is structured.

My overriding conclusion at the end of this chapter is that achieving the goal of gender equal workplaces requires nothing less than the destruction of the system of patriarchy as experienced by both women and men. I find myself wishing that there was a vaccine that could rid us of the 'patriarchy virus.' But sadly, it will be up to each and every one of us to challenge any residual sexist beliefs and assumptions that are still lurking within us, so that together we can enjoy the value of gender diversity and parity in every aspect of our lives.

Chapter 18

It was not always so

H aving examined the impact of patriarchy on men in the last chapter, I'm handing over to Megan Young, a friend and colleague, who takes us back to earlier times when patriarchy did not rule the world. Megan writes:

I grew up in a family of women where my widowed mother, sisters and I did everything ourselves, including mowing the lawn. I topped the advanced mathematics class in high school. It therefore came as a shock to me when I commenced my work life at 19 years of age in a large corporation that was 90% male, and was told by a manager that he would not employ a woman to do a customer facing role because he thought she would cry if a customer yelled at her and that wouldn't be acceptable.

This made no sense to me: how could all women be excluded from certain jobs based on a generalised assumption? Why did he view natural emotional responses to aggressive behaviour as wrong, and needing to be controlled? This was the start of my education in patriarchy and discrimination.

Eight years later, and still working in the same large corporation, I was asked to take on the newly created role of Equal Opportunity and Affirmative Action Co-Ordinator for Women. I researched other corporation's strategies hoping to find the answer to workplace discrimination. I discovered that no answer had been found, so there was no choice other than to trust my own intuition in developing a program.

After a comprehensive staff survey and a range of new policies and programs in response to the findings, the hoped-for organisational culture change did not happen. Women were still resigning at rates up to five times that of men in senior roles, and I encountered resistance to even small changes, which I found extremely challenging. I reflected on why this was, and finally had an 'aha' moment. It became clear to me that I could not bring my whole self to work, but rather had to operate from the neck up to fit in to the corporate environment; and while I then complied with this unspoken rule it felt uncomfortable, unhealthy, unsatisfying, and unsustainable.

My soul, which is traditionally seen as feminine, was feeling disturbed. As David Whyte said in his 1994 book, *The heart aroused: poetry and the preservation of the soul in corporate America*, quoting Dante Alighieri, 'in the middle of the road of my life I awoke in a dark wood where the true way was wholly lost'.[306]

I was working in a high-rise city building and was instinctively drawn to walking in the local forest after work to restore my equilibrium. I'd been conditioned by society to value thinking over feeling, doing over being, and to suppress my inner life – my emotions, feelings and intuition, which are the language of the soul. I had learnt to always be 'in control' and the discomfort I was experiencing showed this was not working.

The other aspect of my 'aha' was that I was a microcosm of the macrocosm. I had been enculturated to actively suppress what I will call the feminine aspects within myself, and value and express my masculine aspects. This led me to realise that discrimination against women in the workplace and the wider society, and things like the high incidence of domestic violence against women, were the end result of our collective devaluing and suppression of 'feminine' aspects including our emotions, feelings and intuition.

Our masculine aspect is analytical and takes action. It is the aspect that wants to fly to the moon and stand on it, to analyse the moon's chemical composition, take measurements and develop formulas to logically explain its magnetic effect on our planet. It keeps statistics to prove things like increases in crime at the full moon. In the extreme case we see this expressed in the current 'race to space' by male billionaires.

Our feminine aspect doesn't need to fly to the moon because it is receptive to and knows the moon's power, without it having to be explained or proven. We all experience it as a deep knowing. We feel the moon's effects on our bodies, our cycles and sleep patterns and emotions; and on the earth in the change of tides. We gaze at the moon and feel somehow different; it stirs our imaginations and we acknowledge life's mysteries. Feminine consciousness is intuitive and grounded in a deep connection and reverence for 'mother' earth and the natural world.

I came to believe that to fix our societal problems at their root, we needed to value and reclaim what has been devalued, suppressed and ignored, both individually and collectively. A healthy relationship between our masculine and feminine aspects requires us to understand we can't control all parts of ourselves or others. We need to 'listen' inside and in doing so we connect not only to our emotions and feelings, but also to our intuitive awareness, allowing creative and inspired ideas to emerge.

I made a decision to learn how to listen to, and respect 'the feminine aspects' within myself, and henceforth to acknowledge and express my feelings and listen to my soul via the vehicle of my intuition. I hoped this new way of navigating life would lead me out of the dark wood, and it did.

I quickly learnt that listening to my feelings and acting on my intuition meant embracing uncertainty, letting go of perceived control, while acknowledging but not catering to my fears. It required an act of faith to listen and then act, no matter what. I chose to, as Susan Jeffers advises in her book of the same name, 'feel the fear and do it anyway'.

My first instinct was to resign from my job even though I didn't have another one to go to. Now that I was 'awake', I could no longer work in a corporate environment that felt 'soul destroying'. I commenced heuristic research via a master degree in social ecology to explore this idea further.

A brief synopsis of what happened for me personally as I took one intuitive, committed step at a time, was that every aspect of my life changed and I was led to more authenticity, creativity and connectivity. I sought connection in a regional community rather than a city, and began connecting to the earth through regular time in nature. An unexpected outcome was that I became more conscious of the way I, and we humans collectively, are affecting the health of the planet, and I began modifying my consumer choices to reduce my consumption of resources. The process continues to lead me toward a life that is balanced, fulfilled and sustainable.

Today the vast majority of cultures are patriarchies, where men are more likely than women to hold positions of social, economic and political power. So has our society always been patriarchal? Have we always valued the masculine way and devalued the feminine? The short answer is 'no'.

Gerda Lerner in her 1986 book *The creation of patriarchy*[307] details the beginning of the patriarchal system of thought that has been passed down through generations, often unquestioned, ever since. In her view this system will come to an end, as it is no longer beneficial for men or women and in many ways it threatens our very survival.

To put our current situation in its largest context I'm going to begin at the very beginning.

Tim Flannery in his 2010 book *Here on earth: An argument for hope*[308] tells us that our universe was born about 13.7 billion years ago in a massive expansion that blew space up like a gigantic balloon. The elements that form us – like carbon, phosphorous, calcium and iron – go back further than the formation of our planet, which formed some 4.5 billion years ago.

Flannery explains that our species, Homo sapiens, evolved approximately 200,000 years ago in Africa and 50,000 years ago began to spread around the earth. Within a few thousand years they arrived in Australia, reaching Western Europe about 32,000 years ago and North America about 13,200 years ago.

We are all closely related – one family in fact. Our genes reveal, as Flannery explains, that due to volcanic and other events the ancestry of every human alive today can be traced back to the same male who lived 60,000 years ago and the same female who lived at least 150,000 years ago. We are one element of a complex, natural living system, which is both uncontrollable and self-regulating.

Before the development of agriculture, which developed independently in five areas of the world, everyone lived in family-sized clans. Towns were established in the area known as the Fertile Crescent in the Middle East by around 11,500 years ago and within 8,000 years humans had spread into Europe, throughout Africa, India and Eurasia.

Riane Eisler in her 1987 book, *The chalice and the blade*,[309] details archaeological evidence that reveals early societies developed over thousands of years and were not male dominant.

Eisler describes the work of University of California archeologist Marija Gimbutas. Gimbutas catalogued and analysed hundreds of archeological finds in an area she defines as the civilisation of old Europe which reveal that between circa 7000–3500 BCE these early Europeans developed complex social organisation that displayed an essentially peaceful character where it is clear that male dominance wasn't the norm. Gimbutas notes numerous indicators that this was a matrilineal society: that is, one in which inheritance is traced through the mother and that women played key roles in all aspects of old European life, including the preparation and performance of rituals in temples and home shrines dedicated to aspects of the goddess.[310]

Eisler writes that James Mellaart, who led the excavations at Neolithic sites at Çatalhöyük in what is now modern Turkey, noted that the sites showed growth of increasingly advanced Goddess-worshipping cultures over many thousand years.

Many early creation stories from around the world revolve around the goddess-mother as the source of all being and in those early societies there was no distinction between the secular and the sacred; they were intertwined. Reverence for the divine feminine, through worship of the religious figure of the goddess and related symbols, was prominent in ancient times.

Despite evidence of the central role women played in both religion and in life, archaeological evidence indicates that pre-patriarchal society was equalitarian. There is evidence of both priestesses and priests, and indications that during the Neolithic period the relationship between women and men indicated linking, rather than ranking, of one over the other. Eisler refers to this as a 'partnership' model of society; that is, neither patriarchal nor matriarchal.

So, what changed?

Eisler details the development of a second model of society, that she calls the 'dominator' model.

From about 4300 BC the peaceful 'partnership' agricultural communities of the ancient world began to experience waves of violent barbarian invasions from nomadic bands who had for millennia survived by roaming the colder, harsher landscapes finding grass for their herds. Over the coming millennia these agricultural societies were transformed into male dominance, warfare and the enslavement of women initially, and eventually men as well. In this region, Minoan Crete was the last and most technologically advanced society in which male dominance was not the norm. It finally succumbed to a patriarchal model by 1100 BC.

Both Eisler and Lerner, who also describes the establishment of patriarchy as a process that developed in the near east during this period, explain that women and children became the first prisoners, and ultimately the first slaves. In chieftain graves dating from the fourth millennium BCE onwards, the skeletons of sacrificed women – the wives, concubines or slaves of the men who died – were found. There is no evidence of this practice before then.

Gerda Lerner writes that the slavery of women and the exploitation of their sexual and reproductive capacity by conquering men marked the initial development of class distinction, and that – as written in an article in the *New York Times* quoting Lerner – 'slave women and children were the first property in these societies'.[311]

The more precarious existence of the nomadic stock breeders and herders fermented a very different ideology, one that worshipped the power of 'the blade' and its ability to take life and so dominate others, rather than the creative and nurturing powers of the universe ideology that developed in the agricultural civilisations who inhabited the more fertile lands.

Eisler explains that the nomadic invaders were led by warriors and priests and one such group were a semitic group we call Hebrews who she says had a fierce God of war. She goes on to explain that religious texts still in use today like the Old Testament and others include statements indicating it is God's will that men rule women, which continues to reinforce the narrative of domination of women by men. She points out that biblical scholars tell us that the writing and re-writing of these texts was by the very people who were solidifying their positions of power over others.

You only have to turn on the news any night of the week to see what is primarily reported and therefore focused on in our modern culture: violence, suffering and death through wars, cars crashes, murders, domestic violence, natural disasters and pandemics, engendering a sense of horror and fear and a focus on life being dangerous rather than creative. A scan of available movies similarly reveals this focus on horror, suffering and violence.

This fairly recent ideology of control and domination that began in the near east about 6,000 years ago expanded around our world, subsuming lands and cultures, consuming the earth's resources, and disturbing the natural world's ecological balance. Not only has mankind sought to control and dominate other people and cultures but 'mother nature' – the natural world – as well.

We can look closer to home and see evidence that the partnership model of society was not only present in pre-patriarchal times in Europe, but was evident in Australia until much more recently. In 1788, the British, as part of their colonial expansion, commenced forcefully taking over Australia from the Aboriginal inhabitants. They had an attitude similar to that of the nomadic tribes of millennia ago, believing that they had a right and 'the might' to take from another society whatever they wanted for their own use. The British encountered the oldest living culture on the planet, who had arrived in Australia not long after the first humans left Africa around 50,000 years ago, and whose society, I believe, fits into Eisler's description of a 'partnership society'.

Bill Gammage, in his 2011 book *The biggest estate on earth: how Aborigines made Australia*, described his study of records from early settlers and explorers and asserts that:

> *Aboriginal Australians collectively managed an Australian estate they thought of as single and universal. ... They damned rivers and swamps. They cut channels through watersheds. They used fire to replace one plant community with another. What plants and animals flourished were related to their management. As in Europe land was managed at a local level. ... They travelled to known resources and made them not merely sustainable, but abundant,*

convenient and predictable. These are loaded words, the opposite of
what Europeans once presumed about hunter gatherers.[312]

Gammage explains that Aboriginals collaborated with the natural
world and each other and that they followed three rules: ensure that
all life flourishes, make plants and animals abundant, convenient and
predictable, and think universal and act local. Coming from a society
that operated on different values and a worldview that favoured control
and domination instead of partnership, collaboration and sustainability, the British didn't recognise, let alone understand, the wisdom in
this approach.

Bruce Pascoe in his 2014 book *Dark emu, black seeds: agriculture or
accident?* wrote of Aboriginal society:

> One of the most striking things is that there are no great conflicts
> over power, no great contests for place and office. This single fact
> explains much else, because it rules out so much that is destruc-
> tive of stability. … There are no wars of invasion to seize territory.
> They do not enslave each other, there is no master, servant relation.
> There is no class division, there is no property or income inequality.
> The result is a homeostasis, far-reaching and stable.[313]

So, what is the world view of a society that can operate sustainably
and essentially peacefully across a large continent for 40,000–50,000
years? Caring for Country is a central tenet of Aboriginal philosophy.
There is no separation, only interconnection. Gammage explains that
for Australia's first inhabitants:

> Theology and ecology are fused … The Dreaming has two rules:
> obey the Law and leave the world as you found it. The Dreaming
> is saturated with environmental consciousness. … Across Australia
> the creation story is essentially the same: God made light, brought
> into being spirits and creator ancestors and set down eternal Law
> for all creation…The universe was made from darkness by God.[314]

Pascoe cites the Australian anthropologist Ian Keen from his book
Aboriginal economy and society. In this book Keen explains that Aboriginal
people from different and at times distant kin groups agreed to live by
a range of shared laws.

Pascoe goes on to explain:

Elders became the equivalent of senior clergy, judges and politicians ... but they didn't assume that position as a result of force or inheritance. They earned the respect of their fellows. All other processes of delivering justice, protecting the peace, management of social roles and the division of the land's wealth were defined by ancestral law and interpreted by those chosen as the senior elders. Of all the systems humans have devised to manage their lives on earth Aboriginal government looks most like the democratic model.

As Flannery explains, Australia's natural environment became less diverse and productive as the Europeans took over.

With the imposition of colonial values, Australia became another patriarchal society – one that mostly has, to date, ignored the knowledge and wisdom of the original inhabitants of this land who managed for nearly 50,000 years to work collaboratively together to sustain both themselves and the natural environment.

Archeological evidence and the earliest creation stories from around the world show that pre-patriarchal and Aboriginal societies acknowledged and celebrated the life generating and nurturing powers of the universe and they broadly worked in partnership, collaboratively and sustainably with each other and the natural world.

A worldview took hold a mere 6,000 years ago and spread around the planet and it underpins patriarchal societies. The idea that the best way to get one's needs met is to control 'the other', which we came to believe includes the natural world. It's based on a mistaken belief that we are separate from each other and from nature: this belief creates a sense of 'other', generating fear and a sense that you have to 'fight to survive'. Remember this control and dominate notion arose from people who lived thousands of years ago in harsh, sparse terrains. The truth is that we are not separate – we are all family and part of a natural connected living system. The trees breathe out and I breathe in.

David J. Tacy in his 1995 book, *Edge of the sacred: Transformation in Australia*, speaks of this fear eloquently. Tacy says the view of nature, in its wild uncontrollable state as something to be feared, mirrors our fear of allowing our own instinctual forces to emerge. The more we try to control both, the more demonic they grow and then the more we try to control them. Tacy says the way out of this bind is for the ego to consciously let go of some control and enter into relationship (partnership) with 'the other'. He says, 'the other is complex, awesome, subtle, many-sided, and must be entered into relationship with'.[315]

I agree with Tacy that the path forward is to let go of some control and enter into relationship with what we perceive as 'the other'. This is needed at all levels of society if we are to restore a healthy balance and live sustainably on this planet. This means, in practice, humans collectively acknowledging we are part of a natural living system, recognising our every action has an impact on the whole, and modifying our current practices to live within nature's laws – by, for example, not continuing to burn fossil fuels. We humans have the ability to both create and destroy and we get to experience the consequences of our choices. The power is in our own hands.

It means men respecting and acknowledging the value and balancing perspective and skills that women bring to every sphere of life, and embracing them as equal partners at all levels of society.

In order to make that happen it means individuals fostering a healthy relationship with their inner world: valuing and developing emotional intelligence, listening to and validating feelings and intuitions and acting wholistically from that internally connected place. Like the natural world the soul is not controllable; however, there is wisdom and wholeness to be found there, as I discovered when I made a commitment to listen to mine.

Everyone has access to their inner knowing, the quiet voice that speaks often with simple, yet clear directions on the path or action to take. The trick is to quieten our busy minds to hear it. I often hear mine when on walks in nature, or engrossed in mundane tasks. We sometimes ignore this voice because of a fear of the unknown. I have learnt in living this way that only the next step becomes clear, and I have to take it faithfully without knowing what the step after that is to be. It requires trust that there is a greater and benevolent wisdom at play beyond my limited understanding.

Fear of the unknown and a lack of faith in the benevolence of life cuts us off from the very medicine we need, to listen to and act on our individual and collective inner wisdom, and collaborate and enter into real partnership with each other and also with the natural world.

A more peaceful and equalitarian and healthy world is a real possibility for our future if we work together, truly collaboratively embracing wholistic ways of being and doing that value both our masculine and feminine strengths.

That manager all those years ago said out loud what is usually left unspoken: that emotions must be controlled. Beliefs like this lurk beneath the surface and influence the decisions made by people who are currently in positions of power. I have spent my life since then trying to answer the questions his unsettling declaration raised for me. I have learnt from my research that it has not always been this way, which means it is in our power to change it.

Chapter 19

Breaking the glass ceiling – are we nearly there yet?

Having learnt from Megan Young in the last chapter that patri-archal cultures are a relatively new phenomenon, in this chapter I'm turning my attention back to how the constraints of current male-dominated cultures continue to affect women in larger organisations in Australia.

Sometime in the early '90s I was invited to speak at a forum for women in management. It was quite a posh affair – at the Sydney Convention Centre if I remember correctly – and the event was called Breaking the Glass Ceiling. I was asked to prepare a seven-minute presentation on my take of the so-called glass ceiling – an invisible barrier preventing women's further progress to the senior levels of Australian organisations.

I'd been invited to speak because of my background as an equal opportunity consultant, but I was by then transitioning my business into providing leadership coaching services to high potential women, primarily in corporate Australia. I dressed carefully for the event. Again, if my memory serves me, I wore a demure cream suit, a turquoise silk camisole and my, by then well-worn, pearl necklace and earrings.

Seven minutes!? I thought long and hard about how I could con-tribute something meaningful on this important topic in such a short time. As I pondered the challenge, the words of one of my coaching clients came back to me. She'd been promoted to a more senior role in the human resources department of one of Australia's four big banks. When I saw her for her next coaching session, she told me that she was feeling somewhat disillusioned. She explained that if what she was seeing at the senior levels of her bank was the cultural norm in all executive suites, she wasn't interested. When I asked her why, she said, 'My values won't let me play the political games I can see being played out there.' That was it. I decided, I'll focus on values in my seven minutes.

And this I did. Where most other seven-minute speakers chose to talk about some of the very many important initiatives that organisations needed to be implementing for women to break the glass ceiling, I told the audience of mainly women that I was going to use my seven minutes talking about women themselves. I then proceeded to explain that in my experience as a leadership coach to high potential women, one reason why women were leaving corporate Australia was because, as they reached more senior positions, they experienced a conflict of values that they found unsustainable. Once they'd worked this out, they were then making the personally powerful choice of resigning. And what did they do next? Many of them proceeded to set up their own small businesses, with help to do so from all the learning they'd gained from their corporate experience and the professional development dollars that had been spent on them over the previous years.

Research

I have in front of me a published research report called *Barriers to women working in corporate management*. In the introduction I can read about progress in helping women advance beyond a certain level, and that the purpose of this study was to further that discussion. The body of the report recommends 10 initiatives that organisations could implement to further women's advancement, but cautions that this could take up to 15 or 20 years to achieve.

The report was published by the Australian Government Publishing Service, Canberra, and the date of the report? 1994. The authors of the report? Patricia Bellamy, a dear friend and colleague of mine, and me, Kate Ramsay.

I've grazed through the pages of the report, and this brings back memories of the fun we had, and the challenges Patricia and I faced while doing this piece of qualitative research. We interviewed women in middle and senior management roles who'd voluntarily left a corporation in the previous three years to find out their reasons for leaving. As I scanned the list of barriers the women in our study identified, I shook my head in dismay because some 29 years later, these same issues are still of concern to women in the workforce – so much for Patricia's and my 15 to 20 years! The barriers identified by the women in our study were:

- *Being treated differently as a woman*
- *Not fitting into the corporate culture*
- *Lack of a career path*
- *Lack of a mentor*
- *Being on the fringe in a support function*
- *Exclusion from male networks*
- *Conflict of personal and professional values*
- *Having children*
- *Having a different management style.*[316]

I've found in my more recent research for this book that the term 'glass ceiling' is not being used much anymore. However, the barriers listed above persist.

Anne Summers in *The misogyny factor* explored the application of the merit principle in organisations as an example of why women leave large organisations:

The merit excuse is laughable, because it is patently inaccurate. ... It is absurd to claim ... in a country where women have for the past forty years received even higher levels of education than men that 'merit' is unequally distributed on the basis of gender. It is simply a further indicator of how entrenched sexism and misogyny are in our thinking. We deny women access and advancement using 'merit' as the filter, and then turn around and say they are undeserving because they have not broken through the 'merit' barrier.

So we come full circle. We argue that the presence of women in ... top jobs is evidence that our society is not sexist or misogynist, but then

> *we treat these women so badly they will most likely be demoralised
> and driven away as well as deterring other women from following in
> their footsteps. So there will be fewer women in these jobs.*[317]

In relation to the findings in the *Barriers* report about women having
children, Annabel Crabb explores in her 2014 book *The wife drought* the
very practical topic of who does the domestic work when both parents
head out the door to paid employment every day. Crabb tells us that 'the
tendency of women to take on responsibility for domestic work, and the
tendency of men not to, is the great rhythm of the Australian workplace
that escapes the naked eye'.[318]

Crabb references the Catalyst 2003 Leaders in a Global Economy
study, in which three-quarters of the men surveyed had a wife or spouse
who didn't work, whereas three-quarters of the women surveyed had a
husband who, like them, worked full-time. And in terms of who takes
more responsibility for making childcare arrangements, this study
found that 57% of the female senior business leaders said they did.
Whereas among the male executives, only 1% gave that answer.[319]

Given the above percentages, finding affordable, convenient childcare is obviously most often the responsibility of working women.
It was not until the early '70s that the Commonwealth government
passed legislation allowing the public sector to develop policy and fund
childcare. Anne Summers wrote in *The misogyny factor* in 2013 that
'childcare is either unavailable, unaffordable, or insufficiently flexible to
meet the needs of large numbers of families.' Summers cited the results
of research undertaken by the Commonwealth Bank that was released
in 2011. The key relevant findings were that 31% of families use paid
childcare and of these, 11% said that their childcare fees outweighed
their earnings, and a further 13%, said that the cost of care meant they
would only break even by working.[320]

An article in *The Guardian* on 25 June, 2020 by Daniel Hurst and
Paul Karp reported comments by Ben Oquist, former executive director of The Australia Institute, on a report written by two economists
at the institute which outlines the economic benefits of free childcare:
'Not only is free childcare a form of fiscal stimulus, boosting consumer
demand by increasing the disposable income of families with young
children, but in the long run it will significantly grow GDP and make
Australia a far more equitable country.'[321]

The *Australian women CEOs speak* research report published in September 2018 heard from the women CEOs interviewed about their different management style from the traditional control/tell style. In particular, the study revealed that these women are less motivated by power than their male colleagues and have a 'strong focus towards working with teams and setting a positive example of openness and transparency, ... but not micromanaging them'.[322]

Just as the 1994 *Barriers* study found most of the women interviewed lacked a mentor, the 2018 Korn Ferry/AICD research found that only two women reported having consistent mentorship throughout their careers. And whereas in the 1994 *Barriers* study most of the women lacked a career path, 75% of the women in the 2018 research said their professional life had included times of 'improvisation'. Some even said they had 'almost entirely unplanned careers and moved into new positions, driven by a desire to learn'.[323]

The phenomenon of the 'glass cliff' or the 'hospital pass' was referred to by 9 of the 21 Korn Ferry/AICD CEOs. I'd not heard of the 'glass cliff' until I read this study. I now know that this is the trend that sees women being handed big opportunities 'when the risk of failure is high – both for themselves and the organisation'. For example, after being recruited for her CEO role, one woman said:

> The board really did want to drive cultural change. I think that's what they saw in me, because the company was in bad shape. Returns were terrible. Staff engagement was horrible. It had really lost its way.[324]

In an article in *The Conversation* on March 19, 2018, Eva Cox, a long-time policy activist for women and an Adjunct Professor at the University of Technology Sydney, was clear about her belief that there is a need for a shift in power balance to achieve gender equality in the workplace and society. She wrote:

> Legal processes, even if based on rights, do not really effect the serious social change to attitudes or power that real gender equity will require. ... Basic assumptions about gender roles still create beliefs about being an acceptable boy (stand up for yourself) or girl (be nice and read peoples' feelings). These offer sure fire paths to toxic masculinity and passive femininity.[325]

Having said earlier that the term the 'class ceiling' no longer has much currency it is referred to, along with its two 'sisters', the 'glass labyrinth' and the 'glass cliff' in Julia Gillard and Ngozi Okonjo-Iweala's 2020 book *Women and leadership*. In chapter 2 the authors tell the reader that their book 'aims to do more than analyse the biases, conscious and unconscious, that swirl in our thoughts about gender. We also look at the structural barriers that hold women back, including the glass labyrinth, glass ceiling and glass cliff':

> *Yes, that is a hell of a lot of glass, and for the women who break through there is always the nasty consequence of being surrounded by jagged, dangerous shards. However, each separate glass barrier does need to be understood.*[326]

I confess that the 'glass labyrinth' was also a new phenomenon to me until I read their book, so was glad to get the authors' definition that this is 'a way of capturing the obstacles that hold women back as they seek to navigate their way up from an entry-level job.'[327]

And while still on the topic of 'a hell of a lot of glass,' I've also heard about yet another glass-related term: this time the 'double-glazed ceiling'. This is being used to describe where a woman of colour, or a disabled woman or a woman from an LGBTQI+ community experiences an added disadvantage as well as her gender, given that most of the time the power pecking order still positions white able-bodied men first, then men of colour, then white women and last of all, women of colour or anyone with a disability or a sexual difference.

The 1994 *Barriers* report comes to mind as I reflect again on the nine issues the women in our study found all those years ago to be such an impediment to their progress that they had left a corporation. We can now bundle all these factors into being part of the glass labyrinth discussed in Gillard's and Okonjo-Iweala's book.

Interviewees

KB, a senior partner in an international law firm, did not use the terms glass ceiling or labyrinth when I interviewed her. However, she did share several barriers to her progression that could well be described in these ways. For example, on being treated differently as a woman in a law firm that she subsequently left, she told me:

You're constantly being reminded that you're a lesser in different ways. For example, there are certain people (who) feel entitled to give you a kiss because you're a (woman). And you get the fish hand-shakes – they're kind of common. … (Further) I think (being called) 'dear' in a meeting is covert discrimination. … Even stupid things like offering to take your bag … it's all part of that condescension.

In terms of having a different management style, KB told me:

I only speak when I need to, so I'm often seen as 'soft' or not strong. I don't fight for things if they don't matter to me as well. … Certain jobs have come through, and I haven't fought to do them even though I've known I'm the better person, and somebody who's less good has got the job, because they're loud and they're male. … I try to be inclusive and collaborate as much as I can because I figure that's what partnership is about, but that behaviour can be seen as soft and gets held against me as well.

KB also talked about the 'language of business' working against women:

Unsurprisingly the rules and language of business are set by males as women are relative newcomers to business, and I don't know how women can change this … but I do think it helps men because it's more natural to them. It's more natural for men to talk about win-ning and losing. Talking about winning and losing is something I've had to learn to do in my job over time, but I think men come to the table with a natural advantage which is learnt in the playground and on the sports field and I don't think that's easy to fix.

On the barrier in the 1994 *Barriers* study relating to having children, JKR told me about the challenges for her when she was juggling mother-hood and a university career in the early '70s:

It was hard. It was before the provision of either childcare or maternity leave and I birthed and raised both my babies without either.

Not fitting into the corporate culture was another finding from the 1994 *Barriers* study. My interviewees for this book had a lot to say about this mysterious thing called culture that is hard to measure or touch or see but pervades organisations as 'the way we do things around here'.

JG, who began her career in HR then moved to consulting, and ultimately became a partner in an international search firm, had quite a lot to say about not fitting into the dominant culture, and being excluded from male networks. As she told me, as well as being talked over at meetings:

> *Then there's the golf game that is planned as the social interaction after meetings and conferences. I don't play golf so I'm excluded from the networking that happens during and after the game. There's still a hierarchy in which I see smarter women in subordinate roles to less able men – the male, pale (white) stale blokes.*

JER, formerly a senior HR professional and now an executive coach, talked about decision-making processes in a male culture:

> *I was in a role and there was to be a merger with mine and another role. I'd had experience in both areas, yet a bloke was parachuted in for the bigger role and I was manoeuvred out without what I would have thought was a genuine consideration of me as a candidate. I think that this was an example of the blokes working out a solution together.*

On the topic of why women leave corporates, JER told me that she's observed that women who are competitive and value status, power and money thrive in corporate environments. However, she went on to tell me:

> *I think women who value different things – more relational, are altruistic, (who) want to make a difference – find (corporate environments) more difficult. … That certainly happened for me. … I think that a lot of women just decide they want to do their own thing because that whole milieu is so incredibly stifling and constraining.*

DP moved from sales and marketing in a male-dominated corporation into consulting to senior teams about leadership. She told me about the wise counsel she gave to another woman who joined the division of the organisation that she'd just left. This woman was struggling to influence her boss through her usually collaborative approach – the same boss that DP had worked for:

She came and asked me how to get through to her boss and I said,
'you've got to behave like a bloke and forcefully say here are the
options – one, two, three and here's what I'm going to do'.

DP also talked about women doing the work, then the boss taking
credit for it:

The guy who led the team used to let the team do the work and he'd
take the credit. There were three women in the team and our work
was his work – would that have happened if there'd been a bloke in
the team doing the work? Probably not.

In terms of a conflict of values found in the 1994 *Barriers* study, DP told
me she left a senior position in her previous organisation because she
worked out you either had to behave like the blokes or leave:

I left when I looked up at the senior group and realised I didn't want
it (because) I'm coming from a different angle, (and I didn't want to
have) to change who I was.

PM, retired health professional and politician, is now a cattle breeder.
She told me about how her caring style was described by her male peers
as 'unprofessional':

I think workplace relations matter for staff and also to the reputation
and integrity of the company. However, when I encouraged the staff
who report to the executive, I was accused of being 'unprofessional'.

LM, a corporate lawyer reflected on how her gender impacted her success in a range of ways in the macho culture of the legal profession:

I've often felt that I was the one doing the work while men were at
the bar or on the golf course networking.

Also, when I was at a law firm, I found out that [my] and other
female lawyer's charge out rates were less than the men. So, if you
think about who you want to promote in the firm, you want to pro-
mote the people who make the most money, so that was a tangible
way that I felt hindered.

I also felt that I was often given very vague feedback because
I was a female and I felt sometimes there were broader or higher

expectations on me. (For example), I've been advised that I need to mentor and support others in activities outside the firm but my male colleagues were not expected to do this.

On reflecting about the resilience of male cultures LM told me:

We recently had a leadership change and quite a few senior women left because of this, and I noticed this made it more difficult for people of diverse backgrounds further down the organisation to be promoted. (After this it became) a much more aggressive perfor-mance management style than when there were some senior women saying I'm not happy with where this company's going. What I've observed is that this makes it harder for women at all levels of the organisation after that – it's almost a falling in line scenario – and so the status quo is maintained.

LM shared her optimism with me that a generational shift will contrib-ute to a shift in culture in the law:

I think there's maybe some generational change coming through. (Some of the) younger men are not prepared to follow the old models of joining the boys/networks. (This is) not just because it's not what they want but (also because) they want to spend time with their children or doing other things, and because they don't believe that this will get them the jobs they want, because they're less certain about their economic future and (there is a) need to be creative and innovative, rather than knowing the right people.

What more can be done?

JS, a former scientist and now business manager at a university, with previous experience as a board member on two boards, ended her interview with two clear structural changes that she believes need to be made to ensure that women get equality of opportunity in employment:

First, women need to be given the opportunity to be considered for any role. And if not appointed, [given] a fair post-interview appraisal with plans for meeting the identified 'gaps' in capability.

And second, once appointed, [there should be] a mentorship program to support the appointee. In fact, it is good HR practice for all new

appointees – men as well as women – to have their needs assessed
and then the appropriate support provided – training, mentoring,
peer support and encouragement of networking opportunities.

To break through the glass ceiling, the *Australian women CEOs speak* study made the following recommendations to women close to CEO level:

- *Stake your interest*
- *Network strategically*
- *Fill gaps in experience and knowledge*
- *Think like a CEO*
- *Stay above dirty politics*
- *Persist.*

And to women in the pipeline this study recommends that they:

- *Seek early roles with measurable results*
- *Objectively size up your organisation*
- *Clarify your vision, values, and core purpose*
- *Volunteer before you feel ready.*[328]

For government and employers, given as quoted earlier that free child-care is a form of fiscal stimulus, isn't it time that both government and policy makers made childcare free in this country?

And finally for senior leaders, it is essential that they not just mentor but also sponsor the high potential women in their teams – and model that to other men throughout their organisations. As former chief of Army David Morrison often said, 'you set culture by the things you ignore or walk past, as much as by what you do', so it is also essential for leaders to walk the walk and talk the talk in everything they do and say.

Conclusions

Are we nearly 'there' yet? 'There' being the end goal of achieving a fully gender diverse workforce in Australia. On my good days I think we are nearly there, but I then remind myself of the gender statistics in corporate Australia: as I've already outlined in some other chapters, there is still a gender pay gap of 13.3%, there are only 21 women CEOs in the top ASX200 companies and only 19% of board positions in the ASX200 group are held by a woman. When I focus on data like these I slump back down as I realise there is still a very long way to go.

The COVID pandemic has sharply highlighted working women's disproportionate disadvantage. As we saw in the research section of chapter 14 about unconscious biases, recent data has revealed that much of the work designated as 'essential services' in, for example, the caring and service sectors, is being done by women. Further, research shows that work in these sectors is more likely to be low paid, casual and part-time. I see this as yet more examples of the fact that we're definitely not 'nearly there' yet.

As I've written elsewhere in this book, we might have some hope in retirement proving to be one way the glass is being shattered in our organisations – be they ceilings, cliffs or labyrinths. As we baby boomers retire we hand over the reins to younger people, many of whom have grown up with strong female, as well as male, role models.

To return to my observations in my seven-minute speech described at the start of this chapter, I saw in my coaching work that one reason many highly skilled and competent women were leaving large organisations to do their own thing was because they found themselves experiencing a conflict of values at the senior levels of organisations. For example, they were typically committed to values such as mutual respect, fairness, openness and loyalty, then once promoted they found that one aspect of the dominant culture at a more senior level was to trust no one. Further, many of them had nurtured their teams to operate in a collaborative way at a more junior level, but then quickly realised that the executive suite was all about win/lose – in other words, a highly competitive environment.

Turning back to my friend's analogy in my conclusions in chapter 17 that 'if you go in the water, you can't help getting wet' – I saw through my coaching work that many senior women did not like the 'water' they were expected to 'swim' in at an executive level. They therefore bailed out and built their own businesses or joined smaller organisations that matched their values. What a loss they were, and are, to those large organisations. Which leads me straight back to my conclusion that a gender diverse workplace is good for workers and good for business.

Chapter 20

Three women CEOs speak

In the last chapter I analysed the barriers women still face at a senior level in large Australian organisations. In this chapter Dr Anne Hartican provides case studies of three women who succeeded anyway.

Anne writes:

Introduction

The legislative changes outlined in chapter 3 reflected the changing attitudes about women's role in society and recognised their rights to full participation in the workforce in the final quarter of the 1900s. These changes made it possible for women entering the workforce in the 1980s, to enjoy a career. I feel fortunate to be one of those women. Unlike my mother and her peers, for most of my career I have not felt professionally constrained by my gender.

On reflection, my gender did hamper my professional progress – predominantly in subtle ways, occasionally in blatant ways. I mostly conceptualised these obstacles as a part of the rough and tumble of organisational life. I believe the fact I did not filter those professional challenges though a gender lens was ultimately helpful. It kept me focusing on possibilities and opportunities rather than on the obstacles I might encounter.

Despite the challenges and the under-representation of women in the senior ranks and on the boards of Australian organisations, there are many women who have succeed professionally on their own terms. Over the past 15 years I have interviewed dozens of senior women leaders who entered the workforce in the 1980s, and while they cite experiences of sexism, I rarely had the sense that any of these women felt significantly constrained professionally by their gender. They found ways to work around this, and are very clear about the factors that have contributed to their professional progress. I think there is something important in this.

In this chapter I present the lived experience of three such women who have achieved professional success in their careers spanning the period from the 1980s to 2020s. Each woman is, or has been, a chief executive officer (CEO) and held other senior governance roles. I provide a summary of each woman's story and then discuss the common themes that emerge from their experiences.

To explore the experiences of our three CEOs, I used qualitative interview questions about the following:

- Family influences and education – We explored the extent to which our CEOs' early life experiences affected them professionally. Specifically, how did the attitudes of their families – parents, grandparents, aunties and teachers – influence our CEOs' career choices and trajectories?
- Reflections on career – We explored our CEOs' experiences in progressing their careers.
- Advice/final reflections – I asked each of our CEOs what advice they would offer young women who aspire to senior leadership roles as they commence their careers.

Introducing our women

- Jacqui Watt, Chief Executive Officer, No to Violence
- Christine Mackenzie AM – Former President, International Federation of Library Associations and former CEO, Yarra Plenty Regional Library

- Jacque Phillips OAM, Chief Executive Officer, NCN Health; former board member, Better Care Victoria

Jacqui Watt, Chief Executive Officer, No to Violence

Jacqui was born in Scotland to parents who experienced world wars and poverty. This undoubtedly influenced her decision to pursue a career in social policy in local government before moving into the fields of social housing and family violence. Jacqui says her mother was her inspiration, in part because of the difficulties her mother suffered. As we outline Jacqui's early life it becomes evident how this period has influenced her career trajectory, leading to her current role as the CEO of No to Violence.

The family

Jacqui recalls that her mother and grandmother enjoyed what working lives they had, valuing the opportunity to express themselves through their work.

> *My granny, my dad's mother, was born in 1893. After the first world war she became a teacher, a job she loved. There was a shortage of men because of the war but my granny married my grandad, gave up work and had 9 children. She always said to her granddaughters, 'you should have a career; don't just get married, have a career'.*

Jacqui explains how her mother inspired her career.

> *My mother was born in 1923. She was a very left-wing, politicised person who grew up in Glasgow during the Depression. These social conditions impacted her life. Mum experienced war and poverty.*

> *Mum loved working with numbers and at the age of 20 she was working for an accountancy firm in Glasgow doing bookkeeping. Mum realised she was working at a higher level than what she was getting paid for so she went to see the boss to ask for a pay rise. The boss said no so Mum resigned and went and signed up to join the army.*

> *The British government were happy to call women into the war effort; there were women in the munition's factories and there were a lot of women manning guns. Many of the women enjoyed those*

roles. My mum enjoyed the freedoms that came with working. When the war was over, all the women were sent back to their homes to have their nuclear families.

Mum was one of those women who married and was stuck at home. She hadn't really wanted to be a mother and struggled caring for her six children. She did not enjoy it. Mum clearly had the brains to do other things and she often expressed disappointment that she had not done more study.

Because of Mum's indifference to parenting, my older sister did a lot of the child raising. Consequently, I wasn't brought up as a little girl. I think this contributed to my sense that I have a right to be in charge. I have always had confidence in taking charge.

Jacqui explains in leaving school she chose to study a degree in social policy and social justice based on her mother's influence:

Both my parents encouraged us to be smart. But it was my Mum who was my inspiration. She didn't push us, but she wanted us to do well and wanted us to be politicised. Mum talked a lot about injustices as she herself experienced abuse, isolation, deprivations and lack of services. Mum imbued in me a sense of social justice – that people should be able to have decent housing, a reasonable wage, a car and to be able to go on holidays. It was no accident that I ended up in social housing working with tenants.

Education

Jacqui was actively encouraged to pursue an education:

Dad always said that getting an education is important; he encouraged me and I enjoyed a good education. The school I attended was famous for high achievement. I had some fabulous teachers. The motto of our high school was 'do well and persevere' and we were indeed encouraged to do well and to ask questions.

Despite the encouragement to achieve academically there was never any discussion at school about having a career. In my mid-teen years – between 14 and 16 – there were some smart girls who got shunted into the secretarial college. When I indicated that I, too, would go to secretarial college my teacher responded, 'no, you've got to do something much better than that'. This teacher said I could do anything and encouraged me to aim higher than being a secretary. I got a lot of encouragement from teachers.

Reflections on career

Jacqui started her professional life in 1984 in Scotland:

My first job was in the HR department of the council. I encountered sexist attitudes and I'd fight back. Looking back, I was informed by feminism and I engaged in a lot of feminist resistance to stereotyped roles for women. I've always been interested in equality and equal opportunity and so I engaged in activism around that cause.

I feel very driven by injustice. As I've previously stated, this influenced my decision to pursue a career in social housing.

I am very energetic. I can be a bit manic, high octane, mad perhaps. I seem to always be in a maverick role taking on things. I have a big vision, and sometimes I forget you need a lot of ducks lined up to deliver it. But someone has to be visionary. I've had bosses who have challenged me over the years: 'you don't have to save the world'. I think my drive comes from my childhood. I have wanted to improve things for people in need. Surely, it is not beyond men and women to make the world a better place.

I haven't had a career break; I don't have children. I grew up in the '70s where we were led to believe we could succeed at being a parent and having a career. I have a friend who worked for a petroleum company in a very senior role. She did it hard: she was a single parent, she was a fulltime carer, and had a fulltime job. She paid a heavy price. She got offered a lot of transfers and promotions but she refused to leave her home town while her daughter was in school. Every time they had a restructure she would end up with another job; she had five jobs. And she'd just do it to prove to them that she could.

I've had a few mentors; I am the sort of person who absorbs mentorship. Anyone who takes an interest in my development – I'm there. I'm hungry for it.

I don't think it is any accident that I have ended up in men's family violence. It does come back to the influence of my parents and what I observed in my own family. Dad was violent.

Advice/final reflections

Jacqui advises young professional women:

Look, listen and learn. Know that you have power and learn to use your power for good, for positive outcomes and change. I grew up with women political leaders like Indira Gandhi and Margaret Thatcher. Thatcher was divisive and hostile to working class people. She talked down to people and took up a model of power that I find offensive – it was the model of power she took up I had an issue with – it's not all about gender.

Jacqui's final reflections:

Strong leaders are powerful. If we are to promote a feminist model of leadership it has to be that we don't entertain the binaries of win/ lose, right/wrong.

I'm not sure I could even relate to my 22-year-old self anymore. I think that has to do with insecurities; the confidence you feel as a 22-year-old can get knocked out of you.

You have to be prepared that people are probably going to disappoint you and so try to not blame them. But then hold people to account. This is what we are trying to do at No to Violence.

Christine Mackenzie AM – Former President, International Federation of Library Associations and former CEO, Yarra Plenty Regional Library

Christine (Chris) Mackenzie was the firstborn of parents who ran a farm in regional Victoria. Consistent with Jacqui's family experiences in Scotland, Chris's family in rural Australia were also affected by the first and second world wars. These family experiences etched a belief deep into the family psyche that women should have a career.

The family

My maternal grandfather had found himself financially supporting his three unmarried sisters as a result of the shortage of young men available for marriage after the First World War and the lack of educational and career prospects for his female siblings. My grandfather was determined his three daughters would not similarly burden his sons if his daughters didn't marry. He wanted his daughters to have a career so he encouraged them to get a good education. Of my grandfather's three daughters, my mum, born in 1927, became a teacher. One of my aunties became a nurse and the other aunt trained as a receptionist and got a 'proper' job.

My Dad also had unmarried sisters. My 'maiden aunts' had a governess and while they did not go to school, they were great readers and became self-educated through their reading. My aunts held fantasies about winning the lottery and travelling to places such as Egypt to see the pyramids. They cultivated wonderful imaginings of the rest of the world beyond Australia. In reality, my aunts travelled as far as New Zealand. It was my aunties who cultivated my love of travel and love of reading.

My Mum adopted her own father's view that girls should have an education. While I was raised on a farm, Mum and Dad sent me to a private school to get a good education and it was this education that had a strong impact on my career choices and professional life. I shared my aunties' love of books and from an early age I loved libraries – the local library and the school library – so it was not surprising that I chose a career in libraries.

Chris had two children and took a career break during their infancy.

I had a three-year career break between the births of my two children who were born 14 months apart. After the first birth I arranged to work part-time. A colleague, who also had an infant, and I worked out a job share arrangement and we went to the boss with a proposal. The boss (female) was agreeable but then I found out I was pregnant again and so I resigned from my position.

After three years off work with my young children, and with my youngest child at 18 months of age, I returned to work on the weekends. I was so happy to be back at work that I would have worked for nothing. I never had any doubt about returning to work. I got a part-time job in a school library and when my eldest child was four years old, I went back to full-time work.

I had to arrange childcare but I was fortunate my husband was a very good dad and was prepared to share the responsibilities of managing childcare. This was critical to my career trajectory. School holidays posed challenges with childcare; you just had to learn to cope. I don't know how you'd do it without a partner who can cook, clean and do the pick-ups from school – unless you had a nanny.

My family never held me back in my career and in fact, they were a help. For example, they'd sit around the kitchen table and put newsletters into envelopes for me.

Education

I recall one of the teachers at my primary school who was also a librarian; she was a very kind person. I would spend my lunch breaks in the library while other kids were outside playing.

In my final year at school, one of my teachers pulled me aside and told me I was capable of doing much better than I was doing and advised that if I didn't start working, I would not pass my final school exams. The conversation was a real wake-up call, I started to really work, did well in my final exams and was awarded a Commonwealth Scholarship. This teacher spoke to me respectfully and kindly and I think it was powerful because someone was paying me attention and cared about me. It made me sit up, take notice and work at my studies as I wanted to go to university. I remain very grateful to this teacher.

I also had a university lecturer I approached for advice in relation to selecting from two job offers. The lecturer advised me to take the more desirable job as it would be much better for my career. I think this helped me realise you have to look after yourself and not get too bogged down by what people might think.

Reflections on career

Chris has devoted her entire professional life to libraries and in that time has been recognised for her leadership in positioning libraries as a critical community asset both within Australia and globally.

> *I was still under 21 when I qualified as a librarian. I started my career at the State Library of Victoria and was surprised at how well I fitted in. I initiated a few small projects that were successful and well received. For example, in the days of card catalogues, when no one could find anything, people would come in and ask for car motor manuals. All the manuals were in the storeroom so I organised, catalogued and listed them. People liked this; I got really good feedback. It was these little projects that I initiated, where I got good feedback, that built my confidence in initiating change and taking a lead on projects. I saw a need and acted. My colleagues gave me encouragement. I enjoyed my two years at the state library. It was a great environment with little pressure; it was a good life.*

> *I never experienced sexism in libraries; the most senior managers were often women. There were plenty of female role models in the smart, effective women I worked with. I never felt being a woman was a problem. I never experienced a glass ceiling. Despite this, it used to niggle me that men dominated the top positions when 90% of the workforce were women. I recall one male librarian explaining to me he selected libraries as a profession because it was feminised and he wanted to get to the top. It was very easy to get to the top if you were a male. But in the early days of my career a lot of women didn't want to be bosses. They just wanted to go to work, do their job and go home.*

Chris reflects on career obstacles she has personally encountered or observed:

> *I think the cost of childcare is the biggest barrier to women's professional advancement; it has become ridiculously expensive. The public service is very family friendly now; that's how it should be.*

> *I can't say I experienced obstacles other than myself. Professionally, my biggest hurdle has been my lack of confidence in selling myself.*

What held me back was I didn't do well at job interviews; I didn't like talking about myself or being the centre of attention. We were brought up – 'you don't blow your own trumpet'. I also have had to really work at overcoming my nerves and developing a relaxed way of presenting.

Chris's dedication to her career and developing her capabilities as a library sector leader is evident in the way in which she embraced opportunities to learn, grow and expand her knowledge and skills:

My job-exchange at Baltimore library for 6 months was life-changing. To participate in the job exchange opportunity, I took my family to the USA for six months. It was a considerable undertaking for my family to pack up and go to the USA but it was a really good thing. My husband took long-service leave at half-pay. The public service recognised the need for employees to support their spouses. My husband earnt more than I did, but in our family my career was always seen as more important.

It was in the USA that I observed a very different approach to library management. They were so customer focused – it changed my way of thinking about how to run libraries and serve people. The Americans were so professional and dedicated to their work. It's a different culture to Australia. I've always loved my work; I love working with librarians. Libraries are good places; they change people's lives.

In the early 1990s as a part of a management program I did a parachute jump. The experience was important in building my confidence; 'after the jump I thought, if I could do that, I could do anything'.

Joining the Bertelsmann [International]Network of Public Libraries and forming international connections has also been important to my career progress; networks are important to career success.

In the 2022 Australia Day Honours awards Christine was awarded a Member of the Order (AM) for significant service to librarianship, and to professional associations through leadership roles.

Advice/final reflections

Chris has been considered in her approach to her career and the type of leader she is, as is evident in taking the advice of Betty Churcher:

I recall reading an article in The Weekend Australian *by Betty Churcher, then CEO of the National Gallery. In the article, Betty advised to always hire bright people and to never be afraid of having bright people reporting to you because they are always going to make you look good. That advice stayed with me and that is what I've always tried to do. I've never felt threatened by the people who report to me. I've just thought, you go for it, then we'll all look good. I look good because I was smart enough to hire this person. I have a lot of trouble understanding people who don't do that because they look petty and the smart people who report to them often feel stifled and unhappy.*

To young women pursuing a professional career Chris advises:

Do your best in the job you've got. Don't always be thinking about the next job. I think it's important that people focus on doing their best in this job. If you perform well in the job, you'll soon get noticed. Take opportunities when people ask you to do things; you never know where it is going to lead. And be brave. Take on projects; think outside the box; step up. Do things that you believe in, put your energy where you want something to happen.

Of the three CEOs interviewed for this chapter, Jacque Phillips appears to have endured higher levels of sexism as she progressed in her career. Her story is therefore more detailed.

Jacque Phillips OAM, Chief Executive Officer, NCN Health

Jacque has also held a number of board positions for organisations including:

- Better Care Victoria
- Victorian Hospitals' Industrial Association
- Goulburn Valley Community Health
- Goulburn Valley Primary Care Partnership.

Jacque has, or currently holds, a number of senior roles in Rotary, including assistant governor.

Jacque Phillips grew up on a farm. For the young Jacque, home was Seymour, a town approximately 100 kms from Melbourne. Jacque enjoyed the encouragement of her parents to get a good education. Her initial training as a nurse set the foundations for a career leading health and community service organisations.

The family

Jacque's family instilled in her a deep commitment to community and to do whatever she did, well.

> *I grew up in a typical, traditional family structure. Mum was a nurse; she stopped working when she married and gave birth to her four children.*

> *My parents had a strong work ethic; they valued work. They expected their children to chip in and contribute to the work associated with running the farm and family household. My parents also instilled in me a commitment to 'do what you do well' and 'do what you say you will'.*

> *Neither Mum or Dad were academically inclined, but they were keen for all their children to get a good education and have a career. They saw equality of opportunity as important and were strong advocates for the rights of girls to an education and career.*

> *Like Mum, I trained as a nurse at Melbourne's Royal Children's Hospital. I carried the 'do what you do well' commitment I had inculcated from my parents into my nursing studies; I studied hard and did well in nursing.*

> *My Dad, while managing the family farm, was also a committed member of the local community and performed a lot of voluntary work. Mum supported Dad's community projects; she provided a considerable amount of voluntary labour through her work in organising and running functions.*

> *While Dad was highly active in the Seymour community, he was a quiet man. Dad would not often make public speeches but consistent*

with the maxim 'always take opportunities when you can', when invited to make a speech he would and he was always impressive.

My parents reinforced the notion of a sense of place and perceptions of a woman's role in community.

Education

My boarding school principal, Dulcie Brookshaw, was an influential role model. Dulcie was a single woman; she was dynamic, short of stature, but with a strong presence. Dulcie also displayed a genuine respect for young women and placed high value on women having a good education and career. Ahead of her time, Dulcie actively promoted the idea of education as a lifelong journey.

Dulcie displayed a proclivity to mentor and coach her students; she would sit with her students. Dulcie instilled in me a belief that success in life is not about privilege but opportunity. I have actively applied this lesson throughout my life taking opportunities as they present.

Boarding school also gave me access to sport, arts and culture; something I would not have been exposed to from my life on the farm.

In my nursing training I learnt to think about interactions with others, to tune into where others are at and consider how to pitch my message. I also learnt how to get the best out of others when they were going off the rails and how to support them to get them back on track. As a consequence, I now approach my leadership role and approach to working with others with an emphasis on learning and development.

Reflections on career

When I commenced my career, my vision for my professional life was to make a difference to the lives of children. This was driven by my understanding of the impact of a child's early experiences on their lives and how child neglect, abuse and removal from a family can adversely impact the trajectory of a person's life. In my work I saw the results of parents who were not able to parent and the impact on children when then they were taken away and deprived of love and nurturing.

From observing the systems designed to protect infants and children I felt there had to be a better way.

When I worked at the Sydney Children's Hospital, children would be flown in from the outback and then decisions would be made about a child's future with no input from the parents. The injustices of the system and the harm that was being caused had a profound impact on me, but at that time I was unclear about what I could do to influence a change to the system.

I was learning about the value of having conversations with people and gaining an understanding of a child's family background, but at that time it was frowned upon to get too close to a patient or client family. I also recall the impact of the AIDs epidemic on babies. I was working in a research ward and I observed how women and babies were separated and ostracised.

In my midwifery ante- and post-natal work, I enjoyed connecting with women and understanding their lives. I established new mothers' groups to create social connections and support networks. Through my work as a child and maternal health nurse I was determined to make an impact on the quality of parenting; I actively promoted the role of men in the lives of their children. At this stage of my career, I had no career goals and no ambition for a managerial role, but I was keen to influence change.

I worked as a maternal health nurse in Shepparton caring for patients and clients in public housing. It was here that I provided care for Iraqi women who had arrived in Australia with nothing. I soon realised I was feeling a sense of disquiet from knowing the rules I had to operate within did not align with my values. That experience galvanised my desire to shape policy. As an example, when I experienced tension between promoting breast feeding and not providing formula to women who could not breast feed, I started to question why the woman and her needs were also not prioritised in policy making.

I ended up spending 10 years in child services working in low socio-economic areas. I loved the work as I could see I was making a difference. I learnt to listen, encourage and assist others to deal with the complexities of their life circumstances.

It was during my time working in local government that I encountered sexist attitudes. When I joined a local government organisation the view was that its primary purpose was to deliver the three 'Rs' – roads, rates and rubbish. It was in this sector that I encountered a highly masculinised work environment with entrenched attitudes to the role of childcare and the value of kindergartens. In other words, childcare and early childhood education services were not valued and there were attempts to remove them as local government services. It was through this period I gained the confidence to challenge the attitudes of those who did not value services for women and children.

During the 1990s, local government organisations were restructured and this provided me with the opportunity to set up and manage a new early childhood program. Unfortunately, I was confronted with the sexist attitudes from one male manager. He was furious when I advised him I planned to take maternity leave, but I persisted. After giving birth to my son; my second child, my manager told me I should be at home with my two kids. I felt so under-valued and undermined by this man. For example, when I was given late notice to attend a lengthy meeting by my manager, I advised him I could attend the meeting but would need to bring my baby to the meeting. My manager responded 'if you must'. Three hours into the meeting I needed to feed my baby. It was suggested I leave the meeting to do this but I determined this was not appropriate as the meeting was at an important stage. I fed my baby in the meeting. After the meeting my manager advised me 'feeding your baby in the meeting was the most degenerating thing you could have done'.

After returning to work from maternity leave, I was never treated with respect by this man. But I hung in there. While this undermining behaviour was occurring, I enjoyed the support of a mentor who worked in community services. My mentor was also a young mum who was tough, fair and values-driven and who had learnt to deal with difficult men and would put up a fight when necessary. Despite getting support from my mentor and others, the constant undermining behaviour of my male manager continued so I left the organisation.

While local government was male dominated and challenging, the experience I gained in that sector was positive; it was where I learnt to be a manager, to take opportunities, to network and to influence. I also learnt a lot about myself and how to hold my own.

After leaving local government I returned to nursing as a Nurse Unit Manager where I worked for 18 months before accepting my first CEO role at Goulburn Valley Community Health Service.

I have three children. I took reducing periods of leave after each birth. I was fortunate I had a supportive husband. We had agreed I would continue my career during and after marriage and children. I have never felt my career stalled as a consequence of having children except for the fact I knocked back offers for roles that would have required my family to move. In health services many CEOs do relocate or undertake a 'fly in/fly out' living arrangement to advance in their careers. I was not comfortable to accept an arrangement if it impacted my family.

I think integrity is my most prominent personal quality along with an ability to hold my own. In my professional life I have regularly been confronted by men or highly masculinised environments where I have been tested by men who have attempted to intimidate me. I do not play political games. I do not network for the purpose of positioning myself to gain in some way. I stay true to myself in my dealings with others including with those in positions of power. Of course, this is not always easy as it can impact on how well you are accepted into a group.

I value the opportunity to use my influence in a positive way and to mentor others. I derive joy in seeing young people grow in their careers. I believe leadership behaviours shape the wellbeing of the team and organisation. It is important to find the balance of flexibility and structure.

As an introvert I have had to work hard to put myself out there. For me, the idea of public speaking used to terrify me but following the example of my father I would take on opportunities to do so, *recognising speaking in public went with the territory of a leadership role. I have taught myself to be confident in expressing myself and, if challenged, I analyse the opinions of others but I'm also prepared to hold to my own opinions where I think it's important for me to do so.*

I have enjoyed a number of career highlights that have contributed to my professional success. Receiving a Medal of the Order of Australia in 2015 for my contribution to community health was a key highlight. The award recognised my efforts in obtaining funding to address the abuse and neglect of children and establishing the 'Best Start' pilot site. My work was accepted and recognised by a previously ambivalent council; this work reshaped the thinking of local government on child services.

I was also recognised in the state of Victoria for leading the effort to rebuild an integrated health care facility and re-establish acute and primary health care after the devastating floods that destroyed the Numurkah Hospital in 2012.

I have enjoyed the support of a mentor who saw potential in me. She valued my thinking and achievements. She supported me in my work in establishing the Best Start program. I have also found the network I formed while undertaking an executive masters at ANZSOG has been valuable. While I was doing this program, I was CEO at Numurkah Hospital; it reinforced that I was in the right place in my career.

Jacque received a Medal of the Order of Australia (OAM) for service to community health in Numurkah. Her nomination focused on her untiring work and dedication to the continuation and re-establishment of services at Numurkah District Health Service after a major flooding event in March, 2012.

Jacque was also awarded the esteemed Rotary's Paul Harris Award in June 2021.

Advice/final reflections

To young women pursuing a professional career Jacque advises:

Don't rush – look ahead but enjoy the present. Harness the present and take opportunities. Make decisions based on what is happening at the time. Don't fear missing out. Value education but also see the value of experience – life and work experience are important to an ability to communicate, form relationships and positively influence others.

Jacque also reflects on the current status of women:

There's still a lot of discrimination and gender bias. There are diverse groups in our communities and there is still a long way to go in achieving equity. What is equality? Equality does not equal 50:50 if you value appointing people on skills and merit. I understand the rationale for targets but I do not associate equality with the achievements of targets. I want to see women valued for who they are and what they offer versus appointing a woman so there is a female in the room.

Anne's reflections

It is not difficult to identify common themes and factors that have contributed to the success of our three CEOs. I have summarised the factors I think are particularly noteworthy and are consistent with the experiences of many other senior women leaders I have interviewed. The themes I want to highlight are:

- social context
- family
- education
- reflections on career
- advice to others.

Social context

In recognising the achievements of our three CEOs it is important to acknowledge they were the beneficiaries of the social conditions into which they were born. The re-activation of the women's movement in the late 1960s and 1970s – the period when our three CEOs were at school – raised awareness of gender inequality and provided the impetus for widespread changes that supported women to fully participate in the workforce. By the time our three CEOs commenced their careers, numerous structural changes had been implemented: for example, the marriage bar had been removed, women had easy access to the contraceptive pill and governments had implemented anti-discrimination laws and a range of policies and programs designed to support women.

Family

Families and childhood provide our first encounter with leadership and the roots of our leadership aspirations and styles.

– Professor Amanda Sinclair[329]

The trajectory of our lives, both personally and professionally, are often shaped by our early life experiences.

Our three CEOs' stories illustrate how their family upbringing and early childhood experiences shaped their career interests, hopes and aspirations, as well as their character: their work ethic, sense of personal agency and confidence. All CEOs cited how they were expected to contribute to the work of the family and did so with a willingness and sense of duty. This work ethic and sense of duty to something greater than themselves appears to have carried forward into their professional lives. Our CEOs all demonstrated a propensity to work hard, to give their best and to persevere when their working lives were challenging.

Another notable theme was that all of our three CEOs displayed a strong and ongoing commitment to their professional fields. Their stories illustrate the power of a sense of vocation and deeply ingrained interest in one's profession. Implicit in our conversations was an alignment between their personal and professional values and the importance of knowing their work efforts resulted in positive societal outcomes. I was struck by their connection to a purpose broader than themselves. These women maintained a focus on their work and its positive impacts versus positioning themselves for the next promotion. That is not to say they weren't conscious of the need to position themselves to advance in their careers, but it did not appear to be their key driver. Again, I consistently talk to senior women who reinforce the power of having a professional vision and sense of purpose associated with their work.

Character, purpose and values matter in sustained professional success. In our three CEOs, these were evidently cultivated during their early years through their experiences in their families and with influential teachers.

In Jacqui Watt we see a reflective and committed activist who has sustained her passion for social justice. Jacqui learnt from an early age to take charge and to use her considerable energy to get things done. Jacqui was encouraged by generations of women before her to pursue a career and her endeavours were supported by her father and teachers.

Chris Mackenzie's family were committed to ensuring women family members were educated and pursued a career. Her husband and children also actively supported Chris throughout her career. In Chris, we see a woman who identified her true vocation and devoted her professional life to developing libraries as a valued community asset. With a genuine love of learning and innovation, and with a strong sense of personal agency, Chris has led many improvements in her sector.

Jacque Phillips was also the beneficiary of parents who were committed to ensuring their daughters had equal access to a good education and career. What is notable in Jacque's story is the extent to which she inculcated her parents' dedication to community service. Jacque is a professional who has the courage to stand her ground with humility and tenacity. In Jacque, we find a truly thoughtful and reflective leader with an outstanding commitment to improving the lives of others through her work.

The other important element of family life was for our two CEOs who had children. For Jacque Phillips and Chris Mackenzie, career breaks did not adversely affect their careers. Both Jacque and Chris were appreciative of their supportive spouses who assisted with the care of their children in their younger years.

As Chris Mackenzie noted, adequate family and domestic support is critical for women participating in the workforce at senior levels. Similarly, most of the successful women I have interviewed acknowledge that supportive partners, domestic help and parental support, along with attitudes of family members that reinforce the woman's career is important and must be supported, are key factors that have enabled women to participate fully in their careers.

Education

It is evident in their stories that our three CEOs were all influenced by parents, grandparents and other significant adults who were progressive thinkers and who displayed an inclination to actively foster a generation of educated, professional women. I was surprised to discover that it was not just parents who supported their daughters to pursue a career, but also grandparents and aunts. These progressive adults, typically born in the 1910s, 1920s and 1930s, had survived a time ravaged by war, disease and depression. As we discovered in our conversations with our three CEOs, the First World War produced a generation of women for whom there were insufficient men to marry. It also stirred within some people a commitment to ensuring their daughters had an education, had the opportunity to be self-sufficient and would not be reliant on a man for their livelihood if they did not marry.

Congruent with the views of our CEOs' parents and grandparents, my research suggests that education is a critical foundation to professional success for the majority of women unless they pursue an entrepreneurial career. In practice, many professions require formal qualifications.

Crucially, teachers can play a vital role in encouraging girls to pursue a career. Our CEOs all commented on memorable teachers who believed in their potential and provided encouragement at the right time. This ensured our CEOs, as girls, were receiving consistent messages about the value of a career and about their individual potentialities.

Reflections on career

The most notable theme for me from the reflections on careers was the propensity each CEO had to having a vision for the changes they wanted to make, and the capacity to identify and leverage opportunities.

Jacqui Watt discussed her capacity to be visionary for social justice and to keep agitating for change. Jacque Phillips commenced her career with a vision to make a difference to the lives of children. Years later she was recognised for her efforts in establishing a pilot site to address the abuse and neglect of children, with a Medal of the Order of Australia.

Throughout her career Jacque Phillips has actively applied the lesson she learnt from her high school teacher that 'success in life is not about privilege but opportunity'. Jacque has consistently stepped up to the opportunities that she has been presented with. Indeed, even when presented with challenges in local government, Jacque described how she used her time in that sector to learn to be a manager and to influence and use her own power effectively, as well as expand her professional network.

Chris Mackenzie, also a visionary leader, became a master at identifying ways to innovate and develop library services. While at times lacking in confidence, she learnt to embrace opportunities that positioned her well for professional success. Chris pursued an international job exchange and engaged in several global networks which culminated in her appointment as the President, International Federation of Library Associations and Institutions.

Advice to others

In summing up the advice from our three CEOs to young women pursuing a career as a senior leader, our CEOs recommend:

Do your best in the role you have and enjoy what you are doing in the present; avoid constantly focusing on the next promotion. At the same time, take opportunities when they are presented, be brave, know what you want to accomplish and learn to use your power to drive positive change. Look, listen and learn.

As our social context and norms change from generation to generation, will the factors that contributed to professional success for women commencing their careers in the 1980s remain relevant for women commencing their careers in 2020? I believe so. While our global and societal challenges become increasingly complex and pressing, and as the emphasis on women's participation in political, business and organisational life continues to gain traction, I consider women – like our three CEOs, who are educated, confident, values-driven and committed to contributing to improving the lives of others – will, despite ongoing sexism and structural barriers, find their place in the senior ranks of our societies and organisations. I pray that they do.

Chapter 21

Where we've come from, where we are now and where to from here?

The success of the three women CEOs outlined in the previous chapter, and how they achieved this, gives me heart, because as I reflect back over the almost 60 years that this book spans – beginning with the first anti-discrimination Act in South Australia in 1966, through to when I began my equal opportunity consultancy in the mid '80s, until now – I find myself asking why there has not been more progress for women in employment over this time. I recall those heady days of the Whitlam era followed by Bob Hawk's affirmative action legislation, and I lament the reduction in services and opportunities for women by recent conservative governments.

Conversely, I carry hope in my heart because at the May 2022 federal election, the new Labor government was soundly victorious with promises of an improvement in the status of women as one of their campaign platforms. Nine so-called teal women independents were elected, all of whom included equality for women in their election promises. As a result of this election 38% of the House of Representatives is now made up of women, the highest proportion of women ever in the lower house; whereas the Senate exceeded 50% women in the last parliament and will maintain this in the new parliament. Surely all these changes will have a positive impact for women at both a legislative and policy level.

Given that at the time of publication there were only 21 women CEOs in Australia's ASX200 listed companies; given that there is still a gender pay gap of 13.3%; given that, in the 2022 World Economic Forum's Global Gender Gap Index (which measures the gender-based gaps of 156 countries around four key dimensions of economic participation and opportunity, educational attainment, health and survival, and political empowerment) Australia ranked 43rd having been ranked 15th in 2006 when the index began; and given the disproportionate social and economic disadvantage that working women suffered during the COVID-19 epidemic in 2020, 2021 and beyond, I find myself wondering how much the mix of legislation and policy that has been enacted over the past almost 60 years has really helped. All these indicators suggest Australia still has a long way to go until it achieves true gender equality.

Research

We have come a long way when we compare ourselves to our much earlier fore-sisters.

As Annabel Crabb writes in *The wife drought*:

The past half century has been a time of extraordinary change for women. Rising levels of education, smaller family sizes, the decline of manufacturing, the rise of the service economy; these are developments that have seen women take on work and accomplishment in a way that has radically changed the expectations we have of ourselves and for ourselves.[330]

Yet not much more than 100 years ago a woman still became the property of her husband on marriage. As Emily Maguire tells us in *This is what a feminist looks like*:

In nineteenth-century Australia, when a woman married, all that she owned ... became the property of her husband. She was his property too, and he could beat, rape or otherwise mistreat her without consequence. Divorce was rare and difficult. For unmarried women, things could be harder still. With no defined role in life, and few education and employment opportunities, it was easy for a single woman to find herself poverty-stricken and desperate. A pregnancy meant social shunning and an end to even the limited opportunities the woman might have otherwise had – either that or risk death or permanent injury at the hands of a 'backyard' abortionist.[331]

On the topic of women and education, Jacqueline Kent, in her 2020 biography of Vida Goldstein called *VIDA – a woman for our time*, tells us that when in 1883 Julia Margaret (Bella) Guerin was the first woman to graduate from an Australian university, *The Argus* newspaper declared that 'too much education would make women uppity, discontented and disinclined to know their proper place'. Kent then wrote that the next hurdle for women was being allowed to study medicine. The view of the medical profession at the time was that attending to the more unpleasant parts of the bodies of women and even more of men, would be unseemly for women. However this belief somehow did not apply to women being nurses, highlighting the fact that this resistance by male doctors was actually about not wanting to share their superior status with women. After many years of argument Kent tells her readers that women were finally allowed to study medicine in 1887.[332]

As referred to above, recent governments have seen severe losses for women's services in Australia. My retired academic historian and bureaucrat sister Janet Ramsay sent me her summary of a conference she attended at the end of 2019 in Old Parliament House, Canberra. It was hosted by the Whitlam Institute within Western Sydney University and was called Revisiting the Revolution: Whitlam and Women. I am choosing to include Janet's notes in this last chapter as a historical reminder that we women must remain ever diligent.

What we have lost from what was achieved back then:
- *Central, well-resourced women's policy machinery, federal and states*
- *Formally required inclusion of gender assessment on all Commonwealth Cabinet submissions*
- *Detailed Commonwealth Women's Budget Statements included among each year's Budget Papers*
- *Equal Employment Opportunity machinery and commitment across all Commonwealth and State government departments*
- *Maintained funding for and commitment to community-based women's services, especially those for women suffering violence*

- *Maintained funding for legal support services on which women suffering violence are often dependent.*

What has yet to be achieved:

- *Equal pay, especially in women majority work areas*
- *Adequate proportion of women in leadership position in politics, business and the community*
- *An end to gender-based violence against women*
- *Return to and increase of adequate funding for community-based women's services.*

I believe that the above four suggested actions alone could serve as an excellent checklist for where leaders throughout Australia might further improve the status of women in Australia.

Over to former Prime Minister Julia Gillard for the final word on the impact of the then ongoing COVID-19 epidemic in late December, 2021. In a piece in *The Guardian Weekly* Gillard wrote:

> *Gender inequality was a persistent feature of our society before Covid and the impact of the pandemic has exacerbated it … Women were more likely to lose jobs, do more unpaid work, and get less government support. At the peak of the crisis, women lost jobs at double the rate of men – almost 8% compared with 4% for men. And they shouldered the increase in unpaid work … in the home … and were forced to give up study in record numbers. As Australia contemplates a life beyond Covid, we must seize the moment to create a more equal playing field. … Gender equality does not only benefit women. It empowers every person to live free from the suffocating constraints of gender stereotypes.*[333]

I join Gillard in this call-out that the achievement of gender equality will benefit us all by freeing us from the bonds of what we should and should not be and do, based solely on our gender.

What more can be done?

If I had any doubts at all before embarking on this book, I am now totally convinced that to achieve gender equality in the Australian workforce much more change is needed. As a result of my many years as an EO consultant and leadership coach thinking about, and then, more recently, researching and writing this book, I've reached the conclusion that for real change to be achieved, a two-pronged approach is needed:

- First, governments, both federal and state, will need to create more innovative policies designed to provide many more support services for women with adequate budgets to make these a reality
- Second, we need enlightened leaders Australia-wide who fully embrace the value of a gender equal workforce and demonstrate this by not only setting policies and practices that will create work cultures that are truly women friendly, but also by 'walking their talk' by modelling an open, fair and collaborative leadership style.

It's now time to review all that I've gathered during the writing of this book – from my own contributions as a feminist activist, from my research about the status of working women in Australia, and from the experiences of my interviewees – to make my summary recommendations about what more can be done.

Let's start at home, where every little girl needs to be raised knowing that girls can do anything. Next, she needs an education that puts up no barriers and reinforces her family message that girls can indeed do anything they choose to do. Things become more complicated once she's joined the workplace, which is the focus of this book. It is here that the now grown young woman and her family alone can't make the necessary changes. At this stage it's up to governments and employers to ensure she can fully contribute her potential.

Nevertheless, here are some practical tips for younger women about how to navigate the current work environment:

- Negotiate your salary – men do it all the time. (And if you find this too hard, get some coaching help to prepare you.)
- Search out supportive men and ask them to keep a watchful eye out for you and, where possible, sponsor you. For example, when you continually get interrupted at meetings, ask a supportive man to help you ensure that you get your say.
- Don't tolerate sexism or misogyny – be prepared to call it out and know where to get support.
- With the current pressure on employers to achieve a more diverse workforce, there are now increased opportunities for women.

If they don't appear to be there in your workplace, ask why not, or change employers.

- Differentiate yourself in some way, and it's not necessarily your professional credentials that will do this. For example, use the opportunity we women have to dress in a professional, yet eye catching way, rather than blending in with the blokes' black and/ or grey suits.
- Never volunteer to set up the room, take the minutes or get the coffee for meetings. Review and approve the minutes and take some ownership this way. But if you're asked to serve the coffee (which sadly still happens), suggest it must be someone else's turn to do so.

All this can help, but it's time we stopped focusing on what women need to be doing differently. My primary message is to the leaders of Australia. I can summarise in three words what's needed in Australia for sustainable change in the status of women at work: leadership, leadership and leadership. Attitudinal change is needed so that all leaders truly embrace the value of a diverse workforce; systemic change is needed so that all barriers to women's progression are removed; and cultural change is needed so that all remnants of the influence of patriarchy are eliminated. My question to leaders across the land is: Are you prepared to take the lead in creating safe and productive work cultures where both women and men can equally contribute and thrive? If you are not, then you should not be in the role you are currently holding.

At a practical level, for starters:

- The Prime Minister and his (and hopefully some time again soon, her) Cabinet must take advice on the impact on women of every new law and policy. To achieve this, they need to raise the profile and size of the Office for Women and allocate adequate funds to enable this unit to function effectively in their role of advising government on what change is needed and on monitoring progress. As well, the remit of every department head should include the responsibility and accountability for the status of women working in their department.
- Leaders in the private, higher education and not-for-profit sectors must fully embrace the value of a gender diverse workforce for

both economic and equity reasons and take a stand to achieve this. Nothing less than this will do.

- Readily available and affordable (preferably free) childcare for all, and gender-neutral parental leave must be provided.
- A bridging of the gender pay-gap and flexible work practices for full-time as well as part-time workers must be achieved.
- Equitable leave policies to increase men's uptake.
- As well as the attitudinal, systemic and cultural changes referred to above, one important yet underrated way that change can happen is for leaders to listen more in order to find out what change is needed. As my interviewee AS, former CEO and now non-executive board director, explained to me, because people are almost always 'managing up' to their CEO they tell them what they think their boss wants to hear. In her interview to me she said, 'It's only when you go out and listen, that you find out what the hell is going on.' So, for leaders to know what's really happening for women in their organisation, it's time to go back to the old idea of 'management by walking around'.

My final reflections

Back in the early '80s, when I was a single mother living in suburban Adelaide and working as a community nurse, I set my first ever two goals: the first was that one day I would live on Sydney Harbour, and the second was that I would make a dent on society to the benefit of society. Yes, I did achieve the former goal for a few years in the early '90s, in the tiniest rental flat in Elizabeth Bay. And my hope is that over my 40 plus years of feminist activism, and as an EO consultant, coach and mentor to dozens of leaders and hundreds of women, I have made a small dent on society to the benefit of working women.

Now I'm relieved and delighted that there are so many wonderful younger women taking over the baton from us ageing feminists. For example, the brave young women I wrote about in the Introduction who spoke out in various ways throughout 2021 are each now taking a leadership role: Grace Tame has established the Grace Tame Foundation with the goal of achieving cultural and structural change to free children and others from sexual abuse; Saxon Mullins is the Director of

Advocacy at Rape and Sexual Assault Research and Advocacy; and Chanel Contos has founded Teach Us Consent to lobby for 'wholistic consent and sexuality education'.[334] This means that two of these three women have had the courage to reinvent themselves having been victims of sexual assault, and all three have become leaders in the field of change for women. Further, as a result, they will undoubtedly be acting as powerful role models to other younger women by inspiring them to speak up too.

I am also mightily impressed by the smart, articulate young women I now see on the panels of ABC TV's *The Drum* and by the articles now being written by younger academics, both women and men, in *The Conversation*. I'm inspired by every one of them as I read, watch and hear all they're saying and doing to report on and keep up the fight for equal rights for women in Australia.

I'm also optimistic that the current Labor government and the teal independents will follow through on their 2022 election campaign commitments to improve conditions for women through legislation and policy. At the time of writing in the autumn of 2023, the Albanese government has made a good start to addressing gender inequality by taking action on the gender pay gap, paid parental leave, early childhood education and care, domestic violence leave, full implementation of the Respect@Work recommendations and a budget that established a women's economic equality taskforce. So far so good.

I hope that this book will inform younger women about where we women have come from and will motivate them to continue to demand equality for themselves and for other women. My optimistic hope is also that they will not be doing this alone, because the leaders in this land – both men and women – will hear their demands.

However, given the glacial pace at which the change still seems to be happening, my pessimistic self fantasises about stepping into an alternative universe where every leader in Australia is already awash with emotional intelligence, awash with empathy and awash with compassion, and clearly sees the sense in creating truly equal and gender diverse workplaces to the benefit of the women and men of Australia and to the benefit of every organisation in this land.

Interview Questions

1. A brief summary of your career thus far.
2. Do you think your gender has helped or hindered your career success? In what ways?
3. Have you experienced overt discrimination or sexual harassment?
4. What about covert examples: the hard to name and describe experiences that you know have happened?
5. If you are a mother, did you or do you experience maternal guilt as you juggle/or have juggled work and family?
6. Have you ever been aware of your remuneration being less than your male peers? And if so, what did you do about it, if anything?
7. Have you had the support of any mentors along the way? And if so, what difference have they made for you?
8. How would you define the term 'feminist' and do you identify as one?
9. Have things improved for women at work over the years?
10. If you've left a large organisation to set up your own business, what were the key reasons for you leaving?
11. I've often been told by my coaching clients that their self-doubt limits them, and that they sometimes fear that they'll be found out as a 'fraud' – the so-called Imposter Syndrome. Have you ever experienced this or have you heard of other women who have?
12. Your thoughts on what needs to change for women's equal representation throughout organisational Australia and how to do this.
13. I've been thinking that the 'elephant in the room' is some men's unconscious biases – do you agree and do you have any examples?
14. Is there anything else you'd like to share?

The Dolphin Forum

Our purpose

We are values-aligned women who enrich each other to be the best version of ourselves for a safer, fairer world. We bear witness to each other's lives – the joy, the pain and the challenge of our hunger for enduring personal growth.

Our values

- **Wisely visionary** – we draw on our inner wisdom to create a compelling vision for the future.
- **Vulnerable authenticity** – we are willing to share what's in our hearts, even when it hurts.
- **Joyful curiosity** – we explore possibilities with child-like wonder.
- **Purposeful courage** – we are courageous in the pursuit of living a meaningful life.
- **Empathic compassion** – we are kind to ourselves and others.
- **Abundant gratitude** – we acknowledge that we are blessed beyond measure.
- **Valuing difference** – we honour difference in the pursuit of the greater good.

Acknowledgements

It's said that it takes a village to raise a child. Similarly, it's taken a lot of supportive people to help me create this book.

In chronological order, I extend heartfelt thanks:

To my interviewees for getting me started, and for their generosity of time and their sharing of experiences.

To my contributing authors Anne Hartican, Lindsay Mackay and Megan Young for each adding a rich perspective to the breadth of the book.

To my sister Janet for her loving support throughout this project, for writing help when I got stuck, for her reframe of feminism from the 'waves' theory to one about a 'persistent underground stream that bursts forth from time to time and is then beaten back down underground', and for her keen eye as my manuscript assessor.

To my editor Sue Pavasaris. We met through a shared yoga teacher at exactly the right time for me. I needed editing help and Sue gave me this and much, much more, often without the metre on.

To my expert self-publishing team at Publish Central: Michael Hanrahan in the foreground and Anna Clemann coordinating all the 'behind the scenes' details, and to Dean Bailey for his superb cover design.

To my photographer/design friend Gaby Borgardts for my portrait picture and my website.

And then there's the support of my family and friends.
My huge thanks:

To my daughter Louise, my son Simon and their spouses Pete and Gilly for being there when I need encouragement.

To my granddaughters Jess, Isie, Pip, Alex and Lila for giving me a reason to write this book.

To my brother Andrew for always being there whenever I need some wise counsel.

To my Book Group – Elinor, Lea, Margot, Nada and Patricia for cheering me on.

To the women in my Dolphin Forum group in Melbourne who have continued to believe in me and my writing for well over 30 years.

To my Friday@4 group who helped me make some crucial decisions about the text and the cover.

To my women's group, the Sun Sistas, for generously listening as the months dragged on, and for encouraging me to change my last paragraph.

To my coffee, wine and zoom friends both near and far for checking in on my progress from time to time. In particular – Alice, Ama, Amelia, Bronwyn, Chrissie, Jann, Megan, Therese and Susanne.

To my loyal dog Bella who sat patiently at my feet throughout the time of writing this book.

And finally, in loving memory of Des Ryan and David Dennis, both of whom taught me so much about life and the challenges of having a feminist partner – me!

Endnotes

Introduction

1   Markus Zusak, *Bridge of clay*, Picador, Australia, 2018.

Chapter 1. Why women too?

2   *Australian Women CEOs Speak: How female leaders rise and how organisations can help.* Korn Ferry Institute in collaboration with Australian Institute of Company Directors (2018), p 46.

3   Richard Denniss, 'Attack of the Clones: Australia's reign by older white men is an offence on us all', *The Guardian Weekly*, October 2019.

4   Annabel Crabb, World-first research shows female CEOs boost companies by $80m on average, ABC News, (https://www.abc.net.au/news/2020-06-19/women-in-leadership-boost-success/12370516), 19 June 2020, accessed 19 June 2020.

5   Workplace Gender Equality Agency, (Rebecca Cassells and Alan Duncan from Bankwest Curtin Economics Centre) *Gender Equity Insights 2018 Inside Australia's Gender Pay Gap*, (https://www.wgea.gov.au/publications/gender-equity-insights-series), 26 March, 2021, accessed 26 March 2021.

6   Ibid.

7   Julia Gillard and Ngozi Okonjo-Iweala, *Women and leadership*, Vintage, 2020, p 35.

8   Kate Jenkins, *The Beijing Platform for Action, 25 years on: Progress, Retreat and the Future for Women's Rights*, (https://humanrights.gov.au/about/news/speeches/beijing-platform-action-25-years-progress-retreat-and-future-womens-rights), 3 December, 2020, accessed 26 March 2021.

Chapter 2. The gang of three – sexism, misogyny and patriarchy

9   Anne Summers, *The misogyny factor*, NewSouth Publishing, 2013, p 7–8.

10   Robert Jensen, *The end of patriarchy*, Spinifex Press, 2017, pp 38–40.

11   Ibid.

12   Ibid.

13   Yuval Noah Harari, *Sapiens: A brief history of humankind*, Vintage, 2011 pp.171-173.

14   Margaret Kelly, *Turning the spotlight on the 'wizard behind the curtain'. How do transgender women experience and navigate male privilege and entitlement, pre-and post-transition?* [master's thesis], Macquarie University, April 2017.

15   Lisa Heap, Women don't speak up over workplace harassment because no one hears them if they do, (https://phys.org/news/2018-12-women-dont-workplace.html), *The Conversation*, 14 December 2018, accessed 17 December 2018.

16   Julia Gillard and Ngozi Okonjo-Iweala, *Women and leadership*, Vintage, 2020, p 269.

17   Susan Fiske and Peter Glick, The science of how 'benevolent sexism' undermines women, (https://neuroleadership.com/your-brain-at-work/peter-glick-on-how-benevolent-sexism-undermines-women/), *neuroleadership.com*, 5 September 2019, date accessed 16 August 2021.

18   Ibid.

19   Anne Summers, *The misogyny factor*, NewSouth Publishing, 2013, p 19.

Chapter 3. What does the law say?

20   From 1902 with the passage of the Commonwealth Franchise Act 1902 (Cth). New Zealand women won the vote in 1893, but New Zealand a colony of Great Britain at the time as discussed in Claire Wright, *You daughters of freedom: the Australians who won the vote and inspired the world*, Text Publishing, 1 October 2018, Author's Note p x.

21   Women's unions lobbied for equal pay from the 1880s and organisations such as the Women's Electoral Lobby pressed for recognition of sex discrimination from the 1970s, but legislation was only implemented much later and after ratification of international treaties. Women won the right to stand for Parliament as a failed tactic to defeat the suffrage bill as discussed in Judith Brett, *From secret ballot to democracy sausage: how Australia got compulsory voting*, Text Publishing, 2020, p 39.

22   The #MeToo movement was started by Tarana Burke sharing her story of sexual abuse and the movement has gained momentum in Australia following the allegation by Brittany Higgins of her rape in a ministerial office and allegations against Australia's Attorney-General Christian Porter as discussed in Jaclyn Diaz, Thousands March in Australia as Another #MeToo Wave Hits the Country,

(npr.org/2021/03/15/977340049/thousands-march-in-australia-as-another-metoo-wave-hits-the-country), NPR Daily, 15 March 2021, accessed 20 March 2021.

23   For example, feedback that affirmative action only represented the interests of a small group of women and would harm the majority of women as discussed in the Hon Susan Ryan AO, 'Fishes on Bicycles' Papers on Parliament, No 17, September 1992. Also see the discussion of opposition in Marian Quartly and Judith Smart, *Respectable radicals – a history of the national council of women of Australia 1896–2006*, Monash University Publishing, October 2015.

24   Australia's defamation laws and lack of constitutionally protected rights to free speech have meant that making allegations of sexual harassment comes with a real risk of liability for those bringing the allegations, as discussed in Vanisha Babani, 'Does Australia have the laws it needs in the #MeToo era?' *Canberra Law Review*, 2020, 17(2).

25   World Economic Forum, Global Gender Gap Report 2022, (http://reports.weforum.org/global-gender-gap-report-2022), 13 July 2022, accessed May 2023.

26   Beth Gaze and Belinda Smith, *Equality and discrimination law in Australia: an introduction*, Cambridge University Press, 24 November 2016, p 22.

27   Ibid., p 52.

28   Ibid., p 23.

29   For example: Attorney-General's Department, *Review of consolidation of Commonwealth discrimination law*, 2011. Parliament of Australia, Senate Legal and Constitutional Affairs Committee, *Report on the effectiveness of the Commonwealth Sex Discrimination Act 1984 in eliminating discrimination and promoting gender equality*, Canberra, 2008. Australian Human Rights Commission, *Discussion paper: priorities for federal discrimination law reform*, 2019 as part of 'Free and Equal: An Australian Conversation on Human Rights' (the National Conversation).

30   Australian Human Rights Commission, *Respect@Work: Sexual Harassment National Inquiry Report* (2020), (https://humanrights.gov.au/our-work/sex-discrimination/publications/respectwork-sexual-harassment-national-inquiry-report-2020) ('Respect@Work Report'), 5 March 2020, accessed 10 March 2020.

31   Australian Human Rights Commission, Free and Equal A reform agenda for federal discrimination laws (https://humanrights.gov.au/our-work/rights-and-freedoms/publications/free-and-equal-reform-agenda-federal-discrimination-laws) 10 December 2021, accessed 21 May 2023.

32 John M. Williams, 'Race, citizenship and the formation of the Australian Constitution: Andrew Inglis Clarke and the "14th Amendment"', 1996, 42(1) *Australian Journal of Politics and History* 19.

33 Helen Irving, The over-rated Mr Clark?: Putting Andrew Inglis' Clark's contribution to the Constitution into perspective, (http://www.aph.gov.au/About_Parliament/Senate/Powers_practice_n_procedures/pops/pop61), Papers on Parliament No 61, May 2014, accessed April 2021.

34 John M. Williams (n 31).

35 For example, *Australian Constitution* ss 51, 127.

36 John M. Williams (n 31).

37 *Australian Constitution* s 117.

38 *Leeth v Cth* (1992) 174 CLR 455. *Kruger v Cth* (Stolen Generations) (1997) 190 CLR 1.

39 Gaze and Smith (No 7), 39.

40 Gaze and Smith (No 7) 42.

41 *Human Rights Act 2004 (ACT)*. *Charter of Human Rights & Responsibilities Act 2006 (Vic)*. *Human Rights Act 2019 (Qld)*.

42 *Human Rights Bill 1973 (Cth)* as discussed in George Williams, The Federal Parliament and the protection of human rights, (https://www.aph.gov.au/About_Parliament/Parliamentary_Departments/Parliamentary_Library/pubs/rp/rp9899/99rp20), Parliament of Australia, Law and Bills Digest Group, Research Paper 20, 1998–99, 11 May 1999, accessed April 2021.

43 Australian Human Rights Commission, Free and Equal A Human Rights Act for Australia (https://humanrights.gov.au/human-rights-act-for-australia) 7 March 2023, accessed 21 May 2023.

44 Ibid, p 7.

45 Margaret Thornton, Challenging the legal profession a century on: the case of Edith Haynes, (https://ssrn.com/abstract=3289410), 23 November 2018, University of Western Australia Law Review 44(1):1 Accessed from ANU College of Law Legal Studies Research Paper No 18.20, accessed May 2021.

46 Rosemary Pringle and Ann Game, Gender at Work [Kindle version], Routledge, 2020, Retrieved from Amazon.com (Location No 105), accessed May 2021.

47 Ibid.

48 Ibid.

49 Ibid.

50 Ibid., Location No 131.

51 *Ex parte H.V. McKay* (1907) 2 CAR 1 ('Harvester Case').

52 *The Rural Workers Union and The South Australian United Labourers' Union v The Employers* (1912) 6 CAR 61 ('Fruit Pickers Case'), 71.

53 *Commonwealth Public Service Act 1902* (Cth).

54 Workplace Gender Equality Agency, Australia's gender pay gap statistics (https://www.wgea.gov.au/publications/australias-gender-pay-gap-statistics), 28 August 2021, accessed 1 September, 2021.

55 The Workplace Gender Equality Agency used seasonally adjusted data to calculate the earnings during the COVID-19 pandemic period and the use of trend data has been suspended (as discussed in Workplace Gender Equality Agency (No 53).

56 Workplace Gender Equality Agency 'Over a quarter of a century until gender pay gap likely to close', [media release], *www.wgea.com.au*, 26 March 2021, accessed April 2021.

57 Gaze and Smith (No 25).

58 *Charter of the United Nations*, art 55.

59 ECOSOC Resolution establishing the Commission on the Status of Women. E/RES/2/11, 21 June 1946.

60 Set as a guiding principle during the first meeting of the UNCSW on 25 February 1947 as discussed in United Nations, The United Nations and the advancement of women 1945–1996, (https://digitallibrary.un.org/record/214867?ln=en), The United Nations Blue Books Series, Volume VI, revised edition, 1996, p 14, accessed April 2021.

61 United Nations, *Universal Declaration of Human Rights, United Nations*, 1948, art 2.

62 *United Nations Convention on the Political Rights of Women* opened for signing on 20 December 1952, 1993 UNTS 135 (entered into force 7 July 1954) arts 1–3.

63 *International Labour Organisation Convention (No 111) Concerning Discrimination in Respect of Employment and Occupation*, opened for signature 25 June 1958, 362 UNTS 31 (entered into force 15 June 1960), art 1.

64 *International Convention on the Elimination of All Forms of Racial Discrimination*, opened for signature 21 December 1965, 660 UNTS 195 (entered into force 4 January 1969).

65 *International Covenant on Civil and Political Rights*, opened for signature 16 December 1966, 999 UNTS 171 (entered into force 23 March 1976).

66 *International Covenant on Economic, Social and Cultural Rights*, opened for signature 16 December 1966, 993 UNTS 3 (entered into force 3 January 1976).

67 United Nations, *Universal Declaration of Human Rights*, United Nations, 1948, art 26.

68 Gaze and Smith (No 25) p 33.

69 Ibid. p 34.

70 Ibid.

71 *Convention on the Elimination of All Forms of Discrimination against Women*, opened for signature, 18 December 1979, 1249 UNTS 13 (entered into force 3 September 1981).

72 Gaze and Smith (No 25) p 37.

73 Prohibition of Discrimination Act 1966 (SA) ss 3–8 as discussed in David Prideaux 'The South Australian Prohibition of Discrimination Act and Racism' (1975) Australian Journal of Social Issues 10(4) p 315 (https://doi.org/10.1002/j.1839-4655.1975.tb00559.x).

74 David Prideaux, The South Australian Prohibition of Discrimination Act and Racism, 1975, *Australian Journal of Social Issues*, 10(4) p 315, doi.org/10.1002/j.1839-4655.1975.tb00559.x, accessed March 2021.

75 'Insurance against Hatred', *The Bulletin*, 17 December 1966, 88 (4528), 20.

76 The Hon Michelle Lensink MLC, Passing the baton, (michellelensink. com/passing_the_baton), [Speech] 10 November 2010, accessed March 2021.

77 Robert Foster, *Turning points: chapters in South Australian history*, Wakefield Press, South Australia, 2012, p 69.

78 Consie Larmour, *Sex discrimination legislation in Australia*, (https://www.aph.gov.au/binaries/library/pubs/bp/1990/90bp28. pdf), Education and Welfare Research Group, Parliament of Australia, Parliamentary Research Service Background Paper, 3 October 1990, p 14.

79 Ibid.

80 Ibid., 15.

81 Robert Foster (No 76 p 70.

82 Consie Larmour (No 77).

83 Robert Foster (No 76) p 69.

84 Consie Larmour (No 77).

85 Equal Opportunity Commission of South Australia, History of equal opportunity In South Australia, (https://www.tiki-toki.com/timeline/ entry/293824/History-of-Equal-Opportunity-in-South-Australia/#var s!date=1831-11-19_20:25:55!)

86 Judith Brett, *From secret ballot to democracy sausage: how Australia got compulsory voting*, Text Publishing, 2020, pp 36–40.

87 Ibid., p 40.

88 Ibid., p 41.

89 *Australian Constitution*, s 41. Official report of the National Australasian Convention Debates, (https://adc.library.usyd.edu.au/data-2/fed0055.pdf), Adelaide, 15 April 1897, 715–17.

90 Gaze and Smith (No 25) p 108.

91 Ibid., p 36.

92 *Convention on the Elimination of All Forms of Racial Discrimination* opened for signature on 21 December 1965, 660 UNTS 195 (entered into force on 2 January 1969) as attached as a Schedule to the *Racial Discrimination Act*. The High Court has held that where a statute gives effect to an international treaty, its terms should be construed in accordance with the treaty: *Koowarta v Bjelke-Peterson* (1982) 153 CLR 168.

93 Ibid. p 37. Direct racial discrimination is prohibited under *Racial Discrimination Act 1975* (Cth) s 9(1) and a concept of indirect racial discrimination was introduced into s 9(1A) in 1990.

94 United Nations Treaty Body Database (www.OHCHR.org) accessed on 19 December 2021.

95 *Convention on the Elimination of All Forms of Discrimination against Women* opened for signature 18 December 1979, 1249 UNTS 13 (entered into force 3 September 1981) art 2.

96 Ibid., art 2.

97 Ibid., arts 13, 16.

98 Maternity leave has now been legislated in the *Paid Parental Leave Act 2010* (Cth).

99 Australian Human Rights Commission, The Convention on the Elimination of All Forms of Discrimination against Women (CEDAW), (https://humanrights.gov.au/our-work/sex-discrimination/convention-elimination-all-forms-discrimination-against-women-cedaw-sex), 2012, viewed 24 July 2020.

100 *Sex Discrimination Bill 1981* (Cth).

101 Commonwealth Parliament of Australia, *Parliamentary Debates* Senate, Thursday, 26 November 1981, Thirty-second Parliament, First Session – Third Period, 2707, Sex Discrimination Bill 1981 Second Reading, Senator The Hon Susan Ryan.

102 Ibid.

103 *Sex Discrimination Act 1984* (Cth) ('SDA').

104 Margaret Thornton and Trish Luker, *The Sex Discrimination Act and its rocky rite of passage*, ANU Press, 2010, p 32.

105 Ibid.

106 Commonwealth v Tasmania (1983) 158 CLR 1 ('Tasmanian Dam case').

107 Thornton and Luker (No 103) p 28.

108 As discussed in 'Scott Morrison credits "quiet Australians" for "miracle" election victory', *The Guardian* 19 May 2019 (Archived from the original on 28 December 2020. Retrieved 23 May 2019).

109 Thornton and Luker (No 103) p 40.

110 Ibid., p 28.

111 Ibid., p 41.

112 Margaret FitzHerbert, *So many firsts: liberal women from Menzies to Turnbull era*, Federation Press, 2009, p 27.

113 The Hon Susan Ryan AO, 'Fishes on Bicycles', *Papers on Parliament*, No 17 September 1992.

114 Only in employment is discrimination on the grounds of having caring responsibilities unlawful (*SDA* (No 34) section 7A and Division 1 of Part II)

115 *SDA* (No 102) s 12.

116 *SDA* (No 102) s 3(c).

117 *SDA* (No 102) Part II Division 3.

118 *Sex Discrimination and Other Legislation Amendment Act 1992* (Cth).

119 *SDA* (No 102) s 106(1).

120 Elizabeth Evatt, 'Falling short on women's rights: mis-matches between SDA and the international regime' in Marius Smith (ed.) *Human rights 2004: the year in review*, Castan Centre for Human Rights Law, Monash University, Melbourne, 2005.

121 *Brandy v Human Rights and Equal Opportunity Commission* (1995) 183 CLR 245 held that the then Human Rights and Equal Opportunity Commission's decisions could not be given judicial power and the *Human Rights Legislation Amendment Act 1995* (Cth) addressed this finding by providing that the Commission can made a determination but this would need to be enforced by the Federal Court.

122 For example: Attorney-General's Department Review of Consolidation of Commonwealth Discrimination Law 2011, Senate Legal and Constitutional Affairs Committee, *Report on the Effectiveness of the Commonwealth Sex Discrimination Act 1984 in Eliminating Discrimination and Promoting Gender Equality*, Parliament of Australia, Canberra, 2008; Australian Human Rights Commission, *Discussion*

Paper: priorities for federal discrimination law reform (2019) as part of 'Free and Equal: An Australian Conversation on Human Rights' (the National Conversation).

123 Beth Gaze, 'The Sex Discrimination Act after twenty years: achievements, disappointments, disillusionment and alternatives', *UNSW Law Journal*, Volume 27(3) 2004.

124 Ibid.

125 *Convention on the Elimination of All Forms of Discrimination against Women* opened for signature 18 December 1979, 1249 UNTS 13 (entered into force 3 September 1981) art 4. Australian Human Rights Commission, The Convention on the Elimination of All Forms of Discrimination against Women (CEDAW), (https://humanrights. gov.au/our-work/sex-discrimination/convention-elimination-all-forms-discrimination-against-women-cedaw-sex), 2012, accessed 24 July 2020.

126 *Public Service Act 1922* (Cth), s 22B.

127 *Anti-Discrimination Act 1977* (NSW), Part IXA.

128 Commonwealth Parliament of Australia, *Parliamentary Debates* Senate, Thursday, 26 November 1981, Thirty-second Parliament, First Session – Third Period, 2707, Sex Discrimination Bill 1981 Second Reading, Senator the Hon Susan Ryan.

129 Sex Discrimination Bill 1981 Part IV.

130 The Hon Susan Ryan AO (No 112).

131 Department of the Prime Minister and Cabinet, Affirmative action for women, May 1984, (https://nla.gov.au/nla.obj-1194380366/view?partId=nla.obj-1200963163#page/n2/mode/1up), Government Printer, Canberra, 1985, Foreword by R.J.L. Hawke, Prime Minister, p 7, accessed March 2021.

132 Ibid., p 10.

133 Ibid.

134 Office of the Status of Women, Affirmative Action Resource Unit, *Affirmative action for women: a progress report on the pilot program July 1984 to March 1985*, Australian Government Publishing Service, 1985.

135 Ibid.

136 Consie Larmour (No 77) p 10.

137 Ibid.

138 *Affirmative Action (Equal Opportunity for Women) Act 1986* (Cth), Part II and Part IV.

139 Workplace Gender Equality Agency, Our story, (https://www.wgea. gov.au/about/our-story).

140 *Equal Opportunity for Women in the Workplace Act 1999* (Cth).

141 Department of Families, Housing, Community Services and Indigenous Affairs, Office for Women, *Review of the Equal Opportunity for Women in the Workplace Act 1999: consultation* report, FaHCSIA, Canberra ACT, 2010.

142 *Equal Opportunity for Women in the Workplace Amendment Bill 2012 Explanatory Memorandum.*

143 *Equal Opportunity for Women in the Workplace Act 2021* (Cth) Part IV, IVA.

144 Workplace Gender Equality Agency, 'New WGEA data shows employer action on gender equality has stalled', [media release], (www.wgea.com.au), 26 November 2020, accessed April 2020.

145 Ibid.

146 Department of Prime Minister and Cabinet, Office for Women Senator the Hon Marise Payne, Review of the Workplace Gender Equality Act, [media release], (https://ministers.pmc.gov.au/payne/2021/review-workplace-gender-equality-act), 20 October 2021, accessed November 2021.

147 *Workplace Gender Equality Amendment (Closing the Gender Pay Gap) Bill 2023.*

148 Jaclyn Diaz, Thousands March in Australia as Another #MeToo Wave Hits the Country, (npr.org/2021/03/15/977340049/thousands-march-in-australia-as-another-metoo-wave-hits-the-country), *NPR Daily*, 15 March 2021, accessed April 2021.

149 Me Too Movement, History and inception [website] (https://metoomvmt.org/get-to-know-us/history-inception/), accessed April 2021.

150 Respect@Work Report (No 29), p 25.

151 Respect@Work Report (No. 29), p 28.

152 Ibid.

153 Human Rights and Equal Opportunity Commission, *Sex Discrimination Act 1984: a review of exemptions*, 1992.

154 Australian Government Attorney-General's Department, A roadmap for respect: preventing and addressing sexual harassment in Australian workplaces, ('Roadmap for Respect'), (https://apo.org.au/node/311776), 8 April 2021, accessed April 2021.

155 *Sex Discrimination and Fair Work (Respect at Work) Amendment Act 2021* (Cth).

156 Roadmap for Respect (No 153).

157 Respect@Work Report (No 29), p 551.

158 Equal Opportunity Act 2021 (Vic) s15.

159 Respect@Work Report (No 29), p 14.

160 Beth Gaze (No 122), 'The Sex Discrimination Act at 25: reflections on the past, present and future', in Margaret Thornton (ed.), *Sex discrimination in uncertain times*, ANU, 2010, pp 109–134, 126.

161 Ibid.

162 Anti-Discrimination and Human Rights Legislation Amendment (Respect at Work) Act 2022 (Cth).

163 Respect@Work Report (No 29), p 33.

164 High Court of Australia, Statement by the Hon Susan Kiefel AC, Chief Justice of the High Court of Australia, (https://cdn.hcourt.gov.au/assets/news/Statement%20by%20Chief%20Justice%20Susan%20Kiefel%20AC.pdf), 22 June 2021, accessed July 2021.

165 Australian Human Rights Commission, *Set the standard: report on the independent review into parliamentary workplaces*, (https://humanrights.gov.au/about/publications), November 2021, accessed November 2021.

166 Crimes Legislation Amendment (Sexual Consent Reforms) Act 2021 (NSW).

167 Premier of Victoria, the Hon Daniel Andrews, Stronger laws for victim-survivors of sexual violence, [media release], (www.premier.vic.gov.au/stronger-laws-victim-survivors-sexual-violence), 12 November 2021, accessed November 2021; Justice Legislation Amendment (Sexual Offences and Other Matters) Act 2022 (Vic).

168 Crimes Legislation Amendment (Sexual Consent Reforms) Act 2021.

169 Criminal Code (Consent and Mistake of Fact) and Other Legislation Amendment Act 2021 (Qld).

170 *The Bulletin* (No 74), 20.

171 Claire Wright, 'A wave of female candidates powered by historic swell', *Meanjin Quarterly* 13, December 2021.

Chapter 4. Equal employment opportunity and me

172 Anne Summers, *The misogyny factor*, NewSouth Publishing, 2013, p 25.

Chapter 5. Changing hearts and minds

173 Julia Gillard and Ngozi Okonjo-Iweala, *Women and leadership*, Vintage, 2020, p 272.

Chapter 6. Affirmative action in action

174 Dr Noriko Amano-Patiño, *What are the Effects of Affirmative Action Regulation on Workers' Careers?*, (https://isps.yale.edu/news/blog/2017/01/what-are-the-effects-of-affirmative-action-regulation-on-workers'-careers), accessed 12 January, 2017.

175 Science News, Scientists show positive effects of affirmative action policies promoting women (https://www.sciencedaily.com/releases/2012/02/120202151711.htm), 2 February 2012, accessed 2019.

176 Julia Gillard and Ngozi Okonjo-Iweala, *Women and leadership*, Vintage, 2020, p 7.

177 Emily Maguire, *This is what a feminist looks like*, National Library of Australia, 2019, p 50.

Chapter 7. We need to talk about quotas

178 Anne Summers, *The women's manifesto: a blueprint for how to get equality for women in Australia*, 2017, p 1.

179 Ibid., p 7.

180 *Australian Women CEOs Speak: How female leaders rise and how organisations can help.* Korn Ferry Institute in collaboration with Australian Institute of Company Directors (2018), p 38.

181 Cliona O'Dowd, 'Turn rejection into an energy to prove doubters wrong: Sherr', *The Australian*, 7 September, 2018, p 30.

182 Nick Toscano, *BHP seeks suppliers to jump-start gender diversity push*, The Sydney Morning Herald, 5 February 2020.

183 Emily's List Australia, (https://www.emilyslist.org.au/about), [website], accessed 28 March 2022.

184 Natasha Josefowitz, *Paths to power: a woman's guide from first job to top executive*, Addison-Wesley, 1980.

185 Dudley Lynch and Paul L. Kordis, *The strategy of the dolphin – scoring a win in a chaotic world*, Arrow Books, 1988.

186 *Australian Women CEOs Speak: How female leaders rise and how organisations can help.* Korn Ferry Institute in collaboration with Australian Institute of Company Directors (2018), p 30.

187 Julia Gillard and Ngozi Okonjo-Iweala, *Women and leadership*, Vintage, 2020, pp 219–20.

188 Ibid., p 213.

189 *Australian Women CEOs Speak: How female leaders rise and how organisations can help.* Korn Ferry Institute in collaboration with Australian Institute of Company Directors (2018).

Chapter 9. The career woman/mother juggling act

190 Katrine Marçal, *Who cooked Adam Smith's dinner?*, Granta Publications, p 61.

191 Annabel Crabb, *The wife drought*, Ebury Press, 2014, p 131.

192 Ibid., p 72.

193 Ibid., p 74.

194 Julia Gillard and Ngozi Okonjo-Iweala, *Women and leadership*, Vintage, 2020, p 196.

195 Ibid., p 193.

196 Ibid., p 193.

197 Anne Summers, *Unfettered and alive – a memoir*, Allen & Unwin, 2018, p 316.

198 Charlotte Grieve, 'Absolutely no progress': Number of female CEOs in Australia is declining', (https://www.smh.com.au/business/companies/absolutely-no-progress-number-of-female-ceos-in-australia-is-declining-20200916-p55w5m.html), *The Sydney Morning Herald* (digital edition), 17 September 2020, accessed 17 September 2020.

199 Australian Bureau of Statistics, Women spent more time than men on unpaid work in May, [media release], (https://www.abs.gov.au/media-centre/media-releases/women-spent-more-time-men-unpaid-work-may), 16 June 2021, accessed 16 June 2021.

200 *Australian Women CEOs Speak: How female leaders rise and how organisations can help.* Korn Ferry Institute in collaboration with Australian Institute of Company Directors (2018).

Chapter 10. Power plays

201 Mary Beard, *Women and power*, Profile Books, Great Britain, 2017, p xi.

202 Ibid., pp 3–4.

203 Ibid., p 4.

204 Ray Hadley, Interview with Tony Abbott, radio 2GB broadcast 1 May 2017

205 Aubrey Allegretti, Ukip leadership contender Raheem Kassam sparks outrage for history of controversial twitter posts, (https://www.huffingtonpost.co.uk/entry/raheem-kassam-ukip-leadership-election-twitter-deleted_uk_580cf387e4b056572d82f392), *Huffpost*, 23 October 2016, accessed May 2021.

206 Kate Burridge and Howard Manns, Shrill, bossy, emotional: why language matters in the gender debate, (https://theconversation.com/shrill-bossy-emotional-why-language-matters-in-the-gender-debate-158310), *The Conversation*, 10 May 2021, accessed 10 May 2021.

207 David Leser, *Women, men and the whole damn thing*, Allen & Unwin, 2019, p 118.

208 Ibid., p 132.

209 Ibid., p 133.

210 Anne Summers, *Unfettered and alive – a memoir*, Allen & Unwin, 2018, p 7.

211 Mary Beard, *Women and power*, Profile Books, Great Britain, 2017, p 19.

212 Ibid., p 34.

213 Michelle Grattan, Part-time work holds women back from executive positions and accentuates gender pay gap: new data, (https://theconversation.com/part-time-work-holds-women-back-from-executive-positions-and-accentuates-gender-pay-gap-new-data-185844), *The Conversation*, June 27, 2022, accessed June 27, 2022.

214 Emily Maguire, *This is what a feminist looks like*, National Library of Australia, 2019, p 191.

215 Jacqueline Maley, 'How Elizabeth Broderick is taking soft-power feminism to the world', *The Sydney Morning Herald*, 9 February 2019, *Good Weekend*, p 21.

216 Ibid., p 162.

Chapter 11. So can women lead?

217 Daniel Goleman, *The New Leaders – transforming the art of leadership into the science of results*, Little Brown, 2002

218 Mary Beard, *Women and power*, Profile Books, Great Britain, 2017, p 94.

219 *Australian Women CEOs Speak: How female leaders rise and how organisations can help.* Korn Ferry Institute in collaboration with Australian Institute of Company Directors (2018), p 20.

220 David Leser, *Women, men and the whole damn thing*, Allen & Unwin, 2019, p 116.

221 Ibid., p 117.

222 Ibid., p 111.

223 Jacqueline Maley, 'How Elizabeth Broderick is taking soft-power feminism to the world', *The Sydney Morning Herald*, 9 February 2019, *Good Weekend*, p 19.

224 Julia Gillard and Ngozi Okonjo-Iweala, *Women and leadership*, Vintage, 2020, p 30–31.

225 Ibid., p 125.

226 Ibid., p 66.

227 Ibid., p 127.

228 Ibid., p 171.

229 Ann Sherry, keynote speech at 2018 Chief Executive Women annual dinner CEW speeches (https://cew.org.au/media-and-research/speeches/).

Chapter 12. Power over at work – the issue of sexual harassment

230 Australian Human Rights Commission, Respect@Work: national inquiry into sexual harassment in Australian workplaces, 2020, pp 10–11.

231 Kate Jenkins, The Beijing Platform for Action, 25 year on: Progress, Retreat and the Future of Women's Rights, (https://humanrights.gov.au/about/news/speeches/beijing-platform-action-25-years-progress-retreat-and-future-womens-rights), Australian Human Rights Commission, 3 December 2020, accessed 5 December 2020.

232 Karen O'Connell, 72% of Australians have been sexually harassed. The system we have to fix this problem is set up to fail, (https://theconversation.com/72-of-australians-have-been-sexually-harassed-the-system-we-have-to-fix-this-problem-is-set-up-to-fail-141368), The Conversation, 26 June 2020, accessed June 2020.

233 Bri Lee B, 'Sexual harassment in the legal profession', The Saturday Paper, 27 June 2020.

234 David Leser, Women, men and the whole damn thing, Allen & Unwin, 2019, p 109.

235 Anne Summers, The fragility of feminist progress and why rage is a luxury we can't afford, (https://www.theguardian.com/world/2018/oct/26/the-fragility-of-feminist-progress-and-why-rage-is-a-luxury-we-cant-afford), The Guardian, 26 October, 2018, p 19.

236 Julia Baird, My experience of the harassment that's been missing from the #metoo debate, (https://www.smh.com.au/opinion/my-experience-of-the-harassment-thats-been-missing-from-the-metoo-debate-20180112-h0h5kd.html), The Sydney Morning Herald, 12 January 2018, p 22.

237 Emma Tseris E and Nicole Moulding, Evidence shows mental illness isn't a reason to doubt women survivors, (https://theconversation.com/evidence-shows-mental-illness-isnt-a-reason-to-doubt-women-survivors-156581), The Conversation, 9 March 2021, accessed March 9, 2021.

238 Australian Human Rights Commission, Respect@Work: Sexual Harassment National Inquiry Report (2020), (https://humanrights.gov.au/our-work/sex-discrimination/publications/

respectwork-sexual-harassment-national-inquiry-report-2020), accessed 5 March 2020.

239 Dr Vivienne Thom AM, Independent Inquiry into matters raised by Ms Rachelle Miller in her statement of 2 December 2021, (https://www.pmc.gov.au/sites/default/files/media-releases/independent-inquiry-into-matters-raised-by-ms-rachelle-miller.pdf), Department of the Prime Minister and Cabinet, 2 December, 2021, accessed December 2021.

240 Julia Baird, 'A single question reverberates throughout the Dyson Heydon affair', *The Sydney Morning Herald*, 27 June 2020.

241 Julian Webb, In the wake of the Dyson Heydon allegations, here's how the legal profession can reform sexual harassment, (https://theconversation.com/in-the-wake-of-the-dyson-heydon-allegations-heres-how-the-legal-profession-can-reform-sexual-harassment-142560), *The Conversation*, 15 July 2020, accessed 15 July 2020.

242 Lisa Heap, Sexual harassment at work isn't just discrimination. It needs to be treated as a health and safety issue, (https://theconversation.com/sexual-harassment-at-work-isnt-just-discrimination-it-needs-to-be-treated-as-a-health-and-safety-issue-144940), *The Conversation*, 28 August 2020, accessed 28 August 2020.

Chapter 13. What on earth is going on?

243 Australian National University's definition of unconscious bias, (https://www.anu.edu.au/files/resource/Unconscious%20Bias.pdf), accessed September 2020.

244 Mary Beard, *Women and power*, Profile Books, Great Britain, 2017, p 59.

245 Ibid., p 96.

246 Victor Sojo and Melissa A Wheeler, 'Why short "unconscious bias" programs aren't enough to end racial harassment and discrimination', (https://theconversation.com/why-short-unconscious-bias-programs-arent-enough-to-end-racial-harassment-and-discrimination-95422), *The Conversation*, 24 April 2018, accessed 24 April 2018.

247 Judith Brett, 'The coal curse: resources, climate and Australia's future', *Quarterly Essay Issue 78*, Black Inc., 2020, p 53.

248 Annabel Crabb, *The wife drought*, Ebury Press, 2014, p 34.

249 Ibid., p 35.

250 Chris Wallace, It's a man's (pandemic) world: how policies compound the pain for women in the age of COVID-19,

(https://theconversation.com/its-a-mans-pandemic-world-how-policies-compound-the-pain-for-women-in-the-age-of-covid-19-144796), *The Conversation*, 24 September 2020, accessed 24September 2020.

251 Ibid.

252 George Megalogenis, 'Women may yet be the PM's downfall', *The Sydney Morning Herald*, 13/14 March 2021.

253 Mike Seccombe, 'The children of gods: how power works in Australia', *The Saturday Paper*, 13 March 2021.

254 Julia Gillard and Ngozi Okonjo-Iweala, *Women and leadership*, Vintage, 2020, p 156.

255 Charlotte Grieve, Absolutely no progress: Number of female CEOs is declining, (https://www.smh.com.au/business/companies/absolutely-no-progress-number-of-female-ceos-in-australia-is-declining-20200916-p55w5m.html), *The Sydney Morning Herald* (digital edition), 17 September 2020, accessed 17 September 2020.

256 Kate Jenkins, Opening address, The Beijing Platform for Action, 25 year on: Progress, Retreat and the Future of Women's Rights, (https://humanrights.gov.au/about/news/speeches/beijing-platform-action-25-years-progress-retreat-and-future-womens-rights), Australian Human Rights Commission, 3 December 2020.

257 Yuval Noah Harari, *Sapiens: A brief history of humankind*, Vintage, 2011, pp 132–3.

Chapter 14. How much are you paid?

258 Michelle Grattan, Part-time work holds women back from executive positions and accentuates gender pay gap: new data, (https://theconversation.com/part-time-work-holds-women-back-from-executive-positions-and-accentuates-gender-pay-gap-new-data-185844), *The Conversation*, 27 June 2022, accessed 27 June 2022.

259 Anne Summers, *The misogyny factor*, NewSouth Publishing, 2013, pp 27–8.

260 Ibid., p 53.

261 Annabel Crabb, *The wife drought*, Ebury Press. 2014, p 27.

262 Leonora Risse, 50 years after Australia's historic 'equal pay' decision, the legacy of 'women's work' remains, (https://theconversation.com/50-years-after-australias-historic-equal-pay-decision-the-legacy-of-womens-work-remains-118761), *The Conversation*, 19 June 2019, accessed 19 June 2019.

263 K Ziwica, Only big moves will speed up the end of the unjust gender pay gap, (https://www.theage.com.au/lifestyle/gender/only-big-moves-will-speed-up-the-end-of-the-unfair-gender-pay-gap-20190815-p52hlu.html), *The Age*, 16 August 2019, accessed 16 August 2019.

264 Emma Williamson, Four home traps that contribute to the gender pay gap, (https://theconversation.com/four-home-traps-that-contribute-to-the-gender-pay-gap-122261), *The Conversation*, 23 August 2019, accessed 23 August 2019.

265 Lyn Craig, COVID-19 has laid bare how much we value women's work, and how little we pay for it, (https://theconversation.com/covid-19-has-laid-bare-how-much-we-value-womens-work-and-how-little-we-pay-for-it-136042), *The Conversation*, 21 April 2020, accessed 21 April 2020.

266 Ibid.

267 Patty Kinnersly, *Our Watch*, (ourwatch.org.au), 31 August 2021.

268 Katrine Marçal, *Who cooked Adam Smith's dinner?*, Granta Publications, 2012, p 120.

269 Robert Breunig and Yinjunjie Zhang, A shocking finding that will change the way you think about gender pay, (https://theconversation.com/a-shocking-finding-that-will-change-the-way-you-think-about-gender-pay-158052), *The Conversation*, 31 March, 2021, accessed April 2021.

270 Amelia McGuire, Gender pay data not transparent, *The Sydney Morning Herald*, October 21, 2021.

271 Workplace Equality Agency, Wages and Ages: Mapping the Gender Pay Gap by Age, (https://www.wgea.gov.au/newsroom/new-age-data-released), June 27, 2022.

272 Brett Gale, Closing the gender pay gap, (https://www.chifley.org.au/publications/closing-the-gender-pay-gap/), Chifley Research Centre's report, 15 August 2019, accessed 15 August 2019.

273 Anna von Reibnitz, Jananie William, Miriam Glennie, Sally Curtis and Sarbari Bordia, Australia has ranked last in an international gender pay gap study – here are 3 ways to do better, (https://theconversation.com/australia-has-ranked-last-in-an-international-gender-pay-gap-study-here-are-3-ways-to-do-better-168848), *The Conversation*, 1 October 2021, accessed 1 October 2021.

Chapter 15. When will they find me out?

274 *Australian Women CEOs Speak: How female leaders rise and how organisations can help.* Korn Ferry Institute in collaboration with Australian Institute of Company Directors (2018), p 32.

275 Ibid., p 29.

276 Jacqueline Maley, 'How Elizabeth Broderick is taking soft-power feminism to the world', *The Sydney Morning Herald*, 9 February 2019, Good Weekend, p 19.

277 Julia Baird, 'Why you should carry yourself with the confidence of a mediocre white man', *The Sydney Morning Herald*, 2016.

278 Julia Gillard and Ngozi Okonjo-Iweala, *Women and leadership*, Vintage, 2020, p 104.

279 Ibid., p 105.

280 Jessica Gildersleeve, Guide to the classics: a room of one's own, Virginia Woolf's feminist call to arms, (https://theconversation.com/guide-to-the-classics-a-room-of-ones-own-virginia-woolfs-feminist-call-to-arms-145398), *The Conversation*, 24 September 2020, accessed 24 September 2020.

281 Julia Baird, 'Why you should carry yourself with the confidence of a mediocre white man', *The Sydney Morning Herald*, 2016.

282 Zoe Kinias, A Simple Exercise Can Help Women Overcome Self-Doubt to Succeed, (https://hbr.org/2016/08/a-simple-exercise-can-help-women-overcome-self-doubt-and-succeed), *Harvard Business Review*, 11 August 2016, accessed September 2018.

283 *Australian Women CEOs Speak: How female leaders rise and how organisations can help.* Korn Ferry Institute in collaboration with Australian Institute of Company Directors (2018), p 32.

Chapter 16. The F word – to be or not to be?

284 Dr Janet Ramsay.

285 David Leser, *Women, men and the whole damn thing*, Allen & Unwin, 2019, p 22.

286 Robert Jensen, *The end of patriarchy*, Spinifex Press, 2017, p 35.

287 Katrine Marçal, *Who cooked Adam Smith's dinner?* Granta Publications, 2012, p 197.

288 Jane Caro, *Accidental feminists*, Melbourne University Publishing, 2019, p 197.

289 Emily Maguire, *This is what a feminist looks like*, National Library of Australia, 2019, p 13.

290 Ibid., p 227.

291 Jess Hill, 'The reckoning – how #MeToo is changing Australia', *Quarterly Essay # 84*, 2021, pp 31–2.

292 Robert Jensen, *The end of patriarchy*, Spinifex Press, 2017, p 3.

293 Ibid., p 153.

294 Ibid., p 154.

295 Annabel Crabb, *The wife drought*, Ebury Press, 2014, p 84.

296 Ibid., p 81.

297 Ibid., p 141.

298 Ibid., p 294.

299 Michelle Stratemeyer, Adriana Vargas Saenz and Elise Holland, How challenging masculine stereotypes is good for men, (https://theconversation.com/how-challenging-masculine-stereotypes-is-good-for-men-114300), *The Conversation*, 28 March 2019, accessed March 2019.

300 Michael Flood, Who is a real man? Most Australians believe outdated ideals of masculinity are holding men back, (https://theconversation.com/who-is-a-real-man-most-australians-believe-outdated-ideals-of-masculinity-are-holding-men-back-147847), *The Conversation*, 8 December, 2020, accessed December 2020.

301 Ibid.

302 Ibid.

303 Annabel Crabb, *The wife drought*, Ebury Press, 2014, p 254.

304 Robert Jensen, *The end of patriarchy*, Spinifex Press, 2017, p 165.

305 American Psychological Guidelines, APA Guidelines for Psychological Practice with Boys and Men, (https://www.apa.org/about/policy/boys-men-practice-guidelines.pdf), August 2018, accessed August 2018.

Chapter 18. It was not always so

306 David Whyte (quoting Dante Alighieri), *The heart aroused: poetry and the preservation of the soul in corporate America*, Articulate Press, 1994, p 1, 26.

307 Gerda Lerner, *The creation of patriarchy*, Oxford University Press USA,1986, p 229.

308 Tim Flannery, *Here on earth: An argument for hope*, The Text Publishing Company, 2010.

309 Riane Eisler, *The chalice and the blade: Our history, our future*, Pandora – an Imprint of HarperCollins, 1993.

310 Marija Gimbutas, *The early civilization of Europe* (Monograph for Indo-European Studies 131, University of California at Los Angeles, 1980).

311 Glenn Collins, Patriarchy: is it intervention or inevitable? (https://www.nytimes.com/1986/04/28/style/patriarchy-is-it-invention-or-inevitable.html), *The New York Times*, 28 April, 1986, accessed 2021.

312 Bill Gammage, *The biggest estate on earth: how Aborigines made Australia*, Allen & Unwin. 2011, pp 1– 2.

313 Bruce Pascoe, *Dark emu, black seeds: agriculture or accident?* Magabala Books, 2014, p 95.

314 Bill Gammage, *The biggest estate on earth: how Aborigines made Australia*, Allen & Unwin. 2011, pp 123–24.

315 David J. Tacy, *Edge of the sacred: Transformation in Australia*, HarperCollins Publishers Australia, 1995, p113.

Chapter 19. Breaking the glass ceiling – are we nearly there yet?

316 Patricia A Bellamy and Kate Ramsay, *Barriers to women working in corporate management*, Australian Government Publishing Service, Canberra, 1994, p 11.

317 Anne Summers, *The misogyny factor*, NewSouth Publishing, 2013, pp 90–91.

318 Annabel Crabb, *The wife drought*, Ebury Press, 2014, p 52.

319 Ibid., pp 46–47.

320 Anne Summers, *The Misogyny Factor*, NewSouth, 2013, p 65.

321 Daniel Hurst and Paul Karp, Extending Free childcare could fuel huge boost to economy, report says, (https://www.theguardian.com/australia-news/2020/jun/25/extending-free-childcare-could-fuel-huge-boost-to-economy-report-says), *The Guardian*, 25 June 2020, accessed June 2020.

322 *Australian Women CEOs Speak: How female leaders rise and how organisations can help.* Korn Ferry Institute in collaboration with Australian Institute of Company Directors (2018), p 18.

323 Ibid., p 24.

324 Ibid., p 34.

325 Eva Cox, #MeToo is yet to shift the power imbalances that would bring gender equality, (https://womensagenda.com.au/latest/eva-cox-metoo-is-yet-to-shift-the-power-imbalances-that-would-bring-gender-equality/), *The Conversation*, 18 March 2018, accessed September 2018.

326 Julia Gillard and Ngozi Okonjo-Iweala, *Women and leadership*, Vintage, 2020, p 32.

327 Ibid., p 32.

328 *Australian Women CEOs Speak: How female leaders rise and how organisations can help.* Korn Ferry Institute in collaboration with Australian Institute of Company Directors (2018).

Chapter 20. Three women CEOs speak

329 Amanda Sinclair, *Leadership for the Disillusioned*, Allen & Unwin, 2007, p 55.

Chapter 21. Where we've come from, where we are now and where to from here?

330 Annabel Crabb, *The wife drought*, Ebury Press, 2014, p 252.

331 Emily Maguire, *This is what a feminist looks like*, National Library of Australia, 2019, p 17.

332 Jacqueline Kent, *Vida – A woman for our time*, Viking, 2020, p 39.

333 Julia Gillard, Australia suffered great trauma during the Covid pandemic – and fixing mental health should be our first priority, (https://www.theguardian.com/australia-news/commentisfree/2021/dec/08/australia-suffered-great-trauma-during-the-covid-pandemic-and-fixing-mental-health-should-be-our-first-priority), *The Guardian Weekly*, 17 December 2021, accessed December 2021.

334 Teach us consent, (https://www.teachusconsent.com).